This essential guide promotes learning through activity-centred adventure experiences, providing advice, skill development, social education and personal development for practitioners, teachers, support staff and youth groups.

This book offers advice and practical guidance on planning, setting up and running adventure education sessions with children and young people. Divided into two parts, it gives an overview of adventure education, explaining how it relates to holistic and outdoor learning and how it encourages active engagement from the learners as well as the instructors.

Adventure Education provides a toolkit of various games and activities that can be used with groups of young children, including parachute games, card and musical activities, and climbing and traversing games. This book will be essential reading for all early years practitioners, primary teachers and support staff wanting to develop their skills and deliver adventure learning effectively, as well as youth groups looking to provide both informal learning and physical opportunities.

Linda Ritson has worked with all ages of children and young people in a range of practitioner roles for many years and is currently employed in Children's Services with Nottinghamshire County Council, UK.

Adventure Education

Fun games and activities for children and young people

Linda Ritson

Routledge
Taylor & Francis Group

LONDON AND NEW YORK

First published 2016
by Routledge
2 Park Square, Milton Park, Abingdon, Oxon OX14 4RN

and by Routledge
711 Third Avenue, New York, NY 10017

Routledge is an imprint of the Taylor & Francis Group, an informa business

British Library Cataloguing in Publication Data
A catalogue record for this book is available from the British Library

Library of Congress Cataloging-in-Publication Data
Names: Ritson, Linda, author.
Title: Adventure education : fun games and activities for children and young people / Linda Ritson.
Description: New York, NY : Routledge, 2016. | Includes index.
Identifiers: LCCN 2015047920| ISBN 9781138119956 (hardback) | ISBN 9781138119963 (pbk.) | ISBN 9781315652016 (ebook)
Subjects: LCSH: Activity programs in education—Great Britain. | Educational games—Great Britain. | Adventure games—Great Britain.
Classification: LCC LB1027.25 .R58 2016 | DDC 371.30941—dc23
LC record available at http://lccn.loc.gov/2015047920

ISBN: 978-1-138-11995-6 (hbk)
ISBN: 978-1-138-11996-3 (pbk)
ISBN: 978-1-315-65201-6 (ebk)

Typeset in Optima
by FiSH Books Ltd, Enfield

Printed and bound by CPI Group (UK) Ltd, Croydon, CR0 4YY

Contents

List of figures

Preface

> Everyone is a genius. But if you judge a fish by its ability to climb a tree, it will live its whole life believing that it is stupid.
>
> (Attributed to Albert Einstein)

We all know that we're different from everyone else – we're individuals and not like everyone around us – so it follows that we will all learn in different ways. Yet when we start school there is the one single method of teaching, which doesn't suit everyone; we simply aren't biologically wired to sit at a desk and listen to a teacher, absorbing and understanding what is being talked at us. A mechanic doesn't learn how to fix cars by listening or reading a book, nor does a hairdresser, a computer programmer, a doctor or a solicitor; there comes a point where the theory has been covered and the learner has to go out and learn by doing, practically putting into use that which they have read and heard. The same goes for school learning. There is a definite place for classroom learning, but subjects and concepts are more meaningful if the learner can get 'hands on', putting them into practice for themselves, perhaps making mistakes and working things through for themselves.

This book is aimed primarily at educators, with the ambition to encourage them to externalise the classroom and develop lessons that are beyond the 'chalk and talk' of tradition. In National Curriculum terms, I see this book as being of principal interest to educators at Key Stages 1 and 2, primarily because there is greater use of external providers at Key Stage 3 and above. However, Part II (the toolkit) is of potential interest to anyone looking for inspiration to add that extra element to their programme that will enthuse and invigorate their learning audience.

PART 1 | THE THEORY

Introduction to adventure learning

Adventure learning is not just something for children or young people, but for everyone, whatever their age. But what does adventure learning mean? Put simply, it means learning through having an *adventure*.

So then, what is an adventure? The *Oxford English Dictionary* defines 'adventure' as 'a chance occurrence or event, an accident; to risk oneself; to venture'. Adventure learning concerns itself with the latter of these: 'to risk oneself, to venture'. Adventure can be considered as an undertaking possibly involving danger and unknown risks. To encounter danger means to expose oneself to the possibility of injury, pain, harm or loss; unknown risk means the nature of the danger is unidentified and the extent is undetermined. So, danger relates to the size of the possible harm (which may or may not be physical) and risk is the probability of that harm happening. These two are variables, shaped by your own perceptions, which may or may not be accurate, but are very real to you. Adventure is therefore created through *your* mental image of what may happen to you if you try this venture and how likely it is that your envisaged consequence(s) may occur. Some people enjoy the thrill of possible harm and actively seek to maximise both danger and risk; others seek to minimise them. Most of us exist somewhere along a middle route, pushing the boundaries of our existence a certain extent every now and again, but not too much.

Adventure is a hugely broad term that does not necessarily mean swinging off a high peak in a remote mountain range or trekking through a faraway jungle, an adventure is relative to *your* life, where and how *you* exist every day. Simply stepping outside of your 'everyday' *is* an adventure, trying something new or engaging with new people; any new experience involves risking the danger of not working out, of not wanting to repeat it, which makes it *an adventure*.

Quite often, the way that people come to be introduced to adventurous activities is through an adventure programme, one or more structured sessions that enable them to learn how to do an activity, and perhaps getting an accreditation or qualification from it. Because of this, adventure learning is often called outdoor education, an active rather than a passive process of learning that requires active engagement from the learners as well as the instructors, linked to use of all five senses within an experience to heighten learning and its retention. There are a number of elements of which an adventure learning programme is composed:

1 *Physical environment:* people respond differently when they are away from their usual environment; they feel less sure of themselves, more nervous in what they are doing, making them more receptive and responsive, they become more willing to try unfamiliar things. This adds to the sense of danger and risk, but also makes their sense of achievement that much greater. When adventure learning programmes are used to tackle group behaviour issues, taking characters into unfamiliar surroundings is a great 'leveller', as people no longer have the same power over others or over the domain; people from closed communities such as housing estates can be 'big fish in a small pond' when on their own 'turf', but in a new environment they become as exposed as all other group members. The increased receptivity can bring transformative changes not possible when working on 'home ground'.

2 *Activities:* rather than the activities themselves, it is the *qualities* of activities that bring about outcomes; the combination of challenge, skill acquisition and success leads to personal growth, rather than doing the activity in isolation. Challenges should be holistic and delivered in incremental stages of difficulty, so as not to overwhelm people early on but allow them to develop and learn as they proceed. While the ultimate goal is success, some failure may be positive in terms of personal and group development; anyone who finds the exercise too easy or too difficult is likely to derive little from it. Participants can learn as much from failure as from success, if they are appropriately supported to understand it. It is also important to remember that the activity becomes secondary in an adventure learning programme. It is less important that you can paddle correctly or tie a figure-of-eight knot every time; what matters is that you learn, progressively if possible, that you understand the concepts being taught and that you develop interpersonal and intrapersonal skills (that is, learning to get along with others as well as understanding yourself and how you appear to others).

3 *The group:* several characteristics of the group contribute to its outcomes. Size can be critical; if a group is too big, it can struggle to function well, but if it is too small then the inherent characteristics of group members may not be allowed to emerge. The gender mix and age mix of the group can play a strong role in performance, as can whether the group members come from the same place and whether they have a positive relationship away from the adventure learning session. The extent to which group members *reciprocate* is important, how much they work together *as a group*, rather than a bunch of individuals.

4 *Instructors:* the presentation, manner, attitude and behaviour of the instructor have

a powerful influence on the way in which the group performs, interacts and achieves its goals, as the members take their lead from the instructor. If the instructor presents themself as a calm, cool character, with a sense of fun and a genuine interest in how the group performs, there will be different outcomes than if the instructor appears as a 'tough he-man' to whom the group members cannot relate. Empathy is critical: the extent to which the instructor can understand what the participant feels or thinks, whether the instructor can 'stand in their shoes'.

5   *The participant:* each person exists with a particular background (their *narrative*) that defines their outlook, expectations and willingness to contribute to the group and to the adventure learning session. This influences group response and therefore performance, enhanced or diminished by existing perceptions, group relations, past experiences and instinctive response ('first impressions') to the instructor.

2 A brief philosophy and history

For adventure to be more than a fun and recreational activity, it must become adventure *learning* and, like all learning, must have a clear philosophical and theoretical basis. Philosophy relates to underlying principles forming knowledge and influencing beliefs, whereas theory categorises those principles and can be used to explain experiences; between them, philosophy and theory guide our thinking and our attitudes.

Adventure learning concerns itself with relationships. First, it is concerned with our relationships with other people (interpersonal) and with the self (intrapersonal). Intrapersonal relationships are to do with the way in which we value ourselves and with how much confidence we enter the world. Second, it is concerned with the relationships we have with nature – both *ecosystemic* and *ekistic* relationships. Ecosystemic relationships relate to the interdependence of objects, such as the food chain and the satisfaction of our needs. Ekistic relationships relate to our interactions with the natural environment and the effect each has on the other, such as deforestation, water supplies and disease. These relationships are expressed through our vision of the world and the way in which we interpret events, experiences and interactions.

How we see the world and the way in which we translate our experiences is defined by our *epistemology* and our *ontology*. Our epistemology is our individual body of knowledge and how we have acquired it; this is embedded in our personal beliefs and how we understand what we know as 'fact', related directly to our understanding and analysis of the world around us. This in turn is all built up from our ontology, our life experiences, understanding and feelings that are the foundation of our personality and interpretation; this comprises the basis of our reading of the events, situations, experiences and encounters of our life. The method through which we come to define our reality and understand our world is known as metaphysics; what and how we learn is embodied in the way we see and interpret our world, thus our epistemology is created through our ontology, which also provides the limitations of our knowledge and understanding. Theories of learning relevant to adventure learning are essentially of three types:

1   *Behavioural:* a passive mode of learning that pays no significant attention to different abilities or learning styles; the learner is directed by and dependent upon the instructor. There is a very empirical (observational), external epistemology, founded on conditioning and control by the instructor, with no recognition of independent thought or personal experience. The learner is not credited with any ability, nor are they expected to contribute to or engage with the learning.

2   *Cognitive:* an active mode of learning that recognises the differences in people; a greater level of rational thought, analysis and recall is credited to the learning, because the focus is on absorbing and remembering information. There is a rational (analytical) epistemology, founded on learner independence and association of existing understanding with new knowledge. The learner is recognised as being able to process the learning, to understand it and remember it.

3   *Experiential:* brings both behaviourist and cognitive learning together, with the learner moving from dependence to independence as they gain in knowledge and understanding, and as their skills increase. There is an inherent assumption of trial and error in learning, with the emotional impact (affective engagement) being given equal credit to physical activity and knowledge progression; experiences are consciously reflected and analysed. The learner is assumed to *want* to learn from their experience, to have the conceptual and analytical capacity to be able to reflect on the experience *and* to have the decision-making and problem-solving capacity to apply the learning elsewhere. While the experiential learner may need support to reflect on and understand the experience, they need sophisticated personal cognitive competency to do so.

Adventure learning uses experiences to bring about learning in a 'demo-mimic-do' process. As the relationship begins, the instructor has to start from the point of assuming the learner has no knowledge or understanding of the experience (activity); so, the instructor takes a lead role in showing the learners what to do, explaining necessary actions and processes. The learners are assumed to have the ability gradually to take over responsibility for the activity, making decisions and working increasingly without direction. They are expected not only to understand what they are doing, but also why something does not work and how they can modify their action to achieve success.

   For adventure learning to become embedded in learning programmes, it needs to be understood as a natural phenomenon that has been around as long as there has been life on earth, rather than a new technique or a passing 'fad'. Let's be clear: once upon a time, life was nothing but an adventure and all learning was activity-based and happened outdoors! The 'outdoors' could be argued to have begun with the 'big bang' some four and a half billion years ago. Although the first creatures that emerged about 3.8 billion years ago could not be said to have been cognisant enough to pass life skills to their young, they were the foundations of the multicellular life forms that evolved into what we would recognise today. These multicellular creatures emerged and evolved with an intrinsic sense of survival that many passed to their young. It is estimated that the first hominid species showed the initial steps towards culture, language and social order around four million years ago.

Human beings as we know them (*Homo sapiens*) emerged only about 200,000 years ago, but have continually evolved, as do the cultural, communal and technological bases by which we understand the concept of 'society'. In those intervening 200,000 years, the beings that became humans developed the inborn instincts to survive, to thrive and to teach their young how to survive and thrive. In the days of the hunter–gatherers, children and young people learned by observing others and putting their observations into practice, learning by trial and error. Human consciousness led to the development of shelters, farming, factory production and organised learning. As humankind has evolved, there has been an increasing attempt to tame nature, make life safe, removing the need for and inherent instinct in humans to meet the challenges of survival with which they were once faced.

A critical distinction between humans and other creatures is that humans have progressed their social capacity such that they have choice; people today do not have to spend their waking hours ensuring they have shelter, can eat, are protected, they have learned to store resources so they may choose the extent and manner of any engagement with 'the outdoors'. Evolution has meant industrialisation and the loss of traditional life skills; people now are disconnected from nature, most fear it or attempt to soften it with modern social comforts.

Adventure learning is a way to foster a re-engagement with nature, allowing partic- ipants to have their learning processes stimulated by experience and within a framework of direction by others, a modern equivalent of a return to the young being taught by the elders! The inherent drive of humans to engage with nature and learn from challenges posed by it, to experience, to survive has not evolved out of our psyche. Controlled engagements with nature allow 'safe' adventure learning, planned and directed but capturing and fulfilling the essence of the core human need for adventure.

Fostering engagement with and understanding of the natural world is nothing new; adventure learning has existed as a concept for many years, although time has evolved its nature to reflect social change. Until the end of the second world war, adventure learning was a 'character building' exercise for public school boys, based on the belief that young men destined for positions of military and social leadership should develop their sense of discipline and social responsibility through outdoor activities and on the school playing field. These were the young men who would forge the British Empire, setting the standards to which lower classes should aspire.

At the same time, increased industrialisation brought an increase in leisure time and a fear that the lower classes would become corrupted with excess, morality would decline and social order would be lost; although there was little central direction, government recognised the need for citizens to retain their association with the natural world. The nature study required in the school curriculum was supplemented with various voluntary and charitable organisations offering holidays in the countryside and outdoor clubs and societies. Many of these charitable clubs and societies were founded in the Church, which considered the outdoors and physical exertion valuable tools in developing healthy, moral, virtuous citizens. The Church worked hard in advocating the need for use of the outdoors in the school curriculum and in developing city parks, health sanatoria and cycling and rambling clubs. The 1944 Education Act ensured Local Education Authorities (LEAs) provided facilities for physical activity at primary, secondary and further education levels. The LEAs went beyond creating playgrounds on school sites, but established camps, play centres and residential centres. The latter were aimed at replicating the public school 'character building' experiences seen as essential for developing social responsibility and addressing juvenile crime.

Following the second world war, a sense of battle weariness and the loss of empire, coupled with a move to a nation focussed on welfare, progressed the focus more to personal development, social education, self-efficacy and confidence-building. Many outdoor organisations had emerged by the 1970s, such as the Field Studies Council, the Outward Bound Trust, the Council for Environmental Education, and the National and Rural Studies Association. Their work was complemented by other youth work initiatives, such as the Scouts, Girl Guides and the Duke of Edinburgh Award.

Self-regulation was assumed sufficient and, overall, adventure and outdoor learning has an excellent safety record, but two incidents reminded the public of the challenges posed by the outdoors and humankind's assumed control over nature: the Lyme Bay kayaking incident of 1993, and the Glenridding Beck drowning incident of 2002.

The Lyme Bay kayaking tragedy prompted the government to end self-regulation for outdoor centres and introduce The Activity Centres (Young Persons' Safety) Act 1995, forming the UK Adventure Activities Licensing Authority (AALA) under the guidance of the Health and Safety Executive (HSE), although schools retained the right of self-regulation. While AALA reinforced the role of National Governing Bodies (NGBs) and was seen to provide an external audit of safe practice, many outdoor centres began to offer only on-site activities from a menu of highly standardised and easily controlled sessions. The consequential reduction of risk was arguably a further attempted taming of nature through increased state regulation and limiting the experiential learning of the young person.

Schools were exempt from licensing, provided they organised activities purely for their own pupils. However, the Glenridding Beck incident highlighted that no organisation can be absolved from a responsibility for properly qualified supervision, adequate planning and risk management.

In September 2011, the government announced its intention to repeal the Activity Centres (Young Persons' Safety) Act 1995 and dismantle the inspection scheme. The proposed changes mean that adventure learning would become self-regulating; once more, the HSE would simply investigate incidents and prosecute breaches of safety law. The changes are yet to be implemented.

While there is no national movement to introduce adventure learning as an embedded part of the curriculum, the Learning Outside the Classroom Manifesto was introduced in 2006 to promote a greater use of the outdoors in the school curriculum; successive governments have voiced their support for the initiative and use of the outdoors remains within the national curriculum. The move to promote independent management of schools through becoming academies and free schools allows school directors to determine their own curriculum and focus alternative methodologies, thus allowing adventure learning to achieve higher focus and become more embedded as a learning tool.

3 | Holistic learning

Traditional education is behaviourist, requiring that the learner sit at a desk in a classroom while a teacher delivers; the assumption is that the learner is 'an empty vessel where the teacher's role is to fill it with knowledge' (Allison and Pomeroy 2000). There are many who advocate that education should cultivate the moral, emotional, physical, psychological and spiritual dimensions equally, a perspective known as *holism*. A holistic way of thinking seeks to encompass and integrate multiple layers of meaning and experience; in other words, seeks to recognise every aspect of a person's life and experience rather than dictates a particular way of being or thinking. We are all unique individuals, with our own experiences and characteristics; our intelligences and abilities are far more complex than our examination results. Holistic education seeks to create an intrinsic reverence for life and a love of learning, advocating there is no single *best* way, but many *paths of learning* that recognise and respect the fact that we are all different.

The foundation of holistic learning is that we, as people, are comprised of a complex and intricate combination of elements – intellect, emotion, motivation, intuition, imagination – and we most effectively learn or progress when all of these are activated and stimulated. There are four modes of psychological being (emotional welfare) that govern the way we think, the way we feel, how we imagine and how we live, which may engage singly or may engage in progressively synchronous partnership. Often we feel before we think and we think before we visualise the outcome; it is only when we have reconciled ourselves to each one and developed an understanding of how each is driven within us, can we practice (or live) in a balanced manner, understanding our emotions and controlling them. Having emotional control and understanding ourselves helps us to learn by allowing us the psychological capacity to become open, receptive to new knowledge. Figure 1 shows the hierarchy of emotions whose incremental synergy establishes the basis of open-mindedness and capacity to develop.

Holistic learning looks to build associations between data items into a network of information chains. These associations develop an underlying understanding (a construct) that can form the basis of a problem-solving solution. Holistic learning proposes that

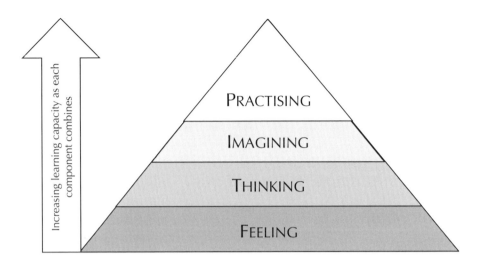

Figure 1 Increasing learning capacity by increasing the senses engaged

when all of our core elements are working, the overall result is better than if only one is engaged (synergy). This contrasts sharply with much mainstream traditional education thinking, where the focus is on intellect, classroom theory and examinations. Traditional (behaviourist) learning relies heavily on rote learning and the memorisation of facts. This encourages 'silos' to form in the brain, lots of separate packets of learned knowledge that are not related to one another, nor are they seen as applicable to anything other than the context in which they were learned. By presenting learning as an holistic methodology, the emphasis moves from a focus on the teacher at the core to the relationship of the learner with the learning situation being the heart of the process, meaning becomes embedded in the process and has an emotional, personal influence on the learner. Every experience has a legacy, adding to how we think and respond in the future, so each aspect of a planned learning experience should exist within a framework that defines and measures capacity, making links between feelings and learning, thereby enabling the learner to identify with their learning, absorb it and apply it elsewhere.

> Holistic learning is the acquisition of cross-curricular knowledge through experiential and multi-modal methods, while developing personally and socially.

In simple terms, this means combining 'delivered' learning (classroom style) with 'discovered' learning (practical experience) so that the person can see, hear, read and put into practice the learning in a social environment (in a group). Rather than school education being shaped by a timetable of discrete subjects taught in isolation, the interrelationship of subjects and their influence on one another enables an holistic (cross-curricular) syllabus.

It is often said that we learn better by seeing and doing than by reading or hearing; it is also said that today's modern world is so full of external stimuli that the average concentration span is decreasing. Most people probably can't remember what they learned in school, unless they have applied it directly to areas of their life, profession and possibly taught it to others. Is that because we genuinely only retain a fraction of what is read or heard? In reality yes, but the reason is less to do with the our ability to concentrate and our brain's capacity to retain information than it is to do with the fact that learning becomes ingrained by it meaning something to us personally and having to engage some degree of effort in acquiring it. The traditional belief among neuroscientists has been that the five senses operate largely as independent systems. However, research suggests that the interaction of the five senses (sight, hearing, smell, touch, taste) are the rule, rather than the exception, so logically the more senses we use in learning and in practising what has been learned, the more pathways are available for embedding the learning and recalling it when necessary.

We are born to learn, the brain has evolved as a machine to explore and learn throughout its lifetime. As humans, we are endowed with the capacity and inescapable impulse to learn, not necessarily as a conscious act, but as a lifelong process of absorbing and transforming experiences, observations and influences into knowledge, skills, behaviours and attitudes. Thus, learning does not necessarily derive from being in a classroom, but allowing the brain to absorb its environment, process it and transform it into learning. In structured learning environments, this can be supported and directed by an instructor. Natural selection has resulted in our brains being able to process data and solve problems in changing environments; when we learn and understand something of meaning to us that we can apply elsewhere and in a different situation, the reward pathway in the brain is activated and gives us a jolt of pleasure (dopamine) so that we will remember and repeat the action when necessary or desired. If the result of the application of learning is something other than what we expect, we are deprived of the dopamine reward, so we learn that application is inappropriate and remember it. Depending on the outcome we do get, either we remember never to try the application again, or we try the application in a different context or situation.

Understanding the way we respond physiologically, we can begin to understand how we learn and then use this to make learning experiences, whether for ourselves or others, deeper and more meaningful, making sure that the maximum amount is derived from each learning opportunity.

Adventure learning is holistic in a number of ways:

1   It relies on practical and visual abilities at least as much as understanding theory; that is, being able to be 'hands on' to see something or handle it, is just as valuable as being able to think through why something should work.

2   It 'levels the playing field' of learning, lesser academic learners can understand concepts and learn through a method more suited to their practical nature. Not all people can follow a lesson through being talked to (or at, most of us have a limited attention span!), so people more suited to watching or doing can understand what is being taught.

3   It allows different subject areas to be brought together. For example, sailing combines mathematics (angle of the sail to the wind) with physics (how a vessel moves through water) and chemistry (compounds to make the vessel). A kayaking session involves physics (what happens when the paddle goes through the water this way or that way); you're out there on the water in all weathers, so you can talk about water cycles, tides and erosion (geography); you see wildlife so you can talk about life cycles, or just identify the diversity of wildlife in the local, urban environment (biology). Getting back to base and writing about their experiences, what was seen, the emotional effect, describing the scenery and colours all brings learners to use language and learn new words; often learners are inspired to research more about an area or topic on their own, so read up on the subject or communicate with others.

4   It brings people of all types of background, abilities and skills to work together so is a massive social education tool. People who would normally never talk or who usually fight can be brought together through a common medium, and the different abilities and strengths of people can come to the fore.

5   It brings people to take on different group roles (Belbin 1993) and learn different strengths, making adventure learning a strong personal development tool. Skills learned can be carried out into everyday life; for example, if young people already have a good understanding of risk assessment from an activity and the way that you delivered it and explained it, they can take that away and choose the right path, risk assessing for themselves and not jumping in a stolen car, taking a substance or disturbing the peace. It can help family relationships by learners coming to understand the drivers of their emotions and the effect their behaviour has on others, thus realising how to control themselves, how to manage different (potential conflict) situations and how to express themselves.

6   It is a physical activity, burning energy and raising the heart rate, thus making it much healthier than sitting behind a desk.

7   It brings a sense of well-being and emotional fulfilment from having participated in an activity, possibly overcoming fears and succeeding in a task or achieving a goal, as well as the associated feelings of wellbeing from physical exercise.

8   It is driven by striving for an outcome, giving the learner ownership over the process and moves the learning relationship towards being a partnership. By assuming control over the pace of learning and progression, the learner develops control over the methodology and the learning.

9   It inspires participants to continue an activity or progress of their own accord. As the learner achieves success, they aspire to more; having control means the learner can direct the path of their future learning.

Adventure learning is not only holistic in enabling use of all the senses; it also requires a physical input, introducing potential further dimensions. This means adventure learning offers an opportunity for lateral learning, to introduce health understanding into the learning equation. In learning and understanding the self, we begin to understand about our drives, our strengths and our weaknesses. This creates a realisation of how we can manage these and gain control of our lives; if we know what makes us happy or causes us distress, we have the ability to direct our lives and our actions accordingly. Programmes can address nutrition and the value of exercise; learning about the body physically and psychologically helps learners understand the value of personal health and how to make the best of themselves.

People learn differently, we all know that, learning can be both a personal and a social process. A lot of literature has been written about learning styles and how we all have a tendency towards one or another (Honey and Mumford 1982; Kolb 1984), but these all assume we only learn in one way. People are complex beings, comprised of a multitude of abilities, which are partially recognised by the theory of multiple intelligences (Smith 2008), but this is still not an accurate reflection of human learning. The reality is that we learn in different ways at different times of the day and of life, according to mood and environment. We are also influenced by the people around us, often copying people we admire or unconsciously aping those with whom we most often socialise. The roles of intentions, choice and decision-making also cannot be underestimated in why and how we learn or act. Adventure learning offers learning in different ways; it is visual and physical; it does not rely on books. While the instructor needs to know and understand the underpinning theory, the participant does not. The instructor must understand the different styles of learning and how to apply them to best effect, as this adds to the 'toolkit' of delivery and to their understanding for developing a programme. Unless it is an aspect of their learning, the learner does not need to know the style applied, simply benefit from the planning and knowledge of the instructor. The art of the skilful instructor is to make a session appear spontaneous and naturally occurring, when it is in fact meticulously planned!

The varied sensory nature of adventure learning provides learning opportunities for people less able to cope with the confines of the classroom. Young people with dyslexia or attention deficit disorder are able to use their stronger senses, such as sight, to understand what is being taught. The ability to learn in a different way opens their world and enables them to operate at the same level as their peers; other (innate) capabilities can come to the fore, such as leadership skills, problem solving or group roles. Having dyslexia or attention deficit disorder does not have to be a barrier to achieving; they are not disabilities but simply mean the brain focuses differently and prefers a different way of absorbing data.

As young people, we have no choice but to take part in school games lessons, yet many young people are not interested in traditional school sport, mainly because if we are not too good at it, we feel self-conscious or become reluctant to participate. For many of us, the idea of running around after a football or a hockey puck does not inspire us in the slightest and as we enter our teenage years we become very aware of ourselves and how we appear. For young women especially, appearance is an integral part of who and what we are; putting it back to ancestral, stone age terms, appearance meant attracting a mate and thus personal survival. This instinct remains inbred in our psyche. Adventure learning offers different sports to try, such as archery, climbing, cycling, mountain biking, kayaking and canoeing. Not only are these intensely physical, they do not necessarily rely on team interaction but can be undertaken in a group setting but achievement is much more about personal capacity and inclination. All these are also Olympic activities, with substantial opportunities for progression if potential and willingness are demonstrated. There is a growing obesity 'epidemic' in the western world that has to be addressed. Providing a range of alternatives to foster an interest in activities and a desire to engage on a regular basis is just one means of doing that and can create wider opportunities, such as joining clubs, making new friends and opening further progressive opportunities.

References

Allison, P. and Pomeroy, E. (2000) How shall we 'know'? Epistemological concerns in research in experiential education. *Journal of Experiential Education* 23(2): 91–97.

Belbin, R. M. (1993) *Team Roles at Work*. Oxford: Butterworth Heinemann.

Honey, P. and Mumford, A. (1982) Typology of learners. In their *Manual of Learning Styles*. London: Peter Honey Publications.

Kolb, D. A. (1984) *Experiential Learning: Experience as the Source for Learning and Development*. Upper Saddle River, NJ: Prentice Hall.

Smith, M. K. (2008) Howard Gardner, multiple intelligences and education. Available at www.infed.org/mobi/howard-gardner-multiple-intelligences-and-education.

3 | Defining adventure and adventure learning

Writers, adventure learning instructors and participants use the term 'adventure' interchangeably with many others: outdoor education, outdoor learning, outdoor pursuits, even physical education. There appears to be no consistency and no clear definition between any of these, which is very confusing for the reader. The common, underlying understanding is that all the terms refer to learning by engaging with nature and being outdoors, but such a broad definition is not really much help. Adventure can be thought of as a branch of outdoor learning, which really is the same as outdoor education, an overarching term that embraces both adventure (adventurous activities) and environmental education.

While Figure 2 may look quite complicated, it shows how the senses are brought together through outdoor learning, which can itself be divided into adventure learning and environmental education, because each emphasises the different relationships people have, but all these relationships are grounded in experience.

An *adventure* is an unusual experience, with some degree of excitement and uncertainty attached; this implies some daring on the part of the participant towards an unknown (risky) outcome. *Learning* is the systematic acquisition of knowledge or skills through study, instruction or experience. Learning itself cannot be measured, but its results and consequences can be. The two apparently incongruous terms come together to define an educative method of experiential, activity-based learning that allows a journey of personal and social inquiry and discovery. Embedding adventure learning within a targeted curriculum, such as school learning requirements, provides a method by which educators can direct the learning, while learners discover the learning. The excitement and uncertainty are embodied in the joy of ownership and unearthing knowledge, the risk is attached to whether the learners will succeed in the given activity. The impact of learning facts through experience is far more powerful than listening about facts discovered and imparted by others.

Adventure and environmental education are both aspects of outdoor learning that holistically engage the senses and involve the spectrum of our relationships

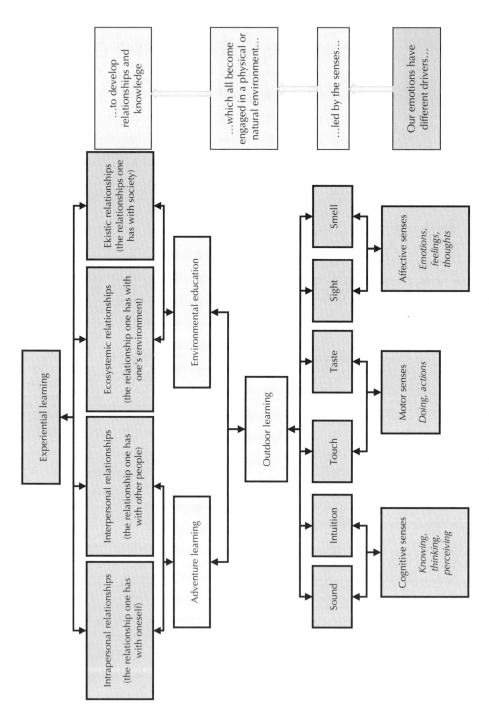

Figure 2 Our emotive drivers of learning

encompassing our environment. Adventure, however, is distinguishable from environmental education in being physical and demanding, encouraging people to think through solutions in order to attain the progression of skills as well as to achieve personal development goals. Because it is physical and personal, there must also be the opportunity provided for people to absorb and reflect on the experience, as the learning cannot be memorised from another source, such as a book and traditional behaviourist teaching has little impact, we have to be able to try an activity for ourselves rather than having someone just talk through the motions of it. Adventure is a really broad term and to say we are *doing* adventure learning does not mean doing something dangerous or in the middle of nowhere, it simply means doing something different.

Uniting the West and the East

Adventure learning has applicability for people of all ages, interests, abilities, lifestyles, environments and occupations. Whatever their cultural, ethnic or environmental background and circumstances, people can learn through adventure, in other words from trying something new. All cultures have an associated philosophy derived from generations of discovery, experience, thinking and theory; both Eastern and Western philosophies are similar in that they concern themselves with human existence, but diverge on their principles and concepts.

Western philosophy looks to a scientific base, with positivist, rational, logical explanations; Western society concerns itself with finding and proving an absolute 'truth'. Life in the West tends to be focused on materialism and centralises the individual, with a clear linear view, based on the Christian philosophy that everything has a beginning and an end; people are driven by individual motives and the search for personal fulfilment. The Western mind-set is most clearly represented by Abraham Maslow (Maslow 1943) and is commonly represented as a pyramid (Figure 3).

Known as the pyramid (or hierarchy) of needs, Maslow (Maslow 1943) argues that there is an order to needs and we are motivated by each in turn; thus lower level needs (survival, security) must be satisfied before we can work on satisfying higher level (personal growth) needs. Maslow identified the lower level needs as 'deficit' needs (if the needs are not met, we are uncomfortable) and the higher level needs as 'growth' needs (we can never get enough of these and are constantly going to be motivated to meet them). If the conditions satisfying lower needs are removed, we regress down the pyramid to satisfy these needs again.

Eastern philosophy has a more subjectivist basis, where people exist as a part of a natural world that has no particular rules but simply *is*; Eastern society seeks to find 'balance', accepting that truth is given and need not be incontrovertibly proven. Life in the East is spiritual, where all events and entities are perceived as interconnected and life is a journey towards becoming part of that interconnectedness through self-knowledge and understanding. Any regularity in the world is the way people organise

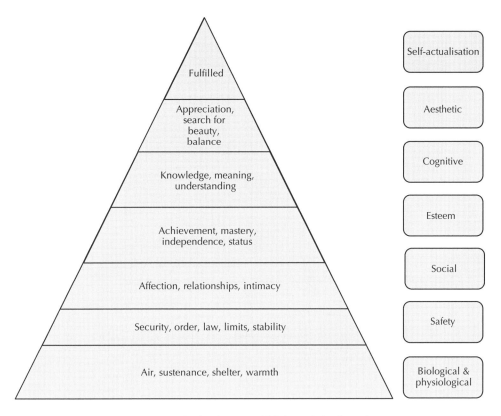

Figure 3 Maslow's pyramid (hierarchy) of needs

and understand their experience, not a proven truth; Eastern philosophy prescribes the nature of reality as being discovered through direct and unplanned experience. The Eastern mind-set is most clearly understood through the 'chakra' system (Figure 4).

The word 'chakra' is derived from a Sanskrit word meaning 'wheel'. A chakra can be thought of as an energy centre and there are seven major ones in the human body working in synchronicity and an imbalance in one will affect others. The chakras are essentially the body's invisible power source that connects your spiritual body to your physical one. Sometimes chakras can become blocked (because of stress, emotional or physical problems) so the energy system cannot flow freely, resulting in physical illness, discomfort or a sense of being mentally and emotionally out of balance. Like Maslow's pyramid, the chakras can be considered a hierarchy of support and control (Figure 5).

In the same way that Maslow's pyramid demonstrates a successive order of need to be satisfied in turn, the ladder of chakras shows the chain of spiritual or emotional needs that must each be met in turn before progressing to the next. Both philosophies see personal development as the path to 'completeness'; for the West the path is more tangible, with materialistic milestones, and for the East it is more ethereal, with emotional

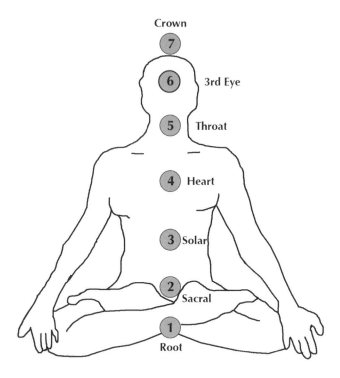

Figure 4 The 'chakra' system

waypoints. So, while the two concepts appear initially to bear no relation to one another, the defining characteristics of each step demonstrate the closeness of their relationship (Figure 6).

Welfare may be translated as 'heart function' as we continue to exist and need our heart to work for us. While Western thinking centres on the physical self and Eastern on the emotional, the body's welfare exists as a permanent balancing act between our emotional, physical and psychological state. Because our emotional, physical and psychological state are all inextricably intertwined, anything that affects one will inevitably have an impact upon another; an imbalance in one element, means another must react to compensate in order to try to maintain the body's equilibrium. The heart exerts a formidable control over the brain and thus the heart affects mental clarity, creativity, emotional balance and personal effectiveness. Elaborate circuitry enables the heart's 'brain' to act independently of the cranial brain – to learn, remember and even feel and sense. By being mindful of, and ensuring, our emotional, psychological and physical welfare, we can exist in equilibrium and control our wellbeing. Thus, Western and Eastern thinking can be considered two sides of the same coin, both striving for the same goal but considering different routes.

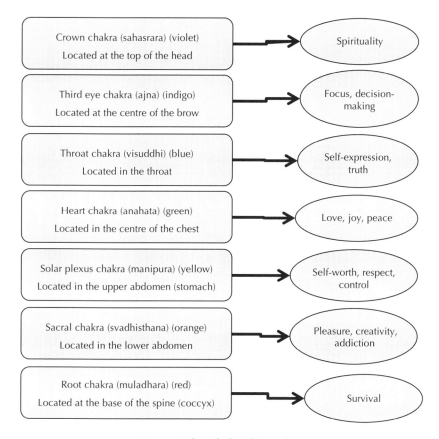

Figure 5 The 'chakra' hierarchy

Whether ascribing to Western or Eastern philosophy, knowing and understanding the attributes of each stage of the elemental hierarchy, we can begin to understand our drivers (motives) and thereby begin to take control of our lives and ourselves. This understanding is often referred to as emotional competency, which focuses on two elements:

1   Personal competence is the art of managing and understanding yourself, your goals, intentions, responses and behaviour (intrapersonal relations).
2   Social competence is the art of managing relationships, understanding others, their feelings and your influence and impact upon them (interpersonal relations).

The level of possession of both competencies determines the extent to which we build supportive networks around us; a low level of emotional competency indicates a poor social capacity where people tend to become isolated, with low motivation to develop positive relationships, thus gaining little personal fulfilment. To *have* motivation and to

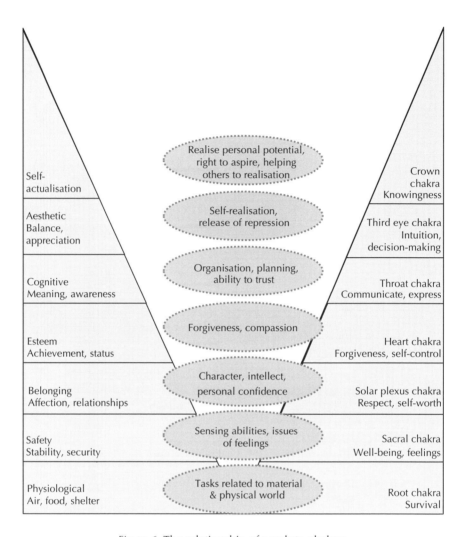

Figure 6 The relationship of needs to chakras

be motivated requires a motive, a stimulus for action (which may or may not be consciously recognised) and a decision to respond to that stimulus, leading to an action (Adair 1996). The implication of this is that to have motivation we must derive some reward, extrinsic or intrinsic, suggesting that motives (hence motivation) are attached to emotions. Physically, the mind and body are interlinked and, being parts of the same cybernetic system, have a close effect on one another. A person's perceptions, emotions, physiological responses and behaviour all occur simultaneously and are driven by the brain, over which the heart has formidable control, so it is possible to control our emotional self through understanding and thought. The heart is far more than a simple pump, but a highly complex, self-organised information-processing centre with its own functional 'brain' that communicates with and influences the cranial brain via the nervous system, hormonal system and other pathways. These influences profoundly affect brain function and most of the body's major organs, ultimately determining our quality of life. Thus, by understanding and controlling how we think, we can change our physiology, feelings or behaviour.

References

Adair, J. (1996) *Effective Motivation*. London: Pan Books.
Maslow, A. (1943) A theory of human motivation. *Psychological Review* 50: 370–396.

6 | Adventure learning and the school curriculum

Adventure learning can be built into almost any sphere of developmental work. Many workers engaged with youth justice programmes, youth work and 'alternative' curricula have taken the activity-based approach, seeing adventure learning as a route to individuals growing healthier emotionally, socially and spiritually through 'informal learning'. The emphasis is almost entirely on challenge and perceived risk, adrenalin experiences followed by supported transformative reflection, whereby learners re-evaluate their previously held beliefs that were based on assumptions derived from and understood through others and through past experiences. There is a school of thought that the outdoor experience should be left as an untainted entity, allowing participants to process the engagement and derive their own unique conclusions from it with little or no external interference from the instructor, other than to support reflection. The learning is assumed to happen naturally, with the individual at the centre of a triangle of life-affirming processes (Figure 7).

This triangular model is two-dimensional, assuming the learner has an innate biological capacity for self-reflection and avoids the extended outcome of taking a more holistic approach to learning, ignoring the possibility and the opportunity to use adventure (the outdoors) as a tool, a 'means to an end'. Children and young people have no choice but to spend a significant proportion of their time in formal learning (about 13% of their life between the ages of 5 and 18 years) because they are legally obliged to be in school. The subjects to be taught are pre-determined through the curriculum and, because they are effectively factories of knowledge, schools have to be efficient, focused in the delivery of that curriculum. This means that structures and systems have to be established so that the teacher can deliver to the mass of pupils and the pupils can gain some knowledge; there is an integral supposition that inevitably most pupils will learn *something*, although they probably cannot achieve their potential. Increasingly this process means that each step of the way is monitored and the learning product measured; that is, a volume approach with directly proportional reliance upon rote learning and examination regurgitation. This system takes the simplistic approach of segregating each

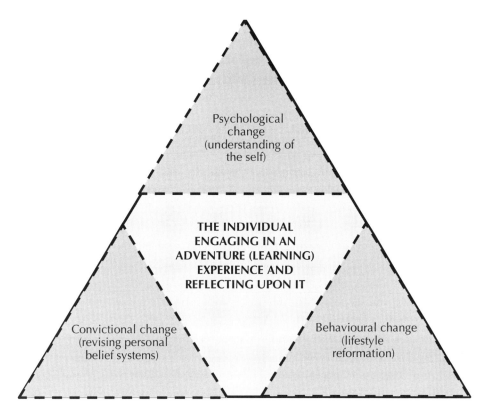

Figure 7 Reflective learning through adventure experiences

subject and teaching it as an isolated entity, with no correlation to another subject or connecting the subject learning into the reality of life (the silo method), in other words school learning does not take a holistic approach. Within the modern world, it is time for schools to move away from this blinkered approach and look to developing more inventive ways to teach children and young people. Life does not exist as a series of unique silos, but as a web of integrated and interacting entities, so children and young people should not be taught to manage it that way. Embedding adventure learning into a (school) curriculum involves curricular, cross-curricular and extra-curricular learning; in other words, adventure learning is holistic, not only teaching a topic in itself, but linking it with other subjects and developing knowledge and understanding beyond that which may lie in the curriculum. The logic behind embedding adventure is the core recognition that people learn in different ways and that when planned as carefully as indoor learning, outdoor learning has equal value to indoor learning. Learning outside the classroom capitalises on and develops different learning styles; experiencing something, as opposed to hearing or reading about it, helps to improve children's and young people's recall and reflective skills, as they can relive the event in their heads. Adventure learning is enhanced by the environment within which it occurs, by the range of adaptable natural resources; fostering the integration of indoor and outdoor experiences brings the educator, be that a teacher or outdoor professional, to consider the experience rather than the use of resources, which allows children and young people to be in control of their own learning.

Ofsted, the United Kingdom's inspection and regulatory body for care, education and skills, views adventure learning as critical to the delivery of a broad and balanced curriculum. School inspections consider the quality and extent of outdoor learning opportunities, whether they are continuous and progressive, their impact on learners, whether they link experience and learning inside and outside the classroom. The clear conclusion from inspection reports is that the greater the level of planning and integration of adventure and classroom learning, the higher the quality and the better the outcomes for learners.

There is an old adage called 'the six Ps': *prior preparation and planning prevents poor performance*. All that it takes for a lesson to move from a passive, indistinguishable endurance, to an active, memorable engagement, is *planning*. All teachers have to do lesson plans, adventure learning simply entails looking to take the learning in a new direction; teachers can team up to plan cross-curricular lessons and so share the burden of innovation. The result is a multi-dimensional, multi-layered programme to address curriculum topics, social education and personal development. The process of reflection and change need not be a protracted, separate component, but an integral element of the activity: a positive remark, a personal perspective, a non-judgmental comment. The reflective process should appear in the activity as unobtrusively as possible, and as a natural part of the overall experience, not a contrived interruption that breaks the flow.

The same approach applies to the off-site experiences that so many schools offer. It seems to have become accepted that schools will offer annual residential experiences at professional outdoor centres, in order to offer a more 'meaningful' outdoor experience. The increasing focus on the technical and safety aspects of experiences seems to have brought about a fear of taking the classroom outside and a belief that expensive opportunities for the few make the experience more powerful and safer. However, too often, these experiences are limited, even marred, by the activity being the focus, with instructors concerned with whether the participant can hold the paddle correctly, tie the figure of eight or understand the compass; the 'supported reflection' then becomes a final, wind-down 'add-on' at the end of the session. When responsibility for the adventure learning session is delegated outside the learning organisation, when it is handed to a professional organisation with a menu of pre-determined activities, teachers can see it as a break from their normal routine and disengage from it. Communication and planning between school staff and instructors would allow a diverse and multi-dimensional programme to deliver a range of subject learning and development opportunities. However, it has to be questioned whether occasional 'big' experiences maximise their potential; many schools seem to have lost sight of the fact that the more meaningful experiences of learning take the outdoors as a natural tool and that lessons can be built into the school grounds, local parks or other open spaces.

The perception of adventure learning is often restricted to an aspect of physical education, with perhaps a bit of social education and personal development attached. Physical education is wedded to adventure learning through the process of actively engaging in an activity, but there the similarity ends; it is an integral part of the school curriculum, but within the silo method is designed towards team sport and competition. Nationally there is recognition that young women particularly are unlikely to continue with physical activity into adulthood, which can have serious and damaging health and lifestyle consequences as they get older. Not only does regular activity improve physical and mental health, but also women play a strong influencing role within their own families and are more likely to be a positive role model to their children than highly publicised sporting events or media profiles. Not restricting the curriculum to traditional methodologies and by using physical activity as a consequence rather than the focus, participants develop a different perception and forget they are 'exercising'.

The National Curriculum of the United Kingdom recognises that different outdoor learning experiences offer additional opportunities for personal and learning skills development in other areas such as communication, problem solving, information technology, working with others and thinking skills. The National Curriculum was introduced into England, Wales and Northern Ireland as a nationwide mandatory programme of teaching for primary and secondary state schools following the Education Reform Act 1988. Its purpose was to standardise the teaching programme in order to enable assessment and thus the compilation of league tables. However, the National Curriculum applies to state schools only, independent and private schools may set their own curriculum and while academy schools are state funded, they are granted significant autonomy in deviating from the National Curriculum. As increasing numbers of schools move away from state to academy status, they become increasingly liberated to develop innovative and laterally conceived frameworks of learning. Learning in the outdoors can make significant contributions to literacy, numeracy, health and wellbeing. In literacy, there are opportunities to use different texts: the spoken word, charts, maps, timetables and instructions. In numeracy, there are opportunities to measure angles and calculate bearings and journey times. In health and well-being, there are opportunities to become physically active in alternative ways and to improve emotional wellbeing and mental health. Therefore, adventure learning offers many opportunities for learners to deepen and contextualise their understanding within curriculum areas, and for linking learning across the curriculum in different contexts and at all levels. A large volume of evidence has built up that clearly demonstrates the benefits for children and young people of acquiring their learning and personal development outside the classroom; this can be summarised as:

- Tackling social mobility, giving children and young people new and exciting experiences that inspire them and motivate them to maximise their potential. Learning in the school grounds, the local area, visiting sites further afield and residential experiences all stimulate interest, curiosity and a passion for 'doing', which broaden horizons and enable children and young people to develop new skills and build relationships. They make young people more engaged with learning and therefore more likely to do well.

- Addressing educational inequality, motivating those who do not thrive in the traditional classroom environment, for example those from disadvantaged backgrounds or with additional educational needs. Regular adventure learning experiences increase self-esteem and engage learners in their education, both inside and outside the classroom.

- Supporting improved standards inside the classroom by improving understanding and context, raising attainment, reducing truancy and improving discipline.

Providing a progressive range of sustainable adventure learning experiences may mean maximising the use of the local area, making repeat visits at different levels to add depth to the experiences, building on and enhancing the learning. From a learner's point of view, each visit, including ones to the same place, will offer a different perspective, enriching the curriculum and providing greater coherence. Effective planning can make the same activity in the same location a completely new and meaningful experience, seamlessly entwining progressive adventure learning with indoor learning. As an embedded part of the holistic (overall) learning experience, the learning begins to happen naturally. The school grounds are generally the first, natural and non-threatening step in taking learning outside. This offers a means of building confidence for teachers and helps to avoid issues of consent and allay safety concerns. The learning context will be changed with the variable context of the group, for example, a rural school may be well acquainted with their 'green' surroundings and adventure learning may be predicated on an urban environment, whereas an inner city school may head to the countryside. While breadth and depth of learning should not be linked to distance from the establishment, environment can be a powerful tool. Learning and meaning in adventure learning occur through 'real life', 'hands-on' activities, which is the combination of what, how and where we learn.

7 Learning and developing

Learning is not simply something achieved by children over years spent in a classroom, but is a lifelong process of growing and developing through experience and understanding. People learn differently for a number of reasons, for example age, level of understanding, motivation or mood. There is an argument that adults and children learn differently because of the difference in life experience and developed thinking (Knowles 1990). While this may be true, there are equally debates as to whether learning and development are related to growing up, to social interaction or to a combination of both. However we may understand the learning process, learning itself can take many forms, the most common of which are formal learning, informal learning and experiential learning.

Formal learning is traditionally classroom learning, a behaviourist process where the learner is inactive, receiving volumes of historically defined data deposited by the teacher through a *product curriculum* driven by rote learning. The objective is to achieve good examination results, with an inherent assumption that the learner has no ability or inclination to think for themselves, has no ownership of the learning and by definition places little value on the learning beyond delivering the demanded product of examination results. A product curriculum is exactly what it says: a generic route to planned outcomes without consideration of the learner, mapped out in a pre-determined technical exercise independently of those upon whom it will be delivered (and often those who will be delivering it). There is no acknowledgement or expectation of any outcomes beyond those defined by the curriculum creators; the product curriculum assumes a 'one size fits all' model, where success is denoted by the ability of the individual to recite learned facts, irrespective of their understanding of them. Listening, memory and the capacity to repeat on demand are the required core skills.

Informal learning is personal development and social education, with a *process curriculum* at the core, advocating working *with*, as opposed to *upon*. Informal learning is more conversationally based than delivered, using conversation to engage and support people in processing their experiences, encouraging their consideration of options, responses and consequences. There is an assumption that the learner grows through understanding. The learner is assumed to be endowed with the capacity and will to appreciate the learning, being able to direct and control it, thereby valuing it and seeking to find opportunities to apply it. A process curriculum presupposes that the individual can think and feel, that they can 'process' given facts and understand, even question, them. The model sees each learner as a unique individual, who can learn through socialised discussion, who can reason logically and, critically, who can draw their own conclusions. The curriculum delivers *opportunities* for learning, so cognitive skills and the ability to reason and explain are the required core skills.

Just as the name implies, experiential learning arises through *lived experience*, progression achieved through personal engagement with something, rather than through received teaching, in an iterative cycle of experience, reflection and action, often referred to as the 'plan, do, review' cycle. Crucially, the learning process is directed by the learner and their engagement, achieved through reflection on action; it is this reflective process that moves the experience into experiential learning. Adventure learning is experiential but combines both formal and informal learning. The instructor must formally teach skills and explain how to perform activities, but equally talks to people, helping them to realise their skill progression and personal development, supporting them to see what concepts are emerging and enabling them to realise what they are learning. Personal ability combines with understanding of the self and social reflected understanding to determine the way in which the individual views the experience and derives learning from it, as they respond to the situation and the environment.

Learning is also derived intentionally, as a deliberate act, or unintentionally, as a result simply of living in the moment of the experience or situation. People interpret their experiences in relation to what they have experienced in the past (their *lived* experience), and in relation to the environment in which the experience takes place and the people with whom they share the experience (their *reflected* experience), a concept known as situated learning (Lave and Wenger 1991). Human evolution has determined that every experience will be translated into an act of learning, even unconsciously. To maximise the move from this accidental learning, the simple learning of skill acquisition from doing the activity into deliberate learning and meaningful life skills, the learner has to be supported to understand and contextualise the experience and to realise its applicability and transferability to other areas of their life. The most effective learning comes from the conscious act of absorption, understanding and deliberate or unconscious future application. Teaching is not the same as learning, for what is taught is not always what is learned. Equally, learning may be temporary, retained only as long as the knowledge is required or it may be more ingrained for repeated future use. Temporary learning has little or no meaning to the learner, such as facts learned by rote for an examination; it bears almost no relation to the learner's 'everyday' life. On the other hand, long-term or permanent learning is understood as knowledge, having meaning and use beyond the context in which it was learned. Passive learning tends towards the former, striving to a defined measurable output; active learning on the other hand tends towards the latter as learners embrace knowledge more readily and feel rewarded (fulfilled) when they can reuse it successfully.

References

Knowles, M. S. (1990) *The Adult Learner: A Neglected Species*. Houston, TX: Gulf Publishing Company.

Lave, J. and Wenger. E. (1991) *Situated Learning: Legitimate Peripheral Participation*. Cambridge: Cambridge University Press.

8 The team and its leadership

In a structured environment, learning will be delivered by a team. A team has to be led and managed, hence there is a need for a designated team leader; yet in the adventure learning context, the members of the team also have duties of leadership and management, as they have to manage the learner experience, the session and the group.

A team is made up of a whole range of cultural backgrounds, ages, knowledge, skills and personalities, as well as an amalgam of relationships and interactions between its members. Human beings are social creatures by nature, but that in itself is insufficient to ensure an automatically successful team. The foundation of the nature of the relationship is the team *culture*, the shared meanings of the group that have developed through their combined values, beliefs and norms of behaviour. Team culture evolves as the team members learn about one another and find a way of working together. The individual members (the workers) find their place within the team, assuming a particular role that suits their character (Belbin 1993). Culture, though, does not develop entirely organically through the workers; it can be created, directed and managed by the leader as they work to mould performance. Culture represents constraints and performance expectations, therefore the power relationships that exist between the tiers of the organisation hierarchy. The leader has a responsibility to ensure that adventure learning sessions are adequately prepared, run on time, are appropriately equipped and that the workers are present as required to deliver the learning. However, the leader also has an emotional responsibility towards their workers, ensuring their morale is maintained, motivating them, encouraging them and keeping them engaged within the team and with the work. Accountability for performance and quality ultimately rests with the leader, but so too do technical skills, role modelling, group process management, judgement and overall decision making.

Newcomers into a team exist initially on the fringe until they learn about accepted behaviour and norms, gaining in familiarity and becoming increasingly accepted by existing members as they become integrated into the fold, a process known as legitimate peripheral participation (Lave and Wenger 1991). However, culture is evolutionary. For teams to thrive, culture must be allowed to change over time; team composition (tenure, age, membership) changes as members leave and others arrive, thinking and attitudes change, or else the team can become 'stuck' and ineffective, out of step with other teams in the organisation or unable to remain productive. Leadership is an emotional relationship as much as a functional one, an association between those who wish to lead and those who choose to be led. From the worker's perspective, their approach to their role is defined by the team culture and the way that they feel about their colleagues, their team leader and the tasks they are required and expected to perform. It is a complex mix of emotional, psychological and material rewards that make this up. Workers have the same responsibility to develop a positive relationship with each of their work colleagues as they do with their team leader. The way people work together dictates how far they can learn together and from each other, which ultimately benefits the team as a whole. However, there is a danger, particularly in small teams, that the unit becomes stable and too comfortable, a homogenous entity that loses the capacity to perform, which sits with allowing the team culture to evolve. Developing existing staff and recruiting new staff brings new knowledge into the team, challenges existing ways and provides opportunities for team learning. Leaders must challenge and question, as well as inspire and support. The leader can challenge the culture of the team, but so can newcomers. The leader deliberately sets out to question and to ensure effectiveness by ensuring the team culture is conducive to performance. Newcomers challenge through simply thinking differently and questioning why the culture is the way it is, why a particular practice exists. A measure of challenge is constructive to ensure active engagement and optimal performance.

A leader is not dictatorial or always directive, but must capture the heart and mind of the individual worker, making them *want to follow*, rather than *having to obey*. Successful leaders concern themselves as much with the people they lead, their motivation and development, as with the operating systems and hierarchical structures. The greatest synergy may be said to exist within a structure that allows interdependence of the worker and the environment in which they operate, with the workers and their leader collaborating closely, co-ordinating behaviour and activity to unite as a whole. Within such a framework, the fate of the worker is associated with the fate of the team and such interdependency is what makes for the most effective performance; when the goals of the worker are synonymous with those of the team, everyone works to maximise performance. There is a lot of literature that explores the nature of teams and groups, and how these may be defined. However, the way in which a group defines itself and whether it defines itself as a team or not is less critical than whether it has a clear purpose, whether it has goals and whether it adds real value to the organisation to which it belongs. The designation does, however, offer an important contribution to unit identity. If the members identify themselves as a single unit, they share objectives and fate, working for collective survival and to the success of the whole; if the members identify themselves as individuals within a disparate collective, their interest is in self-preservation, rather than unit success. The leader plays a crucial role in developing the culture such that the workers see themselves as a part of a bigger entity and not isolated individuals.

Work forms a large part of life for most individuals and this is the arena in which people tend to seek to achieve the highest recognition they can. All workers have their own unique objectives for performing, their motives to work, hence the basis of their *motivation*; when these objectives align with those proposed by the leader, shared objectives are created. Motivation derives from personal fulfilment and the satisfaction of needs (Maslow 1943). However, satisfaction of need and motivation are not always synonymous as people also act through free will, which by definition cannot be manipulated. Historically, pay (extrinsic reward) was the prime form of reward, with little or no regard for whether a worker found emotional or psychological fulfilment. The role of the leader was to elicit absolute compliance without question. In modern society, pay is no longer an adequate motivating factor, there has to be intrinsic, as well as extrinsic, reward (emotional and psychological fulfilment).

The unique objectives of individuals define their psychological needs and denote their drive to follow a particular life path: a profession or a vocation. It is likely that within a team working within the same field, all will have similar drives, although each will experience varying degrees of the different drivers (Herzberg *et al.* 2008). It is the leader's role to manage these into a symbiotic and effective model of team working. Being a leader can be a lonely role; the leadership function demands personal strength and awareness, the vision, self-confidence and stamina to argue for what is right for the team or the organisation, not necessarily for what is popular. The leader has also to have the confidence to delegate, having trust in others to do what they should, as they should and when they should. Without this, the leader does not show the competence and inspiration that workers seek when they are deciding whether to engage in the relationship. Workers seek mutual respect with their leader and want them to demonstrate confidence and credibility; inspiring a shared vision of performance in which all can share and to which all can contribute.

In the same way, the participants to the adventure learning experience seek leadership from the adventure learning instructor, who becomes a leader in their own right 'in the field'. The instructor exists in a 'community' alongside adventure participants, while engaging in an activity, becoming a situated *leader* but that position is negated in the context of their existence within the wider team, where they must defer to the designated leader. The appointed leader must be recognised as such and retain their authority and control, or else the complex and fragile affiliation between leader and worker can break down. Such shared leadership is known as 'distributed leadership' (Harris and Spillane 2008) and may be considered necessary for teams involved in activities such as adventure learning to function, but strong trust relationships are essential, for permitting too great a devolution of power down to the workers risks workers becoming disengaged from the team, resulting in outcomes failure. To succeed, however, part of the development of the individual worker must consist of fostering necessary leadership capacity, or else the system can fail. Within a professional partnership, there have to be clear roles and accountability; communication in a functioning partnership fosters positive working, openness and honesty. Otherwise, it becomes too easy for a partner to withdraw; learners can only derive the most from their engagement if they know that all elements of the partnership are interlinked and that all are supportive of them, watching them, helping them and experiencing the session alongside them.

References

Belbin, R. M. (1993) *Team Roles at Work*. Oxford: Butterworth Heinemann.

Harris, A. and Spillane, J. (2008) Distributed leadership through the looking glass. *Management in Education* 22(1): 31–34.

Herzberg, F., Mausner, B. and Snyderman, B. B. (2008) *The Motivation to Work*. New Brunswick, NJ: Transaction Publishers.

Lave, J. and Wenger. E. (1991) *Situated Learning: Legitimate Peripheral Participation*. Cambridge: Cambridge University Press.

Maslow, A. (1943) A theory of human motivation. *Psychological Review* 50: 370–396.

9 The adventure learning instructor

The instructor plays a critical role in the success of an adventure learning session. The participants take their direction from them, feed off their energy and build their view of the session from the instructor's behaviour, which defines the extent to which they engage and how much they interact. The adventure learning instructor is like an orchestral conductor, establishing the limits, expectations and guidelines for the experience. Effective practice rests on values; the adventure learning instructor has to develop a personal ethical base, developing their own framework of values. That is not to say adventure learning instructors have to set themselves apart from others, but should have considered responses to a range of issues and situations because of the nature of their work and the way that adventure learning operates.

The instructor represents 'adventure' as a concept and becomes the activity personified, entrusted by the participant with their personal and psychological safety; this can bring the participant, particularly if they are young and vulnerable, to see emotional and personal aspects to their interactions with the instructor and the perception of something other than a professional relationship can emerge. The adventure learning instructor may potentially be in a situation alone with a group and must know (and respect) the limits of their relationship. The instructor has a professional duty of care, and both adventure learning instructor and participant need to understand the limits of their relationship and what language, behaviour and interaction is acceptable. The instructor may be the only positive role model in the life of a young, vulnerable or emotionally immature participant. Developing a relationship involves trust, honesty, respect and revealing thoughts and feelings; building a relationship means an emotional commitment. Participants can feel particularly close to an adventure learning instructor, as they share a seemingly hazardous activity or a remote location, resulting in emotional safety that does not depend upon threat and intimidation. In that situation, it is easy for the participant to forget the instructor is a professional, an empathic mentor, not 'one of the gang'. Equally, the adventure learning instructor has to be mindful of their working role; they must maintain authority, credibility and adopt the highest standard of ethical behaviour. The nature of their work brings adventure learning instructors to be *like* friends, but with defined boundaries to the relationship and with distinct differences. To be a friend is to be open and empathic, but instructors are not 'friends' because the young people are not a part of their everyday (social) life. Participants seek advice and guidance from a trusted instructor, often telling them things they would not tell their family or friends; these revelations can often be sensitive and highly personal, the instructor must be clear what is acceptable to be told, when revelations may be kept confidential and when they must be passed elsewhere. In all instances, instructors must be open and honest with participants about how they will treat revelations and never be drawn into apparent collusion or be seen to condone inappropriate behaviour.

On a practical level, the instructor has operational responsibilities beyond the control of their leader. The instructor has to supervise the group appropriately, a responsibility that begins at the start of the encounter, which is not necessarily at the adventure venue, but on the journey to reach the venue or perhaps even before. The instructor must be aware at all times of the environment so that they can ensure the safety of members while managing the externalities of distractive landscape and wildlife. The group members will have a particular dynamic, with needs and interactions that must be managed appropriately. At the same time, the instructor has a responsibility in respect of protecting the environment, making sure that there is no litter or damage and that no harm befalls wildlife.

10 | The adventure participant

The principal focus at first contact is to engage participants in the adventure learning session, to draw them out of themselves because leading participants is a process of influence and encouragement. Very quickly, at the start of the engagement, the adventure learning instructor has a lot to do; they have to evaluate the mood, abilities, focus and interactions of the group, and simultaneously there are routine administrative tasks, such as checking consent forms, finding out if any participants have particular conditions of which the instructor should be aware (asthma, diabetes, heart conditions, mobility issues) and issuing any equipment. At the same time the participants will be excited or anxious, wanting to know what is in store for them, where they can change, where the toilets are, where they can get a drink, and so on; they will be asking questions, chattering, wanting to explore. The first few minutes of an adventure learning session are frenetic and a lot has to be accomplished; the instructor has to be prepared, organised and not disengage the participants by being snappy or ignoring them, while getting necessary tasks done so that they can deliver a safe and enjoyable session.

Adventurous activities can engage and stimulate the most recalcitrant young person by providing adrenalin 'rushes' akin to those of less socially acceptable activities; the aim of adventure is to capture the imagination and harness energy. The informal learning principle of working *with* rather than *on* people allies with the adventure concept of challenge by choice: participants *impelled* not *compelled* to participate, able to withdraw or decline participation if they so wish. This gives participants ownership over the engagement, empowering them to make an informed choice. The decision to engage is embedded in motivation; for motivation to exist, participants have to believe in themselves and their ability to achieve, and the associated learning from an adventure encounter has to have meaning to them personally in a context beyond that of the immediate learning situation. Yet challenge by choice has itself to be managed by the adventure learning instructor. The decision to decline participation has to be questioned, the instructor has to explore why the person is not participating. Quite often, the reason is simple nerves, not wanting to be seen to fail or 'in group' relationships are not positive.

The instructor has to encourage participation, gentle persuasion can be powerful and realising 'having a go' does not mean immediate expected aptitude is often enough. An instructor should never be forceful and demand participation, but equally must be persistent and persuasive.

First impressions are really important, so the initial introduction (briefing) to the activity is fundamental in building anticipation and preparing participants for what is to come. The challenge for the instructor is to create the sense of challenge and to inspire participants to want to take part fully and achieve the set challenge, be that individually or as a group. As the session proceeds, the participants will hit difficulties and may not achieve the goal the first time, perhaps not even the second, third or fourth time; the point is that they should be inspired to want to carry on and keep trying. The instructor supports this by *appreciative facilitation*, which essentially means focussing on what the individual or group get right, not what is going wrong. The participants will be spending enough time getting frustrated at themselves and will be looking at what is *not* working, the art of the adventure learning instructor is to re-focus their minds on the positives, what is working well and where they are succeeding. This maintains the motivation to persevere when the adventure challenge becomes difficult. Adventure has an inherent perception of risk and danger and the challenge should stretch the participants, so for maximum outcome, the adventure learning instructor must balance (perceived) risk with competence (see Figure 8); the higher the level of risk at low competency, the less success can be achieved; the greater the degree of competency, the less risk is apparent and the achievements become more rewarding.

Figure 8 highlights how the interaction of competence and (perceived) level of risk bring about the quality of the experience. As the individual moves from initial experience (low risk, low competence) to self-directed learning (high risk, high competence), they become less reliant on the instructor and the potential rewards are that much greater. There is a point at which the participant engagement matches the instructor input and learning is maximised. It could be said that Figure 8 represents also the interaction of the individual with their environment, as competence is an individual concept concerning personal capacity, mood and skill and risk is an environmental concept concerning the environment, the challenge and the complexity of the challenge.

Rarely does a participant engage in adventure learning alone, more often engagement is in the context of a group. Groups evolve through a developmental process to develop a dynamic (Tuckman, 1965). There is a strong argument that people will learn through interaction (Bandura 1977), as people watch one another, mimic one another and (sub)consciously develop their way of being. The development of this culture is the basis of collective cohesion that defines the way that the participants face the activity (and the instructor); it can be positive and lead to success or it can become misdirected and need subsequent refocus. Participants are individuals, each with their own character, narrative and emotions; yet they are going to arrive as a part of a group. The instructor has to develop an ability to treat the participants equally, making a rapid assessment of their

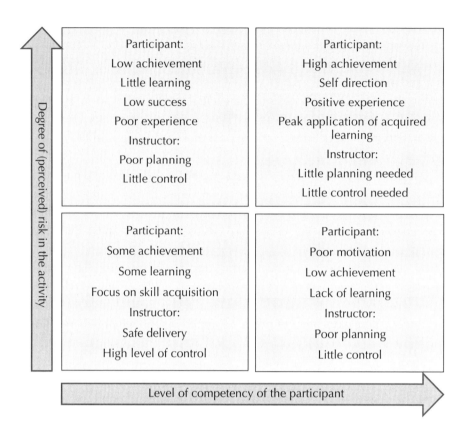

Figure 8 Learning through balancing risk with competence

abilities, but without stereotyping them unfairly. Gender, cognitive ability, physical ability, medical conditions, past adventure experience, culture and ethnicity can all affect the interaction of the participants with each other, as well as the leader. At all times the leader has to be aware of their language and body language, and the effect these can have on the group.

Reference

Bandura, A. (1977) *Social Learning Theory*. Englewood Cliffs, NJ: Prentice Hall.

11 Risk assessment

An adventure can be defined as an exciting or unusual experience that is bold, involves a certain amount of risk and has an uncertain outcome. A risk means potentially losing, against potentially gaining, something of value; it can also be defined as intentionally undertaking something with an uncertain outcome. The risk in question can be physical, psychological or emotional; by their very nature, adventurous activities appear to have the potential for physical danger but they can also hold psychological and emotional danger as people work together and reveal aspects of their personality and ability.

Everyone has a certain *risk perception*, a level of subjective judgment about the severity of the undertaking and its possible outcomes, which is different for everyone. Everything in life carries some measure of risk, but some things are riskier than others are. Adventurous activities create psychological arousal, which can be interpreted as negative (fear) or positive (flow). Fear is an inhibitor, preventing logical thought and stifling progression; it can be triggered by the thought or expectation of the activity, rather than the activity itself. Flow is the opposite; it is a stimulant that brings clarity and psychological reward. Performance increases with psychological arousal, but only up to a point; when levels of arousal become too high, performance decreases. The management of risk, therefore, is a fine balance between the two.

Whether it is physical, psychological or emotional, risk is a critical ingredient of learning by doing (experiential learning). By placing participants in the outdoors, they are placed into a much less controlled (and controllable) environment than exists in a more traditional learning environment. This brings with it fear of injury and litigation. While not being able to alleviate all risk from activities, much of what is delivered in adventure learning centres is *perceived*, rather than *real*, risk: an emotional reaction where the notion of risk is determined by life experience and current circumstance, engaging the senses in such a way that the participant is focused and engaged, a result of careful instructor planning that places participants in unfamiliar environments and situations, rather than in the path of actual, physical hazard.

The potential for physical harm cannot, however, be ignored, and cost-effectiveness cannot be allowed to compromise safety. In Britain, the principal mechanism of quality assurance within the adventure field is national regulation, a framework for protecting participants from harm that encompasses individual adventure learning instructors and their practice, although this is currently under review.

The deaths of two girls in Soham in 2002 highlighted the lack of systematic control over the employment of adults associated with young people. Any adventure learning instructor applying for a paid or voluntary position that involves working with young people or vulnerable adults has been required since 2002 to apply for either a standard or an enhanced check that highlights any previous warnings or convictions. Equally, previous practice of adventure regulation reliant upon common sense and good practice has been rigorously strengthened.

Despite five participants and an instructor dying in Scotland in the 'Cairngorm disaster' of 1971, it was not until 1993 that reform appeared, when four participants died in a kayak incident while participating in an adventure programme in Lyme Bay. The launch of the Adventure Activities Licensing Scheme (AALS) in 1996, making (renewable) licences and regular external inspections (similar to the principles of Ofsted) compulsory for those organisations that charge for the delivery of adventure services to participants aged less than 18 years. Many in the industry welcomed regulation, but equally many argued that much of the 'thrill' had been removed by organisations receding from the wilderness to the safety of their own grounds and seeking higher levels of control. Schools and voluntary organisations remain exempt from licensing when undertaking delivery themselves in respect of their own participants. Such regulation is essential so that participants (and, where relevant, their parents and carers) can have confidence in standards but some see this as purely a reduction in risk, lowering potential learning opportunities.

Licensing requires that adventure instructors should hold National Governing Body (NGB) qualifications and remain active and up-to-date in their elected activities. Similarly, adventure organisations must demonstrate a robust framework of delivery, monitoring and safety. However, licensing can only assure adherence to safety guidelines and good management practice at the point of inspection; it is no measure of quality of delivery. Ultimately, the inspector, although experienced and qualified in the field, makes a judgement as to competence of the provider and their compliance with law. In reality, there are very few litigation claims and even fewer successes.

Risk assessing and emergency planning are a two-stage process in adventure learning. The team, under the direction of the leader, can draw up a set of generic risk assessments and safety processes for the conduct of activities. For example, the team can agree a 'no consent form, no activities' rule, or 'all karabiners are scrapped after 100 times of being used'. However, the instructor has to be imbued with a risk responsibility beyond this, the responsibility for operational delivery. On the day, the instructor has to be responsible for the running of the session, and even whether the session goes ahead. They are accountable for these decisions and must be able to justify them, but must equally be allowed the freedom to adapt and change as weather, conditions or group behaviour dictate. The responsibility placed upon organisations, leaders and workers for ensuring that activities are safe appears broad but given that the activities carry *perceived* rather than *real* risk, adopting an approach of common sense thinking will suffice. The process of risk assessment and management, whether the leader considering organisational and generic risks or the worker considering local (site-specific) risk should be proportionate, simple and reasonable, keeping the risk and associated control measures in perspective.

12 The adventure curriculum

Remember the adage of 'the six Ps': *prior preparation and planning prevents poor performance*? Anyone can head off to the hills for a walk or down a river in a canoe. This is not adventure; it may be *adventurous* but it is not a structured experience that leads to learning. Building the framework of a learning experience demands planning and preparation; understanding the theories that underpin the learning, the processes that come into play as people undergo the adventure experience and learn from it, are important in being able to plan a meaningful session that moves the activity from an experience to learning. The activity itself does not deliver learning, it is the way in which the educator communicates and draws out the learning. A taster kayak session of splashing and games teaches participants that getting wet is fun (or not, depending on how they feel about it), but building skills towards independent paddling teaches them that they are strong enough to set themselves goals and achieve them. It requires not just providing the experience but also re-living the stages of it, talking through what happened and why, exploring what worked and what went wrong. The processing of the experience can be more important in the long term than the experience itself.

A well-constructed, well-run adventure session is enlivening, motivating participants to want more and making them feel rewarded, both psychologically and emotionally satisfied. Well-constructed adventure programmes move people from their 'comfort zone', where they exist in equilibrium into their 'stretch zone', where learning potential is maximised as the senses become enlivened to stimulate focus and concentration. The states of learning existence may be represented as a series of concentric circles, with the person in the centre (Figure 9). Without challenge, a person remains within their comfort zone, calm, relaxed, even bored. New experiences cause disruption to the comfort zone, threatening the existing balance of life. As something new appears, the person enters their stretch zone, interested, curious and receptive to learn, senses become stimulated. However, if the disruption poses too much of a challenge, it becomes a threat and the person moves straight through their stretch zone into a state of panic, where senses become volatile and no learning occurs; there is too much for the brain to absorb and the senses freeze.

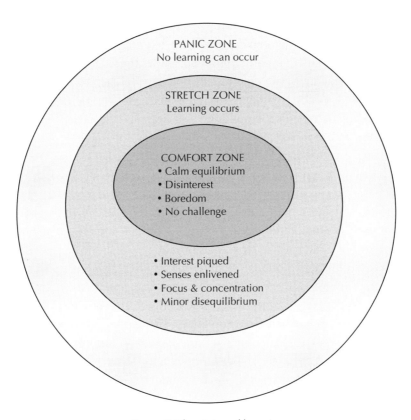

Figure 9 The states of learning

Learning is a fine balance of new opportunities and experiences; the receptivity of the learner is dependent upon the way the activity is presented, how the disruption to their comfort zone is introduced, how they are supported to engage with the activity and challenge offered and how they are empowered to learn from it. Poorly devised programmes either do not move people out of their comfort zone (high competency, low risk) or moves them straight into the panic zone (high risk, low competency), where they feel stressed, frightened and cannot think or act logically.

However, the idea of moving people into their stretch zone has its limitation. Instructors should not assume that they immediately could launch into activities that are highly challenging and raise stress levels on their first encounter with the group. They need to know something of the group members, their abilities and their responses. The model assumes that placing people into a challenging situation will bring them naturally to 'rise to the occasion', that they can overcome hesitancy to grow and learn from participation. It also assumes that the adventure learning instructor can competently assess and manage each individual's locus of comfort and, more critically, the point at which they will move from one sphere to the next. The model should be thought of more as a *process* that demonstrates the concept of adventure learning, not a framework by which instructors should build programmes based on learning through stress. Adventure programmes should challenge participants but allow them to advance beyond their comfort zone only when they are emotionally and psychologically ready to do so.

A framework of learning is designed to engineer a holistic process of meaningful learning and reflection towards the building of (transferable) knowledge; the skills used help to shape the way in which people view themselves, their level of self-esteem, their aspirations and the extent to which they then control their lives. Many participants in learning are young people, upon whom rests the welfare of the future. With no investment by society, the young will fail to attain the capacity to sustain the infrastructure and development of the nation and fail to develop the social awareness and moral fortitude that makes communities thrive as safe, supportive and engaging places to live. An important part of building that capacity is providing a platform for social education. People from different backgrounds, of different abilities and with different ways of thinking can be brought together with the common task and focus of the adventurous activity. By having contact with people outside of their usual group, participants come to new understanding and develop new alliances. Challenging activities can be used to address social and urban problems, such as gun and knife crime, gang culture or social hierarchies, by bringing groups together who do not normally engage or who would customarily engage on a negative basis. An important outcome for society of adventure is the development of self-awareness. This self-knowledge can be used to develop social justice programmes. As adventure produces learning and develops understanding among groups, it brings tolerance. With that come altruism and the impetus to develop fairness. As participants are brought to understand themselves, they realise their underlying propensities and the consequences of their actions, bringing them to a more enlightened existence. Similarly, health issues like obesity, asthma and diabetes can be addressed through activities outdoors, as participants experience different forms of exercise, learn their capacities and learn the extent and limitation of their engagement. Young people need to learn that they are individuals; they need to develop emotional stamina and a moral compass of their own.

The media is a pervasively omnipotent force and for decades, globally successful films have presented a (skewed) picture of reality that has become perceived as *the* way to be. People nowadays are confronted with constant visual and audio stimuli, being constantly entertained, informed or connected to others in some way. To young people with a developing but immature sense of self, these images are attractive and become the embodiment of how they should look and act and how their lives should play out. These images become the quintessence of conditional positive regard (Rogers 1959) and the representation of how young people imagine the world and their existence and interactions within it. The sense of inadequacy can stay with young people and influence them for the rest of their lives. People have become exposed to remote role models and less reliant on close physical contact for their personal development and social education. Television, films, magazines, the internet, computer games, mobile telephones: all are visual and have the ability to portray a vision of a perceived perfection to which young people feel they must strive, but provide nothing in the way of emotional or psychological guidance. Over generations, social and family life has changed, there is less structure and inter-generational influence in the raising of young children. This opens the door to pervasion by the media, which may manifest itself in an aggression of body image, stereotyping or through poor physical health or psychological development. Without the psychological literacy to question the images that traditionally came through cross-generational family support, people are left powerless and exposed to unrealistic role modelling. The informal learning aspect of adventure learning offers support, engaging participants to learn about themselves and how to manage their existence within the world. Processing their experiences, understanding how they react, recognising what triggers various responses and developing strategies for handling these enable people to seize control of their lives and to feel comfortable and confident in themselves, rather than being overly concerned with the perceptions of others.

Adventure learning does not have to take place in wild, remote or challenging terrain. The planning of an adventure learning experience can be progressive, incremented according to a range of 'zones' that begin with the familiar, perhaps the school grounds. The experience may then progress further afield to be more challenging physically and geographically, perhaps a local park. The experience and terrain can be built up in this way towards increasingly remote and challenging experiences, to a day on the moors, at an adventure centre and even on to a residential experience. Launching into too extreme an experience too soon can be damaging to the participant and threaten their immediate and long-term experience. The process can start in school, with subjects harnessed to adventure learning in a way that makes them fun, interesting and memorable, yet also increase the impact of the learning associated to make it more ingrained in the memory of the participant.

1   Reading and writing can be encouraged through bringing nature into the classroom or going outdoors. Simply being in a different environment can bring participants to listen differently or see the world differently.

2   History can be combined with geography and geology to show the natural world and the development of the landscape. Phenomenology refers to the attempt to see the world through the eyes of another, so being out in the natural environment enables participants to think more easily about how their ancestors may have understood the world, how they may have lived their lives and how they may have used the environment around them.

3   Biology and ecology are closely linked, allowing participants to witness and understand life cycles, the balance of nature, symbiosis and conflict. They can observe and measure changing life through the seasons, which can then be linked to history to understand how the seasons affected past lifestyles.

4   Physics and chemistry have important natural associations and emerge throughout the natural world in the forms of density, mass, gravity, balance and friction. Visual experimentation and demonstration are infinitely easier to understand when they can be related to the 'real world' and what participants see and experience every day than presented as a science lesson in a classroom.

5   Mathematics again has significant association to the natural world in terms of length, distance, height, weight, volume and angles. Like physics and chemistry, mathematics can be applied to 'real world' environments and gain impactful meaning.

Adventure learning, even when simply taken into the school grounds, harnesses curiosity and can be linked to underpinning theory and provide a real inspiration to learn. A cycle develops, whereby participants enjoy learning something and can see how they may apply it elsewhere, they then *want* to learn something more and so seek further learning; as their knowledge base grows, they develop cognitively, but in a structured adventure learning context they are with others, so learn from one another's experiences also. As the learning experiences continue, the participant becomes more comfortable with their knowledge and their learning, and less concerned with the way they appear to others. The result is a knowledgeable, balanced individual comfortable with themselves and understanding of the world in which they live.

Reference

Rogers, C. (1959) A theory of therapy, personality and interpersonal relationships as developed in the client-centered framework. In S. Koch (ed.), *Psychology: A Study of a Science, Vol. 3: Formulations of the Person and the Social Context*. New York: McGraw-Hill.

13 Delivery of adventure learning

Every experience carries a legacy into the future, so the adventure experience should exist within a framework to define, enable and measure capacity and development. Competent adventure programmes offer opportunities to develop knowledge and skills by making links between the experience, the emotions arising and the learning that influence personal values, decisions and actions, relative to the individual's past knowledge, experience and current life. Such programmes concern themselves far less with whether people can belay correctly or navigate accurately than with the overall experience, what learning can be derived from it and where or how this applies elsewhere, be that to a classroom topic or in life.

A popular view of the way an adventure session should be run is the 'adventure wave' (Schoel, Prouty and Radcliffe 1988). The idea is that the three components of any adventure activity should be the briefing (framing), the 'doing' (activity) and the debriefing (reflection). The briefing (Figure 10) is the initial trough, critical to set the scene and define expectations; this lead-up builds anticipation and prepares participants for what is to come. The crest (Figure 11) is the 'doing', the activity itself that forms the peak to the wave. Participants engage in the activity, having had their anticipation built up by the briefing and having emotionally, physically and psychologically had the opportunity to prepare themselves for what is to come. The final trough is the end debrief (Figure 12), the stillness of reflection after the wave has passed, leading to the learning as participants review the process of the activity and reflect upon their engagement, their emotions, their high points and what they would have changed. This is the point at which participants begin to relate the experience to their own personal lives, their past experiences and how they can apply new learning and understanding in their everyday lives.

The three elements come together to form a wave that define the process and essential elements of a successful adventure learning session (Figure 13). While the wave demonstrates the construction and content that should comprise a meaningful adventure learning session, it must be used with some degree of common sense and caution. It presents the adventure session as a single, unique entity, existing in isolation from

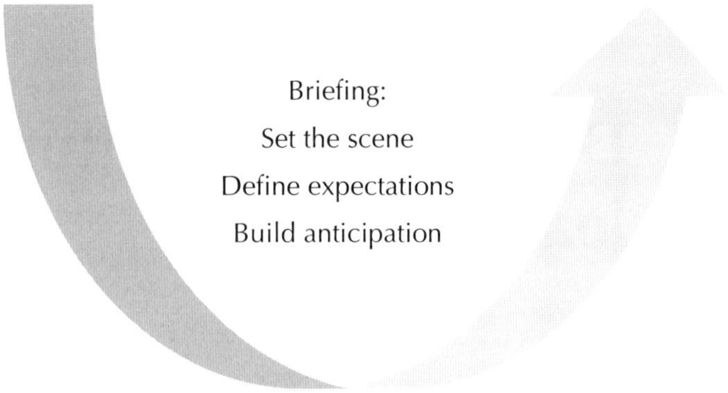

Briefing:

Set the scene

Define expectations

Build anticipation

Figure 10 The briefing phase

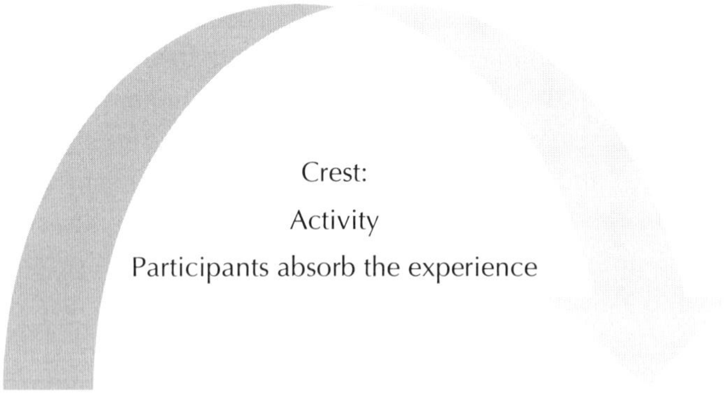

Crest:

Activity

Participants absorb the experience

Figure 11 The crest phase

Debrief:

Reflection

Review

Learning

Figure 12 The debriefing phase

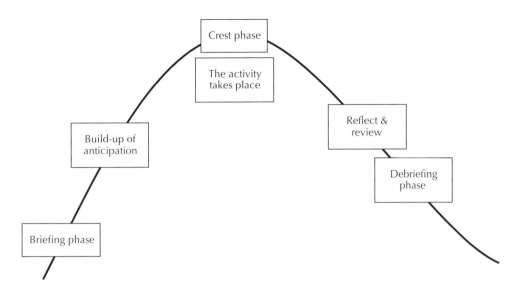

Figure 13 The phases form a wave

external influences, which it clearly is not. The wave depicts the elements that should make up a session, but the planning process has to embody links between any sessions that have gone before and any prior work that may have been done with the group elsewhere.

For example, the adventure programme could be part of a wider school curriculum and there could have been lessons delivered in preparation of the learning to be drawn from the adventure session(s). The foundation of a positive and effective learning experience is in its preparation, planning precisely how each element fits together, sequencing a progressive experience. Each group has different needs, so the plan must be flexible, with staged accomplishments to enable achievement if the core or full activity is not fully accomplished. During the activity itself, participants will have a wide spectrum of reactions, they may relax, learn to trust, try new approaches, ways of thinking or they may rebel against the activity and even the leader; every reaction should be anticipated and an acknowledgement prepared by the adventure learning instructor. Following the activity, the group moves into a time of reflection. This involves discussing all aspects of the activity, supporting understanding and learning. The debriefing session is what makes the activity a meaningful learning experience for the group.

Reference

Schoel, J., Prouty, D. and Radcliffe, P. (1988) *Islands of Healing: A Guide to Adventure Based Counseling*. Hamilton, MA: Project Adventure.

14 Outcomes of adventure learning

Adventure outcomes can be categorised as either formal (skill development, the achievement of recognised adventure qualifications, as contributory factors in achieving outcomes elsewhere, such as school examinations) or informal (gaining greater personal awareness, learning to work with others, developing leadership or team skills). The longer a programme or the more a person participates, the more sustainable are the outcomes. Very often, adventure learning programmes focus on *either* the formal *or* the informal aspect of learning but in reality, both occur simultaneously. The nature of adventurous activities is such that participants naturally will develop skills in the activity itself and it is but a short step to build accreditation into a programme or relate the skills to other fields. Equally, participants in adventurous activities have no choice but to work with others and make decisions, so informal learning is embedded in any programme. The skill of the instructor is to provide the supporting platform that helps people realise the learning and transfer it to other aspects of their life or to a wider programme.

Another way of looking at adventure learning outcomes is that they are tangible or intangible. Tangible outcomes are the formal accreditations and qualifications gained by the participants, whether this is in the form of adventure national governing body awards or in school (or other) certification. Intangible outcomes are the confidence, self-esteem, self-awareness, tolerance and social learning that come from engagement and achievement. The concept of tangible and intangible outcomes take us back to the notion of a product or a process curriculum, explored earlier. A product curriculum provides the 'hard' outcomes that are easily measured in terms of examination results and the recitation of facts or figures to a pre-determined standard and in a prescribed manner. A process curriculum provides the 'soft' outcomes that are unique to each individual and therefore difficult to measure or evidence; often these developmental changes can appear as the maturing of the individual and are not apparent for weeks, months or even years. However, both are critical for human development and learning.

Both formal and informal learning are necessary in life, as people need a common body of core skills and knowledge but also people need to learn from one another for society to evolve. In this way, people can become motivated and aware adults who can and will contribute positively to society and support thriving communities. Formal learning provides the knowledge and basis of qualifications and accreditations, the product outcomes on which tiers of professional life and community functioning rely. Not everyone can achieve the highest levels, and not all would want to, so therefore, by natural selection, society maintains a balance of individuals to make its every aspect function. Informal learning provides the process that enables people to learn about themselves and how to exist, how to live and work alongside others, to be motivated to contribute to society and their community. An objective of adventure learning and an outcome of informal learning is that people have a greater awareness of themselves, and people who understand themselves more fully, relate to others more effectively and have a greater propensity to foster such understanding in others.

15 | Theories associated with adventure learning

In this chapter we will look at:

- cognitive development;
- conditional positive regard;
- emotional intelligence;
- group dynamics;
- hierarchy of need;
- holistic learning;
- learning styles;
- operant conditioning;
- situated learning;
- social construction of reality;
- social development theory;
- social learning theory;
- theory of learning.

Cognitive development

Jean Piaget (1973) was the first psychologist to undertake a systematic study of cognitive development, describing his work as 'genetic epistemology' (the origins of thinking). Piaget defined learning as the sustained re-organisation of understanding in children as they learn and understand, redefining understanding through discovered discrepancies within the framework of their biological maturation and environmental experiences.

According to Piaget, children are born with a genetically inherited mental structure on which all subsequent learning and knowledge is based; learning is biologically progressive, as cognition evolves with age and experience and as the individual actively seeks to learn. The theory of cognitive development focuses on mental processes such as perceiving, remembering, believing and reasoning. Piaget identified four stages in the development of cognition:

1   *Sensory-motor stage* (birth to age two): during this stage, senses, reflexes and motor abilities develop rapidly, with intelligence first displayed as reflex movements become more refined, such as an infant reaching for a preferred toy. The infant understands the world through perceptions and objects they have directly experienced and learns to repeat actions to obtain the same results. Memory begins to develop and the infant begins to understand there is more to the world than themselves.

2   *Preoperational stage* (age two to seven): the child is not able to think logically but begins to learn language and understand the world through mental images and symbols. This is a period of curiosity but limited life experience places the child at the centre of their world, unable to relate well to others.

3   *Stage of concrete operations* (age seven to eleven): the child begins to develop cognitively, thinking about physical actions that were previously performed and increasing in understanding. Operations are labelled 'concrete' because they apply only to those objects that are physically present. The primary characteristic of concrete operational thought is its reversibility; for example, a child can trace their route to school and then follow it back home, or picture where they left a toy.

4   *Stage of formal operations* (age eleven to sixteen): Piaget's final stage coincides with adolescence, and marks the start of abstract thought and deductive reasoning. Thought becomes more flexible, rational and systematic as the individual conceives alternatives and understands different points of view. The adolescent develops a personal value system and a moral code.

Piaget's theory differs to others in the field because his focus is on the development of children, not on learners or learning generally, and because he proposes stages of development, rather than accumulated competency.

Jean Piaget

Born: 9 August 1896, Neuchâtel, Switzerland
Died: 16 September 1980, Geneva, Switzerland
Professional description: genetic epistemologist

Relating the theory to adventure learning

The theory allows instructors to plan sessions appropriately according to an understanding of the age-related ability to reason and remember. As adventure learning may be applied to any stage of an educative curriculum, the instructor has to be able to focus the learning accordingly. Piaget's theory posits the construction of learning as biologically progressive because he contended that cognition could only evolve with age, and that as a child matures, they seek to learn. Primary socialisation occurs as the cognitively immature brain of the child observes and mimics the actions and values of their predominant influencers. In the case of adventure learning, this means that the child will copy the instructor and thereby learn activity skills and the consequential transferable learning is limited by the restricted capacity of the child to relate activity skills to anything else in their life. Positive reinforcement will indicate to the child that safety is important and that there is a certain way to undertake an activity, but this will be the limit of their capacity. Activities need to be age-appropriate, demanding a suitable level of reasoning and calculation.

Conditional positive regard

Positive regard is the emotional fulfilment that humans naturally crave: love, affection, attention, nurturing. Rogers posited that human beings exist as active, creative, experiencing beings, who live in the present and subjectively respond to their current perceptions, relationships and encounters. Carl Rogers (1959) believed that nature provides the senses needed to survive; however, humans have evolved so that society now teaches them to overcome natural instincts with a developed but perverted sense of conditional worth. The preconscious mind dictates how people respond to the influences that surround them; people only feel emotional fulfilment when they are 'worthy' of it, rather than because they need or want it. Rogers termed this 'conditional positive regard'.

Rogers essentially agreed with the basis of Abraham Maslow's hierarchy of need, but extended the foundations to say that for a person to develop, they must exist in an environment of openness, self-disclosure, acceptance and empathy. Without these, relationships and emotional health will not develop. It was Rogers's belief that every person has the capacity and the propensity to achieve their goals, wishes and desires, to achieve ultimately self-actualisation (the latent motivating force in all people to maximise their potential). However, people inherently need positive regard to thrive and this conditioning is so powerful that people adapt, led not by organic actualisation, but by social expectations, which may or may not have their best interests at heart.

Over time, this 'conditioning' leads people to have personal conditional positive self-regard, people like themselves only if they meet the standards (they believe that) others apply, rather than when they are truly realising their potential. Since these standards are created without regard to individuals, more often than not individuals cannot meet them and therefore cannot maintain self-esteem. The ambition of adventure is to create *un*conditional positive regard, to teach participants to strive to their potential, they have value and their inherent worth does not depend upon social perceptions. The strength of Rogers's approach lies in part in his focus on relationships, which is the foundation of adventure. He advocated that no one could teach another person, only facilitate their learning. Rogers believed that individuals know what causes psychological imbalances in their lives and that, within their subconscious, they also know what they need to do to regain equilibrium.

Carl Rogers

Born: 8 January 1902, Oak Park, Illinois
Died: 4 February 1987, San Diego, California
Professional description: humanistic psychologist

Relating the theory to adventure learning

The process of engaging with adventurous activities brings individuals to understand themselves better. The challenge of adventure, overcoming fears and believing in oneself, coupled with the improved holistic understanding of learning concepts being presented in a new way, enables individuals to maximise their potential, to make the most of who they are and what they can do. Most importantly in respect of Rogers's theory, the individual learns to value themselves and take responsibility for their actions and life without reference to the perceptions of those around them (unconditional positive regard). As the individual takes ownership of their actions and choices, they become unfettered by the visions of perceived perfection imposed by environmental and social expectation.

While Rogers's approach can be argued as being egocentric, the group-oriented nature of adventure learning forces a social element to the development of personal knowledge and control, allowing the individual to redefine themselves in a social context, as opposed to a purely personal one. Thus, they learn to value themselves but also gain a sense of appreciation and understanding of others.

Emotional intelligence

Daniel Goleman (1995, 1998) argued that existing definitions of intelligence needed to be reworked because while intelligence quotient (IQ) was still important, intellect alone is no guarantee of proficiency in knowing or understanding personal emotions or responses, of oneself or others. Goleman claimed that a special kind of intelligence was necessary to process emotional information and use it effectively. He named this emotional intelligence, and devised an emotional quotient (EQ), which is the ability to identify, use, understand and manage emotions in a positive way to manage negativity such as stress, conflict and challenge, as well as to communicate and empathise. The five components of emotional intelligence are:

1   *Emotional self-awareness:* knowing your feelings and understanding how your moods affect others.

2   *Self-regulation:* being able to control or redirect your emotions, able to consider the consequences before acting and not acting on impulse.

3   *Motivation:* using emotional factors when working to achieve goals, enjoying the learning process and persevering when difficulties arise.

4   *Empathy:* sensing and understanding the emotions of others.

5   *Social skills:* managing relationships such that we can inspire others and achieve what we want from them.

Emotional intelligence is closely related to informal learning; the outcomes that arise from personal development and social education are the basis of developing emotional intelligence, which in turn provides the platform to reduce bullying, disciplinary problems and violence. Equally, the motivational aspect of emotional intelligence supports learning through stimulating curiosity and the associated feelings of emotional fulfilment. Emotional intelligence starts developing very early in life and its development will vary widely, depending on each child's environment. However, it can be fostered, and teachers must be able to support children in building their emotional literacy. Teachers should be ready to talk about feelings in the classroom, advocating that no emotion should be considered 'wrong', but that there are certain ways of expressing emotions or acting on them that are inappropriate and the discussions must be presented using age-appropriate language and contexts.

Daniel Goleman

Born: 7 March 1946, Stockton, California
Professional description: psychologist, author, science journalist

Relating the theory to adventure learning

Quite closely related to Rogers's theory, emotional intelligence provides the social extension that moves conditional positive regard from self-obsession to altruism. As an individual develops their emotional intelligence, their personal awareness (their drivers, triggers and effect on others) increases. The experiential nature of adventure learning means people learn how they behave or react and their associated emotional responses.

In turn, the reaction of others to their behaviour is apparent and the individual learns how lack of positive emotional control is detrimental to individual and team success. The theory advocates that emotional literacy is not fixed and can be developed through experience and challenge. Using adventure learning as a tool to develop personal awareness and self-esteem, the individual becomes able to manage their emotions, which facilitates their capacity to effect change and influence others by maintaining positive relationships. Similarly, individuals develop their understanding of emotional drivers, enabling them to empathise with others and tolerate different perspectives better.

Group dynamics

Bruce Tuckman (1965) stated that teams need time to develop before they can become effective. Initially the group comes together, members are very polite to one another, the atmosphere is civil and little is achieved, as members are wary of one another because relationships are embryonic. The group goes on towards conflict and challenge as members find their way forward, setting boundaries and establishing the group culture. The most effective groups follow on to stability and cohesion, performing synchronously to achieve goals.

- *Stage 1 – forming:* a very directive phase, with high dependence on the recognised leader. Individual roles and responsibilities are undefined, as are systems and processes. Group members begin to challenge all aspects, bringing their range of experiences and assuming their way is 'the best way'.
- *Stage 2 – storming:* indecision and dispute are common, as team members try to define their position and establish their identity in relation to one another and to the recognised leader, who might themselves find their position challenged. Clarity of purpose increases but there is still a high degree of uncertainty. The power struggles, relationship issues and emotional process can be distracting as the group tries to begin working towards its goals.
- *Stage 3 – norming:* as agreements are reached and consensus begins to form, the leader relaxes into a more facilitative mode. Roles and responsibilities become more clearly defined so a decision-making process emerges. Commitment and unity improve as the team develops its processes and working style.
- *Stage 4 – performing:* the team becomes strategically aware, as its processes and systems become embedded and succeed. A shared vision emerges and the members operate more independently from the leader. Although disagreements still occur, they are resolved amicably within the team, with process and structure changes becoming evolutionary. The team can simultaneously work towards achieving goals while maintaining relationship, style and process cohesion. The leader intervenes only

when requested to do so by the instructors, but adopts a more paternal role of instructor personal development.

- *Stage 5 – adjourning:* Tuckman refined his theory around 1975 and added a fifth stage (also referred to as 'deforming' or 'mourning'). This stage is different in that it is relevant to the group members, but not with managing and developing the team, or even goal attainment. 'Adjourning' is the break-up of the group, after the task is completed, the goal(s) achieved and the members move on. Organisationally this stage can be important as members may feel vulnerable, somewhat aimless and suffer a sense of loss, especially when the group has been successful and the members closely bonded.

Bruce Tuckman

Born: 1938, New York City, New York
Professional description: educational psychology

Relating the theory to adventure learning

When a group of participants comes together, the instructor will be aware of any pre-existing relationship(s), but not necessarily the nature of these. The instructor needs this knowledge because it is a critical indicator of the way that the group is likely to perform over the session/programme. As the group culture is unformed and members do not know one another well, the instructor will have to manage the chaotic individualism of members vying for position and learning how to relate to one another. There will be more failure than success in the activities, so the instructor must manage group emotions carefully in order that motivation is not eroded. As group culture establishes, and relationships form, a working structure develops and the instructor can progressively cede responsibility and autonomy.

Hierarchy of needs

While working with Harry Harlow on his attachment behaviour experiments with rhesus monkeys, Abraham Maslow (1943) noticed how some needs take precedence over others. From these observations, he developed his theory of needs, whereby he defined the drivers of behaviour as people strive to satisfy these needs. Maslow's hierarchy of needs is commonly portrayed as a pyramid, although Maslow himself never used a pyramid as a descriptor.

The lowest tier represents the most fundamental and a prolific need, and then each successive tier of the hierarchy represents fewer needs that are harder to satisfy. The bottom four tiers contain what Maslow called 'deficit needs'; lack of satisfaction of these

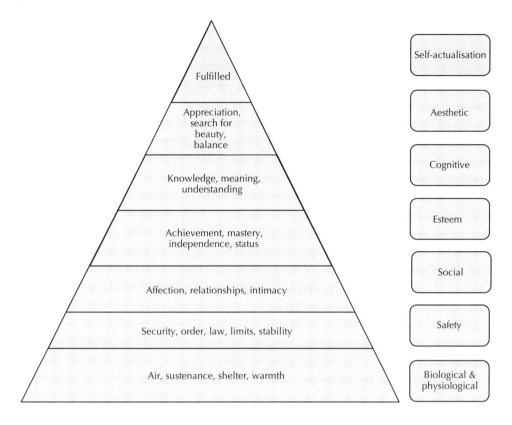

Figure 14 Maslow's pyramid (hierarchy) of needs

leads to anxiety, stress and personal discomfort. Maslow coined the term 'metamotivation' to describe the motivation of people who go beyond the scope of the basic needs and strive for constant betterment.

One starts at the lowest level: physiological and survival. As the individual succeeds in meeting these needs, they proceed to the next level. Maslow's theory suggests that the most basic level of needs must be met before the individual will have any desire or motivation to explore satisfaction of higher-level needs. If the conditions satisfying lower needs are removed, the individual regresses downwards to satisfy these needs again. All individuals have the capacity, latent potential and desire to move up the hierarchy, but progress is often stalled by an inability to satisfy one set of needs.

Stress can also force people to regress down the pyramid, working to satisfy needs that they know they can address, rather than face the testing task of working to meet more challenging needs. When severe progressional challenges make satisfaction of one level particularly complex, individuals can fixate on that level, obsessing at maintaining satisfaction and preventing themselves from progressing.

Maslow noted that relatively few achieve the highest level, self-actualisation, because of the stress involved in achieving and maintaining satisfaction of the tiers below.

Abraham Maslow

Born: 1 April 1908, Brooklyn, New York
Died: 8 June 1970, Menlo Park, California
Professional description: psychologist

Relating the theory to adventure learning

The most obvious application to adventure learning is that activities are outdoors, therefore the primary concern is the satisfaction of basic needs; if group members are cold, hungry and wet, they will have no capacity for learning. Beyond this, the members need to know the rules of the session, what is expected of them and what they can expect. While group members need to feel a level of safety, their learning capacity at this stage will be piqued by a perception of risk, so 'safety' may relate at this point to an understanding of the equipment and what it does. From this point, higher level needs become relevant, as group members begin to experience emotional and psychological fulfilment. By managing the satisfaction of needs appropriately, the instructor directs the capability of the group to focus on the desired learning. As competence develops, higher level social and esteem needs may be addressed and individuals may progress on to seek satisfaction of even higher needs.

Holistic learning

There is no single theorist who can be credited with the notion of holistic learning; over many years, it has been posited that education is about more than a production line of future workers, but that it should evolve to become the cultivation of the moral, emotional, physical, psychological and spiritual components that make up the human being. The advocacy of this encompassing approach became known as 'holism', a way of thinking that seeks to recognise more than standardised test scores. Holistic learning advocates the provision of a product and a process curriculum as the way to develop young people and enable them to achieve their potential.

Holistic learning sees many routes to the learning outcome, each one specific and unique to the individual learner, entwining new knowledge with what is already known and understood. The learner receives new facts, processes them in their mind and absorbs them in relation to what they have learned in the past. Traditional schooling takes learning as a series of discrete subjects, which encourages discrete 'silos' of knowledge without connection to one another and bearing no relation to the reality of the individual, whereas holistic learning allows pieces of learning to become appended to one another in an intricate web of knowledge, constructs applicable throughout life. This process allows the individual to relate the learning to their own 'world' and contextualise it; as individuals, we grow and develop our personal values through our relationship with every element of the world around us. Holistic learning recognises the differences in people, that adults and children learn differently and that, as unique individuals, we all learn and conceptualise differently at different times and stages of life. Ultimately, holistic learning aims to foster an interest in learning itself and advocates learning as a lifelong process, not a stage of childhood. Some advocates of holistic learning are briefly described below.

Amos Bronson Alcott

Born: 29 November 1799, Wolcott, Connecticut
Died: 4 March 1888, Boston, Massachusetts
An American teacher, writer, philosopher, reformer, abolitionist and advocate for women's rights, Alcott pioneered new forms of student interaction, with a focus on conversation and avoidance of punishment. His belief was that the route to perfecting the human spirit was through veganism and pure living.

The second of his four daughters was Louisa May Alcott, who fictionalised her family life in her novel *Little Women* in 1868.

Fritjof Capra

Born: 1 February 1939, Vienna, Austria
A physicist, educator, activist and author, Capra advocates holism and the inter-connectivity of all parts to any system.

John Dewey

Born: 20 October 1859, Burlington, Vermont
Died: 1 June 1952, New York City, New York
An American philosopher, psychologist and educational reformer whose ideas have fundamentally influenced education and social reform, Dewey is considered one of the founders of functional psychology, advocating democracy in all aspects of life.

Dewey believed that schools and society both required attention and reconstruction for intelligence and plurality to flourish.

Ralph Waldo Emerson

Born: 25 May 1803, Boston, Massachusetts
Died: 27 April 1882, Concord, Massachusetts
An essayist, lecturer, poet and transcendentalist, Emerson promoted individualism in the face of social pressure.

Jiddu Krishnamurti

Born: 11 May 1895, Madanapalle, India
Died: 17 February 1986, Ojai, California
A speaker and writer on philosophical and spiritual subjects, Krishnamurti and his brother were adopted by Dr Annie Besant. Besant, president of the Theosophical Society, believed Krishnamurti was to become the world teacher whose coming had been predicted by the Theosophists. To prepare the world for his coming, the Order of the Star in the East, a global group, was created with young Krishnamurti its leader. However, in 1929, Krishnamurti renounced the role, dissolved the Order and returned all the money and property that had been donated. Krishnamurti thereafter belonged to no religion, sect or country, nor did he ascribe to any single political or ideological belief, maintaining these as the roots of conflict and war.

Maria Montessori

Born: 31 August 1870, Chianavalle, Italy
Died: 6 May 1952, Noordwijk, Netherlands
A physician and educator, best known for the philosophy of education that bears her name, Montessori concerned herself with writings on scientific pedagogy. The educational approach emphasises independence, limited freedom for self-discovery and respecting the natural psychological, physical and social development of the learner.

Johann Pestalozzi

Born: 12 January 1746, Zurich, Switzerland
Died: 17 February 1827, Brugg, Switzerland
A pedagogue and educational reformer who founded several educational institutions. His motto was 'learning by head, hand and heart'.

Francis Parker

Born: 9 October 1837, Bedford, New Hampshire
Died: 2 March 1902, Harrison County, Mississippi
A pioneer of the progressive school movement in the United States, Parker believed in mental, physical and moral education. Called the 'father of progressive education' by John Dewey, Parker strove to devise a curriculum centred on the whole child, rather than standardised lessons and rote learning. He aimed to prove that education meant independent learners who think for themselves.

Charlene Spretnak

Born: 1946, Pittsburgh, Pennsylvania
A speaker and activist, Spretnak is concerned with dynamic interrelatedness and proving that the body and mind are far more dynamically interrelated than recognised.

Rudolf Steiner

Born: February 1861, Murakraly, Austria–Hungary (now Donji Kraljevec, Croatia)
Died: 30 March 1925, Dornach, Switzerland
A mystic, philosopher, social reformer, architect and esotericist, Steiner looked for a connection between science and spirituality.

Henry David Thoreau

Born: 12 July 1817, Concord, Massachusetts
Died: 6 May 1862, Concord, Massachusetts
Described as an American author, poet, philosopher, abolitionist, naturalist, tax resister, development critic, historian and transcendentalist, Thoreau is best known for his writings on natural history and philosophy.

Theodore Roszak

Born: 15 November 1933, Chicago, Illinois
Died: 5 July 2011, Berkeley, California
Roszak was the first to label the 'counterculture', the communitarian experiments, cults, spiritual entrepreneurs and competing new-age psychotherapies of San Francisco and Berkeley in the late 1960s.

Ken Wilber

Born: 31 January 1949, Oklahoma City, Oklahoma
A writer, philosopher and public speaker, Wilber writes and lectures on philosophy, sociology, ecology, developmental psychology, spirituality and mysticism. He founded the Integral Institute in 1998, a group that aims to gather and integrate the perspectives of a number of major fields of knowledge, with the overriding foundation that the different perspectives are all true but partial versions of actual reality.

Relating the theory to adventure learning

Adventure learning is experiential, participants learn through doing, unlike the rote memorisation required by classroom learning. To move the experience from activity to learning, participants are encouraged and supported to make sense of the experience by processing their engagement through the unique lens of what they already know and have experienced in the past (their ontology). This is holistic learning, the enhancement of existing knowledge by appending new knowledge, therefore deepening understanding or creating new awareness.

By developing adventure learning programmes as an embedded component of a formal learning curriculum, concepts are presented as physical and visual mechanisms, which support the verbalisation of the classroom. The multi-modal approach facilitates mental models to be created in the mind of the learner, forming the basis of that which is then mentally connected to what they already 'know' (an experience, an emotion, an understanding) and subsequently redefine into greater awareness, understanding or knowledge. Later application of this redefinition, whether to a similar adventure learning experience or to a different situation, will reinforce the redefinition or lead to further adaptation.

Learning styles

A *learning style* is an individual's natural or favoured pattern of acquiring and processing information in a learning situation. The idea of individualised learning styles originated in the 1970s, and has greatly influenced education. Theorists associated with learning styles include Peter Honey and Alan Mumford (1982), Howard Gardner (1983) and David Kolb (1984).

Proponents of the use of learning styles in education propose teachers assess the learning styles of each learner and alter their teaching to accommodate each learner's style. Although there is ample evidence for differences in individual thinking and ways of processing various types of information, there is no solid evidence to support the use of learning styles in practice or to show that identifying the learning style of a participant leads them to better outcomes; the opposite can be argued to be true (i.e. that labelling a participant as a particular type of learner may lead them to only be provided one method, which can damage their learning).

However, it is widely recognised that people learn differently and that a group of learners will require a range of styles (or methods) to optimise everyone's learning. Learning styles, at best, group common ways that people learn. Some people may find that they have a dominant style of learning that they prefer almost all the time, with far less use of other styles, while others may find that they use different styles in different circumstances or at different times. There is no right mix and nor are styles fixed; people can develop an ability in a less dominant style, as well as enhancing a preferred style.

Using multiple learning styles and multiple intelligences for learning is a relatively new approach that educators have only recently started to understand. Traditional education focuses on predominantly linguistic and logical methods, relying on classroom teaching, repetition and examinations. This results in those tending towards these learning styles being labelled intelligent and those who tend towards other styles finding themselves in lower level classes, with sometimes lower quality teaching. This can result in learners 'living down' to a label and restrict them striving for their potential.

By recognising and understanding your own learning styles, you can use techniques better suited to you, improving the speed and quality of your learning.

Both Honey and Mumford (1982) and David Kolb (1984) produced very similar models to explain the learning process, each with its advocates and critics. The greatest weakness of both models is that neither accounts for the impact of social interaction and the extent to which humans ape or learn from each other. In addition, cognitive capacity, goals, purposes, intentions, choice and decision-making are not acknowledged. However, both provide focus and offer a model of facilitation, which apply as the goals of the adventure learning model. Figure 15 shows the two models combined; inside the circle are the types of learner and around the edge are the processes most appropriate to that style.

Both sets of theorists perceived four types of learner, along a spectrum of cerebral to practical preferences. While Honey and Mumford focused on styles, Kolb's cycle demonstrates a *process of learning* as well: concrete experience (Honey and Mumford's

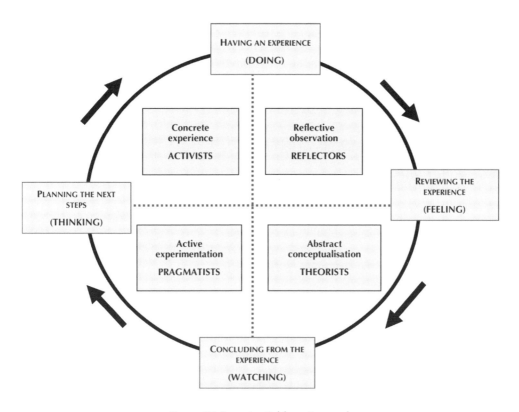

Figure 15 Experiential learning cycle

Source: adapted from Honey and Mumford (1982) and Kolb (1984)

'hands-on' approach), provides a basis for reflective observations. Reflective observations (Honey and Mumford's cerebral learners) are processed into abstract conceptualisation (Honey and Mumford's theorists). This, in turn, produces actions to be tested (Honey and Mumford's practical people). This testing creates new experiences as new learning is applied to different situations.

Gardner supplemented the work of Kolb and of Honey and Mumford with his theory of multiple intelligences, proposing all individuals possess a degree of a number of intelligences, combining uniquely to delineate how individuals internally decide to do or watch, while deciding to think or feel. The result of these two decisions produces the preferred learning style. Thus, people choose their approach by watching others and reflecting on what happens or through just going straight into the task or experience (Kolb 1984). Simultaneously, one emotionally transforms the experience by intangibly analysing or by tangibly feeling (Kolb 1984).

Peter Honey

Born: Oxford
Professional description: occupational psychologist, management trainer

Alan Mumford

Professional description: management development adviser

David Kolb

Born: 1939
Professional description: educational theorist

Howard Gardner

Born: 11 July 1943, Scranton, Pennsylvania
Professional description: development psychologist

Relating the theory to adventure learning

Just as learning is a personal *and* a social process, how each individual arrives at their learning is unique. The way that people learn is a function of the way in which they perceive and process what is being taught and that is a complex amalgamation of the subject, cognitive ability, motivation, emotional state, expectations, environment and personal narrative (personal past history). Nobody learns by one fixed method, so nobody has a single lifelong learning style. However, knowing the process through which people learn enables the instructor to become a more efficient facilitator. During the activity (concrete experience), the instructor can observe the roles played, looking at dominant characteristics of individuals. Intervention and reviewing (during or after the activity) can then be focused upon the prevailing nature of the learner(s) (reflective observation). As participants move to absorbing and relating their experience (abstract conceptualisation) the instructor helps learners to put the knowledge into their personal context, shaping it within the framework of their existing knowledge, understanding and experiences. Finally, participants look to redefining their existing framework in the context of that which they have just processed (active experimentation). The instructor has to be able to target theoretical, visual, verbal and physical tools appropriately in order to maximise the learning for the prevailing style of the learner(s). Through the multi-modal methodology of combining the verbalisation of the classroom with the physical and visual platforms offered by adventure learning, participants can be supported to maximise understanding and achieve their potential.

Operant conditioning

It was Burrhus Frederic Skinner's belief that free will is an illusion and that actions are founded on the learned consequences of experience (Skinner 1948): if the consequence of an action is negative, the action will not be repeated, but if the consequence of the action is positive, repetition is likely. He called this the principle of reinforcement.

Skinner also believed it was more productive to study observable behaviour rather than try to define internal mental processing because the best way to understand behaviour was to look at the causes of an action and its consequences. He named this approach operant conditioning, which means the changing of behaviour by the use of a reinforcement mechanism given after the desired response. Skinner studied operant conditioning by conducting experiments using animals, which he placed in a 'Skinner Box', also known as an operant conditioning chamber, a piece of laboratory apparatus to study animal behaviour. The chamber teaches a subject animal to perform a certain action at the command of a certain stimulus; if the animal behaves correctly, a reward is received and some experiments deliver a punishment for an incorrect behaviour. Skinner identified three types of responses (operant) that can follow behaviour.

1   *Neutral operants:* responses from the environment that neither increase nor decrease the probability of a behaviour being repeated.
2   *Reinforcers:* responses from the environment that increase the probability of a behaviour being repeated. Reinforcers can be either positive or negative.
3   *Punishers:* responses from the environment that decrease the likelihood of a behaviour being repeated. Punishment weakens behaviour.

We can all think of examples of how our own behaviour has been affected by reinforcers and punishers. As children, we try out a number of behaviours and learn from their consequences; for example, if a child tries smoking at school and the chief consequence is that they become part of the 'in' crowd, they are positively reinforced (i.e. rewarded) and are likely to continue. If, however, the main consequence is that they were caught and punished, they are consequently much less likely to continue smoking.

Burrhus Frederic Skinner

Born: 20 March 1904, Susquehanna Depot, Pennsylvania
Died: 18 August 1990, Cambridge, Massachusetts
Professional description: psychologist, behaviourist, author, inventor, social philosopher

Relating the theory to adventure learning

Closely related to conditional positive regard, operant conditioning presents a way to define behaviour. The delivery of overt positive and negative rewards should never form the basis of an adventure programme, which seeks to enhance the latent positive potential and personal awareness of the individual. It does, however, demonstrate a mechanism by which the instructor can underpin learning during the review phases of a session or programme. By encouraging participants to give examples of 'reinforcers' and 'punishers', the instructor can exemplify the nature of conditional and unconditional positive regard. It also enables the planning of adventure learning delivery by fostering a practice of encouraging achievement. Through appreciative facilitation, the instructor emphasises the positive achievements of individual participants and the group, namely strengths such as risk analysis, decision making, collaboration, leadership, team work, meaning successful steps in the attainment of their goal. This provides the basis for building confidence to repeat the behaviour and try it in other contexts. In this way, participants distinguish positive action and begin to adjust their thinking and mind-set accordingly.

Situated learning and communities of practice

Situated learning, as the name implies, proposes that learning is unintentionally achieved (tacit learning) through engagement in an activity, context or culture. It assumes gradually increasing empowerment of the individual towards ownership and control, which chimes with the adventure approach of moving participants from behaviourist to cognitive to experiential learning, and the adventure learning instructor from instructor to facilitator, a process named 'legitimate peripheral participation' by Jean Lave and Etienne Wenger (1991). The process does not, however, recognise a situation where the participant is already familiar with the environment and has moved beyond peripheral participation.

Their implication may be that such an individual has reached a point of saturation, but this would sit in opposition to Berger and Luckman's (1966) advocacy of learning being never-ending.

Communities of practice are principally a process of social learning that occurs when people with a shared (vested) interest in something work in partnership in sharing ideas, understandings, jointly working out and testing solutions to issues that arise. The group may not intentionally come together, but their collaboration is the key and any learning arises as a related by-product of their social interaction.

Three core factors define such collaboration as a *community of practice*:

1   A community of practice is not simply a collective of people, there needs to be a shared interest, known as a *domain*. The domain may be a shared professional arena (in this instance, adventure learning and a particular adventurous activity). Membership of the community provides an inherent implication that the individual has a commitment to the domain.

2   A community of practice requires a *community*; it is essential that the members of the group interact, participate in the shared activity and help each other, sharing learning and understanding. The core of the community is that the members build effective working relationships that enable sharing and learning; this is more than simply a group of people doing the same job, there is a shared intent to commit to the evolution of the community and the empathy that supports all members to learn.

3   A community of practice requires a *practice*; having an interest in the field is insufficient, the members must actively be engaged in the arena to be able to contribute from experience, that is, the members are *practitioners*.

Communities of practice develop from a range of bases, centred either on problem solving and need or on actively seeking to develop and further practice. Both involve learning, which is central to human identity and evolution. The central tenet of learning within a community of practice is learning through social engagement, where the individual actively participates in the community, rather than engaging because they are required to be there (for example, because they work in the field) and in this way actively constructs their identity through their engagement. People are social beings and we naturally and continuously seek to create a shared identity, which is relative to and defined by the way in which we engage in and contribute to society and the practices of communities. The motivation to become a more central participant in a community of practice can provide a powerful incentive for learning.

Jean Lave

Professional description: social anthropologist

Etienne Wenger

Born: 1 July 1952, Neuchâtel, Switzerland
Professional description: educational theorist

Relating the theory to adventure learning

A group of participants exists as a community of practice for the duration of the adventure learning experience. Generally, the group will form at the start of the experience and remain as a unit throughout. As the group grows in confidence and competence, they progress from peripheral to core participation, with the shared interaction, learning and understanding that come to define them. The community is unique in that the experience is theirs alone. This bond forms the basis of the situated learning that subconsciously creates the group culture and possibly extends beyond the existence of the community into the 'everyday' lives of the individuals. The instructor has a strong role in directing the community and shaping it, as they take an initially directive role in the activity. This initial 'lead' will shape the way in which the group identifies itself and forms the community that takes progressive responsibility for the activity and the actions of the group.

The instructor belongs to the community of practice of the adventure learning team. Members learn from one another, develop joint practices and devise collaborative solutions to arising issues. The shared interest of adventure learning and the common practice of delivery bring the team together, creating a more powerful and effective collaborative unit than if each instructor operated in isolation.

Social construction of reality

Peter Ludwig Berger and Thomas Luckman (1966) provide capacity for both social and cognitive development, distinguishing between primary and secondary socialisation. Primary socialisation (Piaget's cognitive learning) occurs through childhood and 'initiation' into society; secondary socialisation (Vygotsky's social learning) is any subsequent process whereby the socialised individual enters new dimensions; primary socialisation is dominated by others (parents, teachers) and is largely uncontrolled by the individual, ending when the individual attains a consciousness that enables them to act independently, become an effective member of society and able to form their own subjective interpretation of experience.

Berger and Luckman advocate that such socialisation is never complete, as social interaction is never-ending; it follows therefore that learning, as a social activity, is a lifelong process. Meaning is continually constructed relative to the individual's narrative (their *lived* experience) and their environment (culture) (their *reflected* experience). The core idea of Berger and Luckman's 'social construction of reality' is that understanding, significance and meaning are developed not separately within the individual, but in co-ordination with other human beings. We all exist as social beings and explain our experiences through our own personal model of our social world. Over time, we develop a shared mental understanding of the way in which those around us in our social grouping think and act, and then eventually these notions become adopted by the whole group and become *the* way to think and act. When this way becomes shared by other social groups, the shared interactions are said to have become *institutionalised* and, in the process, meaning is embedded in society; reality becomes defined by the knowledge and understanding people have of it and thus becomes entrenched. Thus, reality is socially constructed.

This central idea seems obvious and simple; we can all understand the notion that the world has been created through human existence, so it is not a great leap to understand that what we have created is because of what we all understand and, had our understanding been different, the creation would consequently have been different.

Peter Ludwig Berger

Born: 17 March 1926, Vienna, Austria
Professional description: sociologist

Thomas Luckman

Born: 14 October 1927, Jesenice, Slovenia
Professional description: sociologist

Relating the theory to adventure learning

Berger and Luckman's theory defines the longer-term implications of adventure learning. Their assertion that social leaning is a perpetual entity defines the application of learning beyond the adventure learning session. Adventure learning occurs as a group activity; therefore, as the activity progresses, it exists within a social context and will be reviewed as a collective experience. The conclusions of the experience, the learning drawn from it and the knowledge (the 'reality') to be applied to the future by the individual will be defined by the shared analysis of the group. That is not to say that all participants will leave with the same conclusion; the individual legacy of the experience will be predicated on their perception of themselves within their world (conditional positive regard, operant conditioning). In terms of the adventure learning team, the social construction of their reality is very closely tied to the creation of their community of practice (Lave and Wenger 1991). The team members collaborate to define their culture, the way they operate, interact and exist, thus establish their reality. The way in which each instructor will deliver activities, work with participants and colleagues and undertake other functions will be defined in the context and by the norms of the communally created team culture.

Social development theory

Lev Vygotsky (1962) felt social learning precedes development; his belief was that the key to human intelligence is our ability to use various types of tools and just as humans use material tools to extend our physical achievements, we have invented psychological tools to extend our mental capacity. These tools are developed within our social culture, rather than genetically inherited, and are the way we communicate and define our world. Vygotsky believed that until children learn to use these mental tools, their learning is controlled by the environment, responding only to the things that are brightest or loudest and remembering things only if they are repeated many times. Vygotsky says learning is a social act, the purpose of which is to introduce children to these cultural tools and help them learn to use them successfully, developing psychological qualities (abilities). The development of abilities leads to the blossoming of personality, independence and social interaction. Many schools have traditionally adopted a behaviourist model, where the teacher 'transmits' information to participants, whereas Vygotsky's theory promotes participants playing an active role in learning, moving the teacher/participant relationship to become more collaborative.

According to social development theory, social interaction is a necessary precursor to development, with consciousness and cognition arising because of socialisation and social behaviour. Vygotsky's theory is one of the foundations of constructivism and is founded through three themes:

1 Contrary to Piaget's theory of child development, where physical development necessarily precedes learning, Vygotsky postulated that social interaction is central to cognitive development and that social learning precedes development.

2 The existence of a more knowledgeable other (MKO), a being with better understanding or greater ability than the learner. The MKO can be the activity instructor but can equally be peers or others within the social group. It is also contended that the MKO could be inanimate, such as a computer.

3 There is a gap between the learner's ability to perform a task under guidance or with a group and their ability to perform alone, known as the zone of proximal development (ZPD). It is in the ZPD, according to Vygotsky, that learning occurs.

Many learning institutions traditionally operate by transmitting data for learners to absorb, but under Vygotsky's theory, learning is most effective where the learner plays an active role in learning. Learning thus becomes collaborative and a reciprocal experience for the learner and instructor.

Lev Vygostsky

Born: 17 November 1896, Orsha, Belarus

Died: 11 June 1934, Moscow, Russia
Professional description: psychologist

Relating the theory to adventure learning

Working in antithesis to Piaget's cognitive development theory, Vygotsky conceives progression as a social phenomenon, whereby the individual learns to exist within the confines of social norms and rituals through mimicry, instruction and collaboration. The assertion of learning as a group process resonates in that adventure learning is a group activity so the whole group finds a way to operate that allows them to tackle the task in hand. Through performing as a group, the different participants will derive personal learning points that are unique to them, (such as learning their leadership potential) as well as the group learning points (such as when everyone talks at once there are no clear decisions). Bearing in mind Tuckman's group dynamics theory, the group almost inevitably will experience failure before success and it is incumbent upon the instructor to manage the emotional impact of that in order for the group to remain motivated to continue in the face of disappointment (a learning point in itself). The instructor can also use the social group perspective to highlight collective success or failure and alleviate the almost inevitable allegations of individual poor performance.

Social learning

According to Albert Bandura's theory, behaviour is derived from observation of the environment; in a concept he named reciprocal determinism, he advocated that the world and a person's behaviour were inextricably linked and caused each other (Bandura 1977).

Social learning theory (SLT) demonstrated aspects of traditional learning theory and Skinner's operant conditioning theory. However, unlike Skinner, Bandura saw the human mind as a powerful and active information processing system that can evaluate the consequences of actions; indeed, he advocated that observational learning (modelling) cannot take place without significant cognitive ability and that behaviour arises out of environmental and social observational learning, not the 'reward and punishment' reinforcement process posited by Skinner.

Bandura's famous 1961 'bobo doll' experiment demonstrated how children observe and learn from the people around them. Children are surrounded by many influential models (individuals), such as parents, siblings, relatives, friends, teachers, television characters, all providing observable and imitable behaviours. Sub-consciously, children absorb their behaviour and mimic it. Bandura observed that children are more likely to mimic people with whom they identify as similar, followed by lesser-known people of the same sex. The mimicked behaviour will elicit a positive or negative response from the people around them; if the response is positive, the child feels rewarded and will continue to replicate the behaviour. The behaviour has thus been reinforced. Of course, negative motivation exists too (punishment, threats), giving reasons not to mimic. Like most traditional behaviourists, Bandura argues punishment does not work as well as reinforcement.

Founded on three core concepts, social learning (observational learning, modelling), can explain a wide variety of human behaviour:

1   People learn through observing those within their environment and mimicking their behaviour, as they perceive that behaviour as the accepted way to behave.

2   Internal mental state is important to learning; intrinsic reward (sense of achievement, pride, gain in confidence or self-esteem) is as influential as the reinforcement methodology in bringing about learning.

3   Learning does not equate to a change in behaviour; people actively choose whether to apply new learning, and this can be on a temporary or a permanent basis.

There is also a correlation between Bandura's social learning theory and writings on organisational culture, such as Lave and Wenger's communities of practice.

Albert Bandura

Born: 4 December 1925, Mundare, Canada
Professional description: psychologist

Relating the theory to adventure learning

Very closely related to operant conditioning and the social construction of reality, social learning presupposes the cognitive maturity to relate actions to consequences. Adventure learning is a group process whose success relies as much on the cohesion of the members as it does on their abilities. The collaborative process of forming a strategy, discussing options, making decisions and working together combine to make adventure learning a valuable social learning tool; peer reaction and action consequence are important mechanisms that embed and reinforce personal development. Having a strong influence on the positivity of reaction to group behaviour and actions, the adventure learning instructor can direct and manipulate this. Supporting participants to realise the nature, extent and applicability of their learning, the instructor facilitates the subliminal decision-making of the individual as to whether or not they want to proceed to Kolb's active experimentation and apply their perceived 'new' knowledge in their 'normal' everyday environment away from the adventure learning setting.

Along the lines of social development theory (Vygotsky), a group of adventure learning participants will mimic one another but, more importantly, will mimic the instructor, perceived as the significant influential model (MKO) within the adventure learning setting. The criticality of the way in which the instructor presents themselves and behaves in respect of the group is thus fundamental.

Theories of learning

Progressive education is essentially a view of education that emphasises the need for experience, to learn by doing. John Dewey (1910, 1938) believed that people learn through a 'hands-on' approach, advocating the idea that experience in itself does not provide ingrained learning; reflection on experience provides lasting learning, which makes the adventure learning instructor's responsibility to the quality of experience infinite. Where traditional education centred upon a curriculum and inherited knowledge for its content, progressive education focused upon the learner as an individual, unimpeded by the educator. Dewey argued that neither viewpoint is adequate because traditional education requires regimentation and avoids consideration of the learner's capacity or interests, but progressive education requires absolute individualism and avoids consideration of the educator's role.

Dewey was a pragmatist, believing that reality must be experienced, that learners must interact with their instructor and their environment, with all enjoying an equal voice in the learning experience. Dewey believed in an interdisciplinary (holistic) curriculum that connected subjects and allowed learners to construct their own paths of learning; the instructor is a facilitator, recognising the propensity of the students and facilitating their next steps. The Dewey-style classroom would be filled with groups exploring differing concepts within subject (topic), conversation and collaboration. Written tests may or may not be evident, but would be supplemented and supported by a range of evaluation techniques.

The term 'andragogy' is ascribed to Malcolm Knowles (1990), but was actually first introduced in 1833 by Alexander Kapp. Knowles's principles of andragogy are arguably a synopsis of the assumptions and values of other theorists of adult educational theory. Malcolm Knowles argued that adults and children learn differently, believing child learning is limited to directive classroom teaching because of limited life experience and less developed thinking, whereas adults independently seek learning and progression. He argued adults are self-directed, responsible for decisions and actions. Adult learning (andragogy) exists in opposition to child learning (pedagogy), as adults enter learning willingly (often voluntarily) because they know and understand *why* they need to acquire the knowledge. On this basis, adult learners engage differently, applying past knowledge and experiences. The educator becomes a facilitator, rather than a teacher, supporting, rather than controlling, input.

Knowles established four differentiating characteristics between andragogy and pedagogy, later adding a fifth:

1   *Self-concept:* individuals move with maturity from dependence to independence, becoming involved in the planning and evaluation of their learning.

2   *Adult learner experience:* increasing maturity brings increasing experience, building a knowledge bank as a resource base on which to ground learning, founded on experience and 'trial and error' learning.

3   *Readiness to learn:* increasing maturity orients learning to the social and professional life of the individual; people are most interested in the subjects that affect them personally or professionally.

4   *Orientation to learning:* increasing maturity makes the need to apply new knowledge more immediate, with the goal of learning being the application of knowledge (problem solving), rather than the knowledge itself (content oriented).

5   *Motivation to learn:* individuals become more motivated to learn as they mature.

Paolo Freire (1996) maintained two views of people:

1   People are objects to be shaped as desired, able to be trained like animals, acting and obeying as commanded, without thought or reflection.

2   People are subjects, independent thinking beings who can shape the world as they desire, able to reflect and strategise.

By his concept of 'banking education', Freire sees the instructor depositing (imposing) predetermined information, without dialogue or negotiation, with no consideration that the learner is able to think or act independently (behaviourist). Freire proposed the alternative of 'libertarian education', starting with the reality of the learner and their right to question and challenge (cognitive). Cognitive learning acknowledges the value of dialogue and the learner–instructor relationship. Freire postulated that learning is never neutral; if people are not passive recipients of knowledge, they are active problem solvers, linking knowledge to action in order to shape their world. According to Freire, the world is comprised of dominant social relations that instil a culture of silent suppression on the oppressed, but the oppressed can develop a critical consciousness that will enable them to recognise this culture and reform the world to overcome it.

John Dewey

Born: 20 October 1859, Burlington, Vermont
Died: 1 June 1952, New York City, New York
Professional description: philosopher, psychologist, educational reformer

Malcolm Knowles

Born: 24 August 1973, Livingston, Montana

Died: 27 November 1997, Fayetteville, Arkansas
Professional description: adult educator

Paolo Freire

Born: 19 September 1921, Recife, Brazil
Died: 2 May 1997, São Paulo, Brazil
Professional description: educator, philosopher

Relating the theory to adventure learning

Learning theories are at the core of adventure learning as an holistic educative tool. Adventure learning is experiential, participants engage in an activity physically and psychologically, they feel the emotional and corporal consequences of their engagement and are commissioned with the discovery of their own learning. The support offered by the instructor is ultimately facilitative, rather than directive, placing the responsibility of success on the participants and their cognitive capacity. The subsequent lateral transfer of knowledge and skills endows the participant with the recognition that they have ownership of its application and may choose when and how they may do so. Taking ownership means understanding and accepting the consequences of actions, making informed decisions, a critical indicator of human maturation.

References

Bandura, A. (1977). *Social Learning Theory*. Englewood Cliffs, NJ: Prentice Hall.

Berger, P. L. and Luckmann, T. (1966). *The Social Construction of Reality: A Treatise in the Sociology of Knowledge*. New York: Anchor Books.

Dewey, J. (1910) *How We Think*. Chicago, IL: D. C. Heath & Co.

Dewey, J. (1938) *Experience and Education*. New York: Touchstone.

Freire, P. (1996) *Pedagogy of the Oppressed*. London: Penguin Books.

Gardner, H. (1983) *Frames of Mind: The Theory of Multiple Intelligences*, New York: Basic Books.

Goleman, D. (1995) *Emotional Intelligence*. New York: Bantam Dell.

Goleman, D. (1998) *Working with Emotional Intelligence*. New York: Bantam Dell.

Honey, P. and Mumford, A. (1982) Typology of learners. In their *Manual of Learning Styles*. London: P. Honey Publications.

Knowles, M. S. (1990) *The Adult Learner: A Neglected Species*. Houston, TX: Gulf Publishing Company.

Kolb, D. A. (1984) *Experiential Learning: Experience as the Source for Learning and Development*. Upper Saddle River, NJ: Prentice Hall.

Lave, J. and Wenger, E. (1991) *Situated Learning: Legitimate Peripheral Participation*. Cambridge: Cambridge University Press.

Maslow, A. (1943) A theory of human motivation. *Psychological Review* 50: 370–396.

Piaget, J. (1973). *The Language and Thought of the Child (Vol. 5)*. Brighton: Psychology Press.

Rogers, C. (1959) A theory of therapy, personality and interpersonal relationships as developed in the client-centered framework. In S. Koch (ed.), *Psychology: A Study of a Science, Vol. 3: Formulations of the Person and the Social Context*. New York: McGraw-Hill.

Skinner, B. F. (1953). *Science and Human Behavior*. New York: Simon & Schuster.

Tuckman, B. W. (1965) Developmental sequence in small groups. *Psychological Bulletin* 63: 384–399.

Vygotsky, L. S. (1962). *Thought and Language*. Cambridge MA: MIT Press.

16 Theories associated with leadership and management

In this chapter we will look at:

- action-centred leadership;
- bureaucratic management theory;
- distributed leadership;
- five forms of power;
- learning organisations;
- management by objectives;
- motivation theory;
- revisionist theory of leadership;
- systems thinking;
- team roles;
- theory X and theory Y;
- transactional leadership theory and transformational leadership theory.

Action-centred leadership

In the early 1970s, John Adair developed the theory that the interaction and control of three core elements of management within an organisation determined effectiveness and success, and that organisational leaders could learn the skills to manipulate these accordingly (see Adair 1996, 1998). Adair's famous 'three circles' model demonstrates the three core management responsibilities (Figure 16).

Figure 16 Adair's 'three circles' of management responsibilities

Adair suggested that skilled leaders should know and understand these three elements of their organisation well and should be able to manipulate each appropriately, according to the situation they are trying to manage. In this way, morale remains high, fostering a positive team attitude and thereby increasing productivity.

Adair identified eight characteristics of leadership ability, the possession of which demonstrate leadership competence:

1   Ability to define the task well, setting clear objectives.
2   Ability to plan, identifying alternative approaches and contingency plans.
3   Ability to brief the team appropriately, building an appropriate environment that brings out the best individual and team performance.
4   Ability to work effectively, getting the best possible outputs from the most efficient use of resources and minimising waste.
5   Ability to evaluate, identifying and understanding consequences and how to improve future performance.
6   Ability to motivate, with the right combination of intrinsic and extrinsic motivators.
7   Ability to organise effectively, both personally and all necessary resources.
8   Ability to set an appropriate example to which workers can aspire.

John Eric Adair

Born: 18 May 1934, Luton, Bedfordshire
Professional description: leadership theorist

Relating the theory to adventure learning

Adventure learning can be likened to an organisation: there is a leader and a group of people working towards achieving a task. The leader has the responsibility of assessing performance against plan, making sure that all necessary work is undertaken correctly, adapting plans towards success, motivating team members, using individual strengths and recognising individual and collective abilities. These functions can be identified within the team delivering the adventure learning and in the participant groups. The leader of the adventure learning team must balance these three elements to maintain team morale and ensure quality of delivery over a long period. The participant group may only be together a short period, perhaps only the one session, but the same elements have to be present for them to be successful; the leader of the participant group may be the adventure learning instructor in the first instance, but leadership may be gradually transferred to a group member (or even rotated around group members) as the session progresses. Important learning points for the group are that awareness of these core 'responsibilities' will enable them to lead any group and that the identity of the leader may be irrelevant to accomplish tasks successfully.

Bureaucratic management theory

Max Weber, writing in the late 1800s, believed that the route to organisational effectiveness and maximising performance lay in a formal, rigid structure of bureaucracy, arguing that bureaucracy was the most logical way to organise human activity efficiently and that routine, systematic processes and defined hierarchies are necessary for maintaining order, working efficiently, avoiding favouritism or bias in the workplace (see Waters and Waters 2015). However, Weber also recognised uncontrolled bureaucracy as a threat to individual freedom. Advocating a highly impersonal structure with a rigid hierarchy, clear rules, legitimate authority and a stringent 'reward and punishment' system, Weber believed that the position an individual held within an organisation provided sufficient authority to command the performance of those below. While undertones of 'theory X' are clear, Weber's theory related to a world of highly labour-intensive workflows that rested on standardisation and a social structure that followed the same hierarchical chain of command. Some of the core elements of bureaucratic management theory include:

1   clearly defined job roles;

2   a hierarchy of authority;

3   standardised procedures;

4   meticulous record-keeping; and

5   hiring employees only if they meet the specific qualifications for a job.

Karl Emil Maximillian Weber

Born: 21 April 1864, Erfurt, Germany
Died: 14 June 1920, Munich, Germany
Professional description: sociologist, philosopher, jurist, political economist

Relating the theory to adventure learning

Implementing bureaucracy while advocating person-centred learning may appear counter-intuitive, but there is a logic to the implementation of systematic process that relates to a team of adventure learning instructors. The nature of adventure learning delivery is such that instructors are often out with groups for much of their time and therefore everyone has to work to the same process in order for the team to function effectively, for example:

- *Job roles:* everyone has to know what they are required to do and when, with which groups they are to work, what activities and support activities are expected of them.
- *Hierarchy of authority:* there has to be an overall leader to co-ordinate activities and ensure all tasks are addressed.
- *Standardised procedures and record keeping:* instructors have to know that equipment is fit for purpose, that the equipment they need is where they expect, damage and incidents have to be logged, accidents and applied first aid have to be recorded.
- *Quality of staff:* instructors have to hold appropriate skills and qualifications to conduct a session safely, colleagues need to know each other's level of competence.

Without such bureaucracy, there is the danger of safety risks, breaches of health and safety legislation and potential threat to life, not to mention chaos and confusion among the instructor team!

Distributed leadership

Distributed leadership is associated with Alma Harris (2005, 2008; Harris and Spillane 2008). Essentially, it focuses on the mobilisation of leadership at all levels in an organisation in a collaborative model, and not relying on leadership from the top, as traditional models. It is about the many playing a role in the leadership function rather than the few, where the emphasis is on *leadership practice* rather than leadership as a hierarchical function and the responsibility of the highest tier(s). The idea of 'distributed leadership' has become popular in recent years and offers an alternative to the many models of leadership that focus on the attributes and behaviour of individuals, defining the characteristics that 'leaders' should portray. Shared leadership provides a more systemic perspective, where the responsibility of leadership is divorced from formal hierarchical roles; the actions and influence of people at all levels is recognised as integral to overall organisational direction and functioning. However, the critical role played by those in formal leadership positions must be recognised, although distributed (shared) leadership proposes that leadership is a collective responsibility, not a responsibility to be deposited on one person. The focus moves from the people to the systems and process, encouraging latent potential to be brought to the fore.

Distributed leadership emerges naturally within the culture as an integral way of operating; it is not a system that can be 'built' or forced. While practically leadership will emerge according to need, not everyone will lead all the time or simultaneously, and some team members will lead more strongly or in more ways than others will. The need for a recognised and credible figurehead to set direction and goals becomes critical within a distributed leadership structure; the leader cannot be seen as purely delegating, avoiding accountability and responsibility.

The distributed leadership relationship can be seen as a partnership of the various parties interested in the outcome(s) of the team. In a holistic learning environment, delivery has to be recognised less as the sole responsibility of the instructor and more of a partnership of relevant and necessary associates from all elements of the learner's life. Within a multi-modal process, it has to be recognised that the instructor cannot deliver expertly in every aspect of the learning. Such partnership working is a relationship of mutual respect for the ability, experience and knowledge of each party, with a professional maturity that enables the sharing of ideas and expertise, and developing a coherent programme that facilitates maximising the learning potential of each programme opportunity. Such partnership working demands common purpose(s), with clear boundaries and goals. To achieve this, the individuals within the relationship have to be clear and comfortable with their own team culture and their position within it before they can navigate their way into and reconcile with an emerging new collaborative cultural domain.

Alma Harris

Born: 21 December 1958
Professional description: educationalist

Relating the theory to adventure learning

Practically, the theory almost follows from Weber's bureaucratic management theory, but has the added necessity of a strong team interrelationship. When clear processes are in place, every member knows what to expect and what is expected, the leader should be able to rely on workers to perform routine functions at least without continued oversight. In an adventure learning team, the leader can rely on the instructors to execute the session safely and make local decisions: whether a group is behaving unsafely, the weather is deteriorating, a piece of equipment must be condemned, evaluative paperwork will be completed. The leader cannot be in attendance at every session to oversee performance, and nor would that be desirable; often there will be long periods between when instructors see their leader face-to-face because of the nature of the work, and the leader may have to deliver activities as well as lead and manage the provision. Therefore, the leader has to be confident that not only will instructors perform adequately, but that necessary tasks will be undertaken as necessary without direction, such as maintenance, fault reporting, equipment replenishment. The involvement of everyone contributes to a smoothly functioning unit where all members feel involved and that they have a stake in its success.

Five forms of power

Leadership and power are closely linked. People tend to follow those who are powerful, and because others follow, the person with power leads. However, leaders have power for different reasons. Some are powerful because they alone hold the ability for promotion, dismissal or reward; others are powerful because they determine the tasks others must perform and control their workload. Yet, while leaders of this type have formal, official power, their teams are unlikely to be enthusiastic or supportive if this is all they rely upon. Alternatively, leaders may have power because they are experts in their fields, or because their team members admire them. People like this do not necessarily have formal leadership roles, but they influence others because of their skills and personal qualities.

One of the most notable studies on power was conducted by social psychologists John French and Bertram Raven (1959), who identified five bases of power:

1   Legitimate power comes from the belief that a person has the formal right to make demands, and to expect compliance and obedience from others, their power being derived from holding a particular organisational position.

2   Reward power results from one person's ability to compensate another for compliance. Reward power is the ability to give other people what they want and demand something in return. Rewards can also be withheld for non-compliance.

3   Expert power is based on a person's superior or unique skill and knowledge; and is a very common form of power.

4   Referent power is the result of a person's perceived attractiveness, worthiness and right to respect from others. Power is derived from followers aspiring to be like the leader.

5   Coercive power comes from the belief that a person will punish others for noncompliance; it is the power of dictators, despots and bullies, derived from fear.

If you are aware of these sources of power, you can:

- understand more clearly why you are influenced by someone, and decide whether you want to accept the base of power being used;
- recognise your own sources of power; and
- build your leadership skills by using and developing your own sources of power, appropriately, and for best effect.

John R. P. French

Born: 7 August 1913, Boston, Massachusetts
Died: 14 October 1995, Ann Arbor, Michigan
Professional description: psychologist

Bertram H. Raven

Born: 26 September 1926, Youngstown, Ohio
Professional description: psychologist, academic

Relating the theory to adventure learning

Within pre-existing groups, adventure learning instructors can often identify the power dynamic that exists among different individuals and use their understanding to break down negative relationships. This can be done subtly, without the group members realising, but to be most effective it is done overtly, using the group relationships as the basis of learning. Often, an instructor will nominate a leader from within the group and in so doing, they must be mindful to observe the group dynamics and pre-existing power bases, as these can materially affect group performance (but form excellent material for group discussion and learning points!).

Within an adventure team, the leader must be aware of their own basis of power and the principle(s) upon which they are achieving compliance. The leader will have legitimate power through their appointment, but there are likely to be others in an adventure learning team with expert and referent power, which can threaten stability in times of challenge. Successful overall performance demands a balance of mutual respect and co-operation; the exercising of coercive power is not conducive to the trust relationships necessary in adventure learning, where instructors and their leader are generally geographically distanced.

Learning organisations

A learning organisation is the term given to a company that facilitates the learning of its members and thereby continuously transforms itself. A learning organisation has five main features; systems thinking, personal progression, mental modelling, shared vision and group learning. The learning organisation concept was conceived by Peter Senge (1990) and his colleagues, encouraging organisations to realign to a more interconnected way of thinking. Learning organisations are more akin to communities with which employees can empathise, as they will then work harder towards success. The underlying principle is that, in times of change, only flexible, adaptive and productive organisations can excel and so to develop accordingly, organisations need to learn how to capitalise on the skills, knowledge, experience and commitment of all members of the workforce. While everyone has the capacity to learn, the structures in which they have to function are often not conducive to reflection and engagement. Further, individuals may lack the cognitive capacity or maturity to make sense of their situation. According to Senge, learning organisations are those where workers continually expand their capacity to achieve, where propensity to learn is fostered, where creativity is nurtured, where collective aspiration is encouraged and liberated and where workers see 'the whole' as opposed to their small function. Senge argued that only organisations able to adapt quickly and effectively can excel; to be a learning organisation two factors must exist: first, the ability to design the organisation to match the intended or desired outcomes, and second, the ability not only to recognise when direction differs from desired outcome, but also to initiate corrective action.

Senge also believed in the theory of systems thinking (discussed further later in this chapter), which has sometimes been referred to as the cornerstone of learning organisations. Systems thinking focuses on how the individual element interacts with other system elements and, rather than focusing on the individual, consideration should be on the interactions within and beyond the system. Systems thinking is a holistic approach to analysis that focuses on the way that a system's constituent parts interrelate and how systems work over time and within the context of larger systems. The systems thinking approach contrasts with traditional analysis, which studies systems by breaking them down into their discrete elements. According to systems thinking, system behaviour results from the effects of reinforcing and balancing processes. A reinforcing process leads to the increase of some system component; if reinforcement is unchecked by a balancing process, it eventually leads to collapse. A balancing process is one that tends to maintain equilibrium in a particular system, therefore attention to feedback is an essential component.

Peter Michael Senge

Born: 1947, Stanford, California
Professional description: systems scientist

Relating the theory to adventure learning

The group undertaking adventure learning activities can be likened to an organisation in that it has members working to achieve one or more goals and must create a functional structure that allows it to do this. The group will continually change and transform in nature as its members find their operating model and develop their strategy. Successful attainment of the set goals will require a range of skills and knowledge, held by most or all of the members of the group and success will demand that all members remain focused and involved in the task in hand. If the group becomes distracted by one element of the activity or one group member, they will not succeed. They need to see the activity 'as a whole' in order to define and achieve each step.

Similarly, in an adventure learning team, the group of instructors has to have a shared understanding of what is to be achieved and should be able to learn new ways to approach a learning topic or deliver an activity element from one another. The acceptance that there is more than one route to success underpins both learning organisation and systems thinking theory; it is essential that individuals work as a cohesive unit, sharing practice, respecting one another and accepting constructive feedback, or the system becomes 'stuck', fixated on one element, which undermines overall success.

Management by objectives

Management by objectives (MBO) is the mutual definition of objectives by leaders and workers so that both agree and understand what they need to do, then get on with achieving the objectives without question or much further direction. Once the targets are set and agreed, the leader can focus on more strategic matters and the worker can focus on achieving the targets. This approach of joint target setting assumes that the involvement of the worker ensures their commitment to achieving the objectives, as the objectives of the organisation become aligned with the objectives of the worker; performance then becomes the comparison of actual against set targets.

In the 1950s Peter Drucker developed a theory in which the need for the different levels within an organisation to co-operate and interact, with common commitment and responsibility; if everyone within the hierarchy understands and agrees to the goals to be achieved, there is a natural common challenge to which everyone rises (Drucker 1999). The system starts at the top, with those at the pinnacle of the hierarchy determining the strategic goals of the organisation, and then each subsequent tier successively identifies and agrees the goals of their tier and shared targets form.

Advantages:

- Objectives are discussed before being mutually agreed.
- The participative approach builds understanding between leaders and workers.
- The worker is better motivated and fulfilled in their role.
- Overall communication and co-ordination within the organisation are improved.
- Organisational goals and those of the individual are aligned.
- All tiers and areas of the organisation have goals they understand and to which they agree.
- Goals can be tailored to specific interests, skills and circumstances.
- Leaders have to spend less time focused on the minutiae of worker performance and can devote more time to strategic development.

Disadvantages:

- It is a systematic process that has to be undertaken in the right order to be successful.
- The emphasis falls on the goal setting, rather than the process or the outcome.
- Individuals and teams can tend to focus on their own targets and not the interaction with others.
- There is no consideration of the external environment in which the organisation operates or capacity to change quickly if the environment changes unexpectedly.
- Goals can become the focus, without being SMART (specific, measurable, achievable, realistic, time-bound) or even of high quality.
- There is no capacity for creativity and innovation.
- Effective target measurement may be difficult to achieve in a synchronous timeframe across the organisation.
- Not every objective is measurable.
- The process is slow to set up, resource demanding and can be inefficient to maintain.
- Resources are managed to achieve targets, rather than evaluating whether it is the most effective use of the resources in the first place.

Peter Ferdinand Drucker

Born: 19 November 1909, Vienna, Austria
Died: 11 November 2005, Claremont, California
Professional description: management consultant, educator

Relating the theory to adventure learning

Considered by some modern commentators as outmoded today, management by objectives (MBO) is simply about communication, each party understanding what they are expected to achieve and within what timeframe. Any group of participants needs that clarity in order to be able to perform the required activity.

While the disadvantages quoted are clearly potential downfalls if the process is used unthinkingly, MBO can be a constructive means of managing an adventure learning team that operates quite remotely and with relatively little peer interaction. Used alongside other leadership and management constructs (such as distributed leadership and bureaucratic management), MBO helps to shape an informed, motivated team, working to its strengths and as a cohesive unit.

Motivators and hygiene factors (two-factor theory)

According to Frederick Herzberg's theory in the late 1950s, there are two critical factors that influence the way people perform: motivators and hygiene factors, where motivational factors will not necessarily reduce, but can increase motivation and hygiene factors will not, in themselves, motivate, but if not present, can lower motivation (Herzberg 2003; Herzberg *et al.* 2008).

Closely linked to Abraham Maslow's hierarchy of need, Herzberg contends that the satisfaction of low-level needs (hygiene factors) is insufficient for motivating people to perform, that is a minimum salary and adequate working conditions are not enough; people also need higher needs (motivators) to be satisfied, such as personal fulfilment, recognition, responsibility, progression. Herzberg's theory added a further element by the proposition of a two-factor model, where one set of work characteristics (incentives) leads to satisfaction at work, while the other leads to dissatisfaction (Figure 17). Thus, he proposed that satisfaction and dissatisfaction are not ends of a spectrum, but are in fact independent and separate factors and to improve motivation both sets of factors must be recognised and satisfied. According to the two-factor theory, there are four possible combinations (Figure 18).

Herzberg contended that job satisfaction and job dissatisfaction are not opposites that cancel each other out, but the opposite of *satisfaction* is *no satisfaction* and the opposite of *dissatisfaction* is *no dissatisfaction*. Remedying the causes of dissatisfaction will not create satisfaction, nor will adding satisfaction eliminate dissatisfaction. If you have a hostile work environment, giving someone a promotion will not make them satisfied and if you create a healthy work environment but do not provide members of your team with satisfaction factors, the work they are doing will still not be fulfilling; you may create peace, but not necessarily enhance performance, as you placate your workforce instead of actually motivating them to improve performance.

Motivators	Hygiene factors
Challenging work	Status
Recognition	Job security
Responsibility	Work conditions
Achievement	Benefits in kind
Personal growth	Work relationships

Figure 17 Herzberg's motivators and hygiene factors

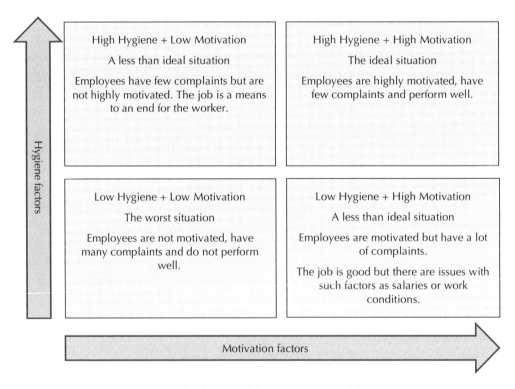

Figure 18 The four possible combinations of factors

Frederick Irving Herzberg

Born: 18 April 1923, Lynn, Massachusetts
Died: 19 January 2000, Salt Lake City, Utah
Professional description: psychologist

Relating the theory to adventure learning

Motivation is critical to performance and to success. Young people are not paid to learn, so the most basic of motivators (salary) is non-existent for them, heightening the importance of more intrinsic rewards. For participants to engage in an activity there has to be a conscious decision on their part (employment of self-will). That decision is based upon their personal objectives (their motives), which may be to have fun, because they want to achieve certain goals, or something entirely different. The point is that the instructor cannot envisage activity performance as the sole impetus to a session, there has to be something else, a (motivator or hygiene) factor that resonates with the participant and makes them want to have a go. If a participant only engages on the basis of 'the sooner I get this over with, the sooner I can be out of here and go home' (the fulfilment of a basic security need), they will never gain the most they can from the activity. However, if they believe in peer respect, personal development and strengthened peer relationships, they will derive so much more.

Within the adventure learning team, a similar psychology exists; workers have to derive personal fulfilment and a sense of worthiness from their role; it can be very isolating to be operating geographically distanced from colleagues, especially with a more challenging group, leading potentially to poor motivation if an instructor does not feel valued, respected or fulfilled.

Revisionist theory of leadership

In the modern business environment, characterised by complexity and constant change, it is neither necessary nor desirable for the pinnacle of the hierarchy to be populated by autocrats. Rather, leaders with more humanistic, democratic styles will achieve better results and maximise performance. According to Warren Bennis, true leaders understand themselves, possessing both a vision and the ability to translate that vision to their teams, which are staffed by workers who trust them and want to follow them (Bennis and Nanus 1985). It was Bennis who coined the phrase 'managers do things right: leaders do the right thing'.

Bennis identified six personal qualities of effective leaders:

1   *Integrity:* aligning words, actions and values, and maintaining these because they are the right course of action for the whole, even if an alternative may be easier or more personally advantageous.

2   *Dedication:* devoting the time and energy necessary to get the job done correctly, not making the job fit into a timeframe.

3   *Magnanimity:* giving praise where it is due, not taking the praise for the work of others and admitting when they are wrong.

4   *Humility:* recognising that others may have better skills, knowledge or experience, rather than assuming that a leadership position means they are right.

5   *Openness:* listening to the thoughts and ideas of others, even when they are completely different, then being willing to discuss the advantages and disadvantages of each without preconceptions.

6   *Creativity:* being able to think laterally and conceive of alternative approaches.

It was Bennis's contention that leadership is a skill that may be learned and that if they were willing, individuals could learn (even from failures) to empathise with their workers, bring them together as a functioning team and create the opportunities for that team to thrive.

Warren Gamaliel Bennis

Born: 8 March 1925, New York City, New York
Died: 31 July 2014, Los Angeles, California
Professional description: scholar, organisational consultant

Relating the theory to adventure learning

The revisionist theory of leadership works alongside theories like distributed leadership in advocating that hierarchical position does not equate to greater knowledge or ability, but rather that leaders can recognise the abilities of others, will consult team members and will happily give credit where due to others for the successful attainment of targets. The adventure learning team leader has many complex responsibilities from session timetables, to session planning, to equipment requisition and maintenance, to personnel management, to future planning. In addition, the geographic displacement of the team (and depending on schedules and delivery type, there could be a significant time displacement too) makes collaborative relationships far more important than rigid command and control structures.

Systems thinking

Systems thinking has roots in the general system theory that was advanced by Ludwig von Bertalanffy in the 1940s and furthered by Ross Ashby in the 1950s. Von Bertalanffy argued that, contrary to contemporary popular scientific belief, systems are more than the sum of their elemental parts by interacting with their environment in such a way that they evolve new properties. While systems thinking is an essential component of a learning organisation (Senge 1990), it brings together principles and concepts from all fields and therefore cannot be ascribed to a single theorist. Systems thinking concerns itself with a holistic entity that may be permanent or temporary. A system is a set of interrelated and interactive parts that interact and affect each other, thereby creating a larger complex whole, a system. Systems thinking is a method of critical thinking by which the interrelationship between the elemental components of a system are studied in order to understand their interaction, thereby gaining a better perspective on the overall system and making more informed decisions.

The defining characteristics of a system are:

- It is composed of a number of parts (elements), which may be physical or abstract.
- All the elements are related in some way.
- Definite boundaries can be identified, in terms of time, space and decision-making.
- It can exist as a part of another system.
- It has inputs that are processed into outputs.
- It is holistic as it has autonomy in that it does not need a third party to activate its processes.

Organisational systems may consist of people, structures or processes, working together to make the overall organisation or they may be the separate components that make up an individual part of the overall organisation. In adventure learning, a system may be an overall adventure centre or it may be one particular activity; thus, a system may be comprised of a number of smaller systems that overlap or exist within one another.

The systems thinking approach as a decision-making and problem-solving methodology advocates identifying and analysing the elements that make up the system, rather than targeting the outcome as the 'problem', which may lead to further issues or consequences. The focus is on the system *cycle*, rather than a linear cause and effect perspective, recognising that an improvement in one element of the system can affect another positively or negatively. This interactive approach encourages communication and co-operation to avoid the silo effect of tackling one element in isolation. By recognising patterns, we can make informed decisions to strengthen or change a pattern towards overall effectiveness and the achievement of objectives.

Some systems thinking theorists are briefly described below.

Alfonso Montuori

Born: The Netherlands
Professional description: transformative leadership consultant
Montuori's multifaceted research has been dedicated to creativity in research in order to make sense of our complex, diverse and ambiguous world. His principle foci are leadership, cultural diversity, education and creative inquiry.

Béla Heinrich Bánáthy

Born: 1 December 1919, Gyula, Hungary
Died: 4 September 2003, Chico, California
Professional description: linguist, systems scientist
Founder of the International Systems Institute and the White Stag Leadership Development Programme, Bánáthy focused his work principally on how people can shape their world through consideration of the systems from which it is constructed. His son, Béla Antal Bánáthy, continues his work.

Debora Hammond

Born: 1951
Professional description: historian of science
Inspired by the outdoors, Hammond believes social justice rests on consideration of the structural systems for inclusive participation and community dialogue.

Eugene Pleasants Odum

Born: 17 September 1913, Newport, New Hampshire
Died: 10 August 2002, Athens, Georgia
Professional description: biologist
Famous for his work on ecosystemic ecology, Odum pioneered the idea of the ecosystem and the interdependence of many different diverse ecosystems as the basis of how the earth functions.

Fritjof Capra

Born: 1 February 1939, Vienna, Austria
A physicist, educator, activist and author, Capra advocates holism and the inter-connectivity of all parts to any system.

Howard Thomas Odum

Born: 1 September 1924, Chapel Hill, North Carolina
Died: 11 September 2002, Gainesville, Florida
Professional description: ecologist
Like his brother, Eugene, Howard concerned himself with ecosystemic ecology, but focused on zoology and meteorology, as the basis for systems ecology. Odum's legacy is vast and covers many fields, including ecological modelling, ecological engineering, ecological economics, estuarine ecology, tropical ecosystems and general systems theory.

Ludwig von Bertalanffy

Born: 19 September 1901, Altgersdorf, Austria
Died: 12 June 1972, Buffalo, New York
Professional description: biologist, general systems theorist
One of the founders of general systems theory, Bertalanffy suggested that thermodynamic laws applied to closed, but not always open systems (living things).

Richard A. Swanson

Born: 1942
Professional description: organisational theorist
Best known for his work on financial research related to human resource development, Swanson focuses on performance improvement through development of staff.

Talcott Parsons

Born: 13 December 1902, Colorado Springs, Colorado
Died: 8 May 1979, Munich, Germany
Professional description: sociologist
Parsons developed action theory, the study of society, based on voluntarism (free will) and analytical realism (considered action). The theory is seen as a theory of social evolution and a means to understand and evaluate world history.

William Ross Ashby

Born: 6 September 1903, Lewisham, London
Died: 15 November 1972, Tockington, Gloucestershire
Professional description: psychiatrist, cybernetics pioneer
Despite being highly regarded and influential within the field of cybernetics and systems theory, Ashby remains less well known than others of the field.

Relating the theory to adventure learning

Systems thinking is also known as 'marginal gains' and has become prevalent in sports coaching. By focusing on small, manageable elements, the individual does not feel overwhelmed, so makes small steps successfully that aggregate into bigger achievements.

Every young person, indeed every participant to any adventure learning session, is comprised of a range of experiences and subjected to a range of influences. The 'system' is the array of environmental factors, past encounters, consequences, family, friends, aspirations and emotions that combine to form the way that the individual relates to the world around them (their ontology, the filters through which they perceive and understand). The instructor has to understand the ontological system in order to influence change in the individual, they cannot focus on one behavioural element in isolation. When adventure learning is used as a part of a programme of social education, the participant has to understand the influences and consequences in their lives and how a change to one part of the 'system' affects other parts. Simply targeting risky or anti-social behaviour, for example, without reference to all the other factors of the individual's life, will not result in behaviour modification.

Team roles

Dr Meredith Belbin (1981, 1993) studied teamwork for many years, noting that people tend to assume different roles when they work together. The team roles that he defined measure behaviour, not personality, but by identifying the particular role we assume in a group, or observing how others behave, we can work to develop strengths and manage weaknesses, thereby improving our own contribution and the overall performance of the team. Teams can become unbalanced if several team members have similar styles of behaviour (team roles); if team members have similar weakness, the team as a whole tends to have that weakness but if team members have similar strengths, they tend to compete (rather than co-operate) for the tasks and responsibilities that best suit them. Belbin identified nine team roles and he categorised these roles into three groups: action oriented, people oriented, and thought oriented; each role is associated with certain behavioural and interpersonal strengths and weaknesses.

Action-oriented roles

1 *Shaper (SH):* people who challenge the team to improve, being dynamic and extroverted, enjoying stimulating others, questioning norms and finding the best approaches for solving problems. The shaper is the one who shakes things up to make sure that all possibilities are considered and that the team does not become complacent. Shapers see obstacles as exciting challenges and want to push on when others feel like quitting. Their weaknesses are in being argumentative, often offending other people's feelings.

2 *Implementer (IMP):* people who get things done, turning ideas and concepts into actions and plans. They are disciplined people who work systematically, being efficient and well organised. On the downside, Implementers are inflexible and resistant to change.

3 *Completer–finisher (CF):* people who see that projects are completed, without omissions and paying attention to the detail. They are concerned with deadlines and will push the team to make sure the job is completed on time; they are orderly, conscientious and anxious. However, a completer–finisher worries unnecessarily, and finds it hard to delegate.

People-oriented roles

1 *Coordinator (CO):* the ones who take on the leader role, guiding the team to what they perceive are the objectives. Often excellent listeners, they recognise the value of colleagues and are calm, good-natured and delegate effectively. Their potential weaknesses are that they can delegate too much and may be manipulative.

2 *Team worker (TW):* the people who provide support and make sure that people within the team are working together effectively. These people negotiate, being flexible, diplomatic and perceptive, prioritising team cohesion. Their weaknesses are in being indecisive and not wanting to commit themselves during discussions and decision-making.

3 *Resource investigator (RI):* innovative and curious, they explore available options, develop contacts and negotiate for resources. They are enthusiastic, identifying and working with stakeholders to help the team accomplish its objective. Outgoing and extroverted, others are receptive to them and their ideas. On the downside, they lose enthusiasm quickly and are overly optimistic.

Thought-oriented roles

1 *Plant (PL):* the creative innovator who comes up with new ideas and approaches, thriving on praise but finding criticism hard to deal with. Plants are introverted and prefer to work apart from the group, being poor communicators and tending to ignore parameters and constraints. Their novel ideas can be impractical at times.

2 *Monitor–evaluator (ME):* best at analysing and evaluating ideas from other people. Being shrewd and objective, they are critical and strategic thinkers, carefully weighing all the options before making a decision. Often perceived as detached or unemotional, they are poor motivators who react to events rather than instigating action.

3 *Specialist (SP):* specialised knowledge needed to get the job done, they pride themselves on their skills and abilities and work to maintain a professional status. Their job within the team is to be an expert in the area, and they commit themselves fully to their field of expertise. This may limit their contribution and be preoccupied with technicalities at the expense of the bigger picture.

Meredith Raymond Belbin

Born: 1926
Professional description: management theorist

Relating the theory to adventure learning

When a group is undertaking an activity, the instructor can identify the roles that the different members assume as they develop their place within the group. This can be used by the instructor to help the group towards success, even if it means moving individuals between groups for a more even balance of characters. The nature of individuals within a group will be particularly influential in longer programmes, as the members of the group have more time to interact and establish a group culture.

In the context of leading an adventure learning team, the different roles that members assume can be considered by the leader within the context of other theories (MBO, forms of power) to develop a balanced team of complementary characters. The longer a group is together, the more the leader can invest in overcoming weaknesses in the team construct in order to create the necessary balance for success.

Theory X and theory Y

Theory X and theory Y, devised by Douglas McGregor (1960, 1966), have to do with the perceptions that managers hold of their employees, which in turn influence their management style. Theory X can be compared with transactional leadership, where managers rule in a 'reward and punish' style that assumed extrinsic reward suffices to define performance. Theory Y and transformational leadership assume that leaders want to encourage the best from their staff, assuming trust, respect and self-motivation. Theory X assumes that people are inherently idle, requiring close control and direction. An authoritative management style within a rigid hierarchical organisational structure is the only way to ensure performance. Workers are assumed to have no ambition and no ability to contribute to organisational planning or objectives.

Theory Y assumes that workers are ambitious, self-motivated and have self-control, that they derive enjoyment from their occupation and want to give the best of themselves if they continue to feel that emotional fulfilment. Workers are seen as having a significant contribution to organisational planning and objectives but are insufficiently exploited in most organisations.

McGregor did not perceive theories X and Y as ends of one spectrum, but as separate phenomena. Inherent in theory X is the assumption that people would rather not be at work and therefore there is the supposition that productivity relies on close supervision. However, theory Y assumes that people have chosen their career and naturally want to do the best they can and progress within the organisation, so the supposition of theory Y is that people do not need supervision in order to perform their job effectively.

Douglas McGregor

Born: 1906, Detroit
Died: 1 October 1964
Professional description: management consultant

Relating the theory to adventure learning

At the start of an adventure learning relationship, the instructor will play a 'theory X' manager, where rules are laid down, standards of behaviour are set and as the participants learn the basics of what they are required to do. Some groups displaying challenging behaviour may not progress away from 'theory X'. For most groups however, as they grasp the concepts of what is expected and the fundamentals of the activity, motivation blossoms with confidence and progression. Thus, the instructor can move to a 'theory Y' style that transfers increased autonomy and responsibility to the group.

For the adventure learning team, the theory serves to reinforce the need for the leader to defer autonomy to the workers. The geographical displacement arising from the nature of the work demands higher levels of trust, mutual respect and self-direction than would exist in other fields of teamwork (for example in a factory leader and workers would be physically together for an entire shift). 'Theory Y' leadership is not just desirable, but unavoidable in an adventure learning team.

Transactional leadership theory and transformational leadership theory

Transactional leadership theory is associated with Bernard Bass (1985), while transformational leadership theory is associated with James MacGregor Burns (1978). These are two seemingly opposing types of leadership: transactional leadership has a focus on the relationship between the leader and follower, whereas transformational leadership focuses on the beliefs, needs and values of the workers.

The transactional style of leadership was first described by Max Weber (1947); it is a style that focuses on the basic management processes of controlling, organising and short-term planning. Transactional leadership assumes that a worker's own self-interest is sufficient to motivate them and that extrinsic rewards hold most, if not all, the power in determining performance. Transactional leaders rely on their given hierarchical formal authority, with the worker having no other responsibility than to obey given instructions (something akin to the behaviourist theory of learning). Transactional leaders are not looking to organisational change, but to maintain existing performance and situations, to operate in a routine, rote fashion, often characterised by micromanagement, where the leader is directive and prescriptive, focused on process. Within the context of Maslow's hierarchy of needs, transactional leadership works at the basic levels of need satisfaction, where transactional leaders focus on the lower levels of the hierarchy.

Transformational leadership is an opposing style, where the leader focuses on change, creating a vision and building the foundation of a motivated team to achieve the vision. The leader becomes the role model to inspire followers, understanding their strengths and weaknesses so that they can delegate responsibility appropriately.

Transformational leaders define achievable and emotional expectations for those below them, stimulating the basis for fulfilling their personal needs; workers feel empowered and nurtured. Transformational leadership is akin to cognitive learning processes, where the learner is credited with individual thought and self-will. Within Maslow's hierarchy of need, the transformational style applies to the meeting of higher level needs. However, given that Maslow's theory mandates the satisfaction of lower order needs ahead of higher ones, there is an inherent assumption in transformational leadership theory that transactional leadership exists simultaneously to address the lower level.

Bernard Bass

Born: 11 June 1925, the Bronx, New York
Died: 11 October 2007, Binghamton, New York
Professional description: leadership theorist, organisational behaviourist

James MacGregor Burns

Born: 13 August 1918, Melrose, Massachusetts
Died: 15 July 2014, Williamstown, Massachusetts
Professional description: historian, political scientist, leadership theorist

Relating the theory to adventure learning

Exactly as 'theory X' applies to the start of the relationship with a group of participants, (and defines the relationship when the group presents high challenge), so too does transactional leadership apply. The participants look to the instructor for direction and structure, deferring to their authority (legitimate power). As confidence and competence grow, the instructor moves to transformational leadership, deferring autonomy and independence.

For the adventure learning team, transactional leadership highlights the functional requirements of team operations, such as work rotas, equipment servicing, funding applications, making sure staff are paid, co-ordinating leave, covering sickness absence ... the list can be almost endless. Transformational leadership defines the strategic visioning that enthuses the team members, explores new activities and programme structures, seeks new client groups and works to provide inspiration and enthusiasm to the workers. Both forms of leadership are necessary, as transactional leadership caters for the functional operating of the team and transformational leadership addresses the emotive caretaking and aspirational planning that provide worker motivation and commitment.

References

Adair, J. (1996) *Effective Motivation*. London: Pan Books.

Adair, J. (1998) *Effective Leadership*. London: Gower Publishing.

Bass, B. M. (1985) *Leadership and Performance Beyond Expectations*. New York: The Free Press.

Belbin, R. M. (1981) *Management Teams: Why They Succeed or Fail*. Oxford: Butterworth Heinemann.

Belbin, R. M. (1993) *Team Roles at Work*. Oxford: Butterworth Heinemann.

Bennis, W. and Nanus, B. (1985) *Leaders*. New York: Harper & Row.

Drucker, P. F. (1999) *Management Challenges for the 21st Century*. New York: HarperCollins.

French, J. P. R. and Raven, B. (1959) The bases of social power. In D. Cartwright and A. Zander (eds), *Group Dynamics*. New York: Harper & Row.

Harris, A. (2005) *Crossing Boundaries and Breaking Barriers*. London: Specialist Schools Trust.

Harris, A. (2008) *Challenging Leadership Practice: Exploring New Forms of Leadership Practice*. Nottingham: National College for School Leadership.

Harris, A. and Spillane, J. (2008) Distributed leadership through the looking glass. *Management in Education* 22(1): 31–34.

Herzberg, F. (2003) One more time: how do you motivate employees? *Harvard Business Review* (January).

Herzberg, F., Mausner, B. and Snyderman, B. B. (2008) *The Motivation to Work*. New Brunswick, NJ: Transaction Publishers.

MacGregor Burns, J. (1978) *Leadership*. New York: Harper & Row.

McGregor, D. (1960) *The Human Side of Enterprise*. New York: McGraw-Hill.

McGregor, D. (1966) *Leadership and Motivation: Essays*. Cambridge, MA: MIT Press.

Senge, P. (1990) *The Fifth Discipline*. London: Random House Business Books.

Waters, T. and Waters, D. (eds) (2015) *Weber's Rationalism and Modern Society: New Translations on Politics, Bureaucracy, and Social Stratification*. New York: Palgrave Macmillan.

Weber, M. (1947) *The Theory of Social and Economic Organization* (tr. A. M. Henderson and T. Parsons). New York: The Free Press.

PART II | THE TOOLKIT

17 | Introduction to the toolkit

This toolkit is essentially a collection of initiative games. The aim of the toolkit is to provide those working with people, whether children, teenagers or adults with a range of activities that challenge perceptions, develop group skills, expand comfort zones, and promote activity-based learning. From the participant's point of view, above all, these games are fun and get them moving around, burning energy or thinking and talking. These games can be used as easy ways to get to know people, to *begin* to look at issues, they can be used as the foundation of wider programmes of learning or they can be used as the core of a development programme. The point is, games are games and, if planned appropriately into a programme, can be used as the basis for an immeasurable spectrum of learning, development and achievement. The limitation is the imagination and creativity of the group leader, but the fundamental tenet is the same: prior preparation and planning promotes performance. Initiative games are not just for children and young people, they are a useful way of any organisation finding out more about people, how they think, who has innate leadership capacity, who sits back and directs while others do the work.

So, what are initiative games? Simply, they are games that involve thinking (inventiveness, resourcefulness). Initiative games are fun, cooperative, challenging games in which the group is confronted with a specific 'problem' to solve and has to work out a solution, sometimes with and sometimes without support from the leader. Many community and youth groups have had to close over recent years, increasing numbers of young people are turning to remote social platforms for their entertainment and there are increasingly fewer areas for outdoor play environments, especially ones where children and young people can play freely, using their imagination and burning energy. All this has resulted in the loss of valuable knowledge and skills in group work and using little materials (and no electronics, computers or other gadgets!) for learning and team building; the growth in social media and reduced opportunities for activity puts society in danger of losing the valuable commodity of human interaction.

Initiative games are valuable for three main reasons:

1   To demonstrate and teach leadership skills, which help to promote personal, emotional and psychological growth;

2   To allow (young) people to learn valuable life skills in negotiating, interacting and decision-making, which helps them to learn about living in a social environment;

3   To demonstrate a process of thinking about experiences, which helps people understand and learn.

In delivering initiative games, you begin by:

1   Planning the programme and understanding yourself exactly what you want the activity to achieve, whether there are staged achievements and how you will guide the group towards the objectives you have for them.

2   Risk assessing the activity and the playing area (prior to commencement!).

3   Clearly explaining the activity to the group.

4   Make sure the rules are understood, including any special elements (for example, the fact that everyone must complete the activity, or a certain part of it, for the group to be successful or a requirement for everyone to take part in some way).

5   Not offering ideas for solving the problem too quickly. Stand back; let the group work, think and experiment, even if they appear to be struggling. It can be really frustrating to watch group members struggle, but you must remember that growth and learning come from trying and making mistakes far more than being provided with the solutions too readily.

6   Don't interfere unless something is unsafe or the group has fallen apart, which includes dropping large, unsubtle hints!

After the experience, reflect on the activity as a whole with the group; reflective practice is a tool used a lot in adventure learning and youth work, and it is important to build time into the session to talk about what the participants are learning during the activity, as well as when the activity has finished.

1   Talk about how effectively and efficiently they accomplished the task(s) and how they got along with each other. Even if the group seemed to have failed miserably in achieving the tasks, a skilled facilitator can always find positives to discuss.

2   Ask open-ended questions to help the group talk about the issues and draw the group into discussion.

3   Don't be judgemental.

4   In asking questions, first help the participants focus on what happened, then ask them to decide if what happened was good or bad. We tend to judge ourselves much more harshly than others do, so be prepared to emphasise and promote the positives!

5   Finally, ask them how this learning can be used elsewhere in life, setting some goals for the future.

The best impact that initiative games can have is for the reflective methods and the associated learning to be used in subsequent activities or in other aspects of people's lives. While initiative games are fun and meaningful, valuable life lessons can be learned and a lasting impact will only be achieved by the person understanding the learning and applying it when they head back to their everyday life, whether it is a young person heading back into their community or a worker heading back into the office. As a role model and adventure mentor, you help people learn to make decisions and solve problems; you teach them the skills they need and let them practice for themselves. Reflective review during and after activities and experiences helps people learn. Get them into the habit of thinking and sharing together as a group.

If a game is too easy or if you have other motives, you can vary the skills of the participants by not allowing some to talk, by blindfolding, by not allowing the use of various limbs, or other 'hindering' tactics.

'Facilitation' means to make something easier or less difficult, to help forward an action or a process and to assist progress; it is often described as the art of making things easy for others, but if you make things too easy you risk returning to the spoon-feeding tradition in which learners passively digest whatever the educator wants them to. In essence, facilitation is an enabling role in which the focus is on what the learner is doing, experiencing and feeling rather than on what the educator does or directs the learner to do. You are there to be a facilitator, the person who is there to ensure a productive group process. The role of the facilitator is to ensure that the group works as a constructive and cohesive unit. When facilitating these activities, it is important to be yourself; you will be most effective when you are being your natural self and expressing your own personality. This has a positive impact on the group; people get permission to be themselves from the way the facilitator behaves, through modelling. If *you* are stiff and formal, the group tends to be like that; if *you* are relaxed and self-expressed, the group will follow suit and relax into the activity. It is also important to know when to stand back and allow natural group processes to operate; just because the group does not think or act in the way or at the speed you would, does not necessarily mean they are wrong! Some common facilitation styles:

1   *Non-directive facilitation:* where you believe that participants can work things out for themselves and where both you and they will find it more rewarding to do so. An impartial stance can also help to encourage discussion, defuse conflict or help participants become more independent and responsible. However, there are always going to be your non-negotiable educational values, about which you should be clear to yourself and to others and on which you should never remain neutral.

2   *Appreciative facilitation:* emphasises what works well and pays attention to success and achievement. At its simplest, it involves catching participants at their best moments and providing positive feedback about what they did or said. You can invite positive comments from participants for each other following a group exercise or just ask, 'what is working well?'

3   *Active facilitation:* emphasises the facilitator's role during a group activity. Sometimes the facilitator may simply be enabling a group to achieve a task in the time available. However, where the purpose of the activity is to generate experiences from which people will learn, the facilitator may want to intervene during the activity in order to influence what is experienced.

4   *Front-loading:* leaves little to chance. The facilitator is in the role of storyteller before participants have had the experiences to fit the story. Even when there is pressure to achieve particular outcomes, it by no means follows that 'predetermined' and 'prescribed' interpretations will be the most effective facilitation strategy. If interpretation precedes experience, the 'experience' is little more than an illustration in the facilitator's story. This is 'confirming through experience' rather than 'learning from experience'.

Our task as facilitators is threefold:

1   *To enhance experiences* – by raising awareness during activities and making it easy for group members to communicate their experiences during reviews.

2   *To enhance reviewing abilities* – initially by encouraging and helping group members to reflect on their experiences from a range of different perspectives.

3   *To enhance understanding of group members' own learning style* – so that they become better (experiential) learners.

18 | **Practical considerations**

Adventure learning is simply taking participants away from the activities in which they would normally engage, offering opportunities for active interaction, then reviewing the process and result. It need not always be large scale, high risk and adrenalin fuelled, but can be smaller, localised and more directly under the control of the group leader. The considerations are the same, irrespective of venue, only the instructor and the group leader are more likely to be the same person. Successful adventure learning sessions do not happen by accident, the instructor has to prepare in advance and plan not only the activities of the session but the surrounding features. This includes:

- equipment to be used, and making sure it is fit for use and in the right place at the right time;
- the process of the session in how they are going to stage the elements of the activity and review them;
- how they will convey the learning from the session; and, of course,
- the instructor must have fully assessed all risk aspects of the session in advance.

Adventure learning is an experiential learning tool, grounded in both formal and informal learning and communication is a crucial part of that educative process. It is essential that the instructor is able to communicate with participants, imparting necessary safety and activity instructions as well as engaging young people in the relational conversations that support their social education and personal development alongside their skill development and cognitive learning.

Participants are not always willing and compliant; the instructor may also be faced with challenging young people and they must have a constructive strategy of dealing with them. Young people become challenging for a number of reasons: fear of the unknown, nervousness at a new situation, wanting to appear a certain way to their peers, wanting to maintain their perceived group status or it may simply be an emotional, psychological reaction (otherwise known as 'being a teenager'!). The instructor has to deal with the challenge in a positive way that does not undermine the young person, reinforces the instructor's position as the authority figure, does not damage relationships with the rest of the group members and retains the adventure learning principle of 'challenge by choice'.

Adventure learning is based as much on conversational interactions as it is on skill development and cognitive understanding; therefore, engaging challenging young people in conversation and understanding the root cause of their behaviour is a far more constructive way of dealing with the situation than becoming irritated or dictatorial. There is an old adage of 'fail to prepare and you prepare to fail' and this is certainly true of adventure learning; the essential core criteria to a successful adventure learning session are *planning* and *preparation*! Plan well and the session will be positive for the instructor as well as the participants, but a terrible plan is just that, no matter how carefully it is undertaken!

A good adventure learning instructor will make a poor activity a memorable and enjoyable experience, but equally a poor adventure learning instructor will ruin the best activity. The core question the adventure learning instructor should consider is whether they would be happy with the quality and quantity of planning and preparation if the activity were to involve their own child. The adventure learning instructor is *in loco parentis* during their time with the participant, meaning that they have to apply the same standard of duty of care as they would in respect of their own child. There are some fundamental points to remember when planning a session:

1   Awareness and understanding underpin quality: knowing the session or programme objectives and having a strong strategy to achieve them make a session meaningful for the instructor and the participants, the learning becomes naturally embedded. Also included in this are emergency planning, knowing accident and emergency procedures and contingency planning.

2   Teamwork builds quality and shared knowledge: no instructor should feel they have to build a session plan alone, it is important to get other views, test the planned process and share responsibility for development. It is good practice to ensure colleagues know the plan, act as a 'base' contact in case of issues and emergencies and are notified when everyone is returned safely so involving these people improves their awareness and their ability to help should the need arise.

3   The participants want to have fun: it is easy to become focused on rules, activity skill level, weather, distracting questions and behaviour, but the participants will learn by enjoying themselves; if fun is absent, so too is learning. A simple way to help minimise the understanding of expectations is to provide a full information sheet with the consent form (which will be required from parents or carers for any adventure learning activity).

4   The opener is critical: in the first 15 to 30 minutes of the encounter, the adventure learning instructor will win or lose the majority of the group. The start sets the impact and defines the extent to which the participants will engage, so this is where the 'bang' has to be!

5   Facilitation makes or breaks the memory: the instructor has to turn disappointment and failure into a positive, valuable learning experience, helping the participants to see their success, however small, in what they have done.

6   The activities have to be appropriate to the group: this is where prior communication comes into play. The instructor cannot assume a certain level of knowledge, skills or abilities within a certain age group, they must have advance knowledge of the group members and any limitations or prior learning so that they can plan appropriate activities associated with required learning.

7   Timings play a central role in success: each stage of the session has to be associated with an estimated time that will allow the overall session timing to be achieved. If participants feel rushed or if one element of the session has to be cut because the instructor has run out of time, then learning can be severely compromised.

8   The environment will affect learning: logistics are an important consideration; if the instructor has to struggle with wind, rain and surrounding noise to impart important safety information or crucial activity direction, the participants cannot be expected to gain the most from their session. In planning the session, the adventure learning instructor should consider their own role and how they will achieve their responsibilities. Researching a venue that is not regularly used means knowing the dangers and boundaries to be applied; if an offsite venue has perhaps not been used for a few weeks or months, a site visit is important to make sure that nothing has changed.

Risk management is a very important part of the background work associated with adventure learning sessions. All adventurous activities must be accompanied by regularly reviewed risk assessments that are understood by the activity instructors as well as their managers. A risk assessment is simply a document that breaks down each activity into its component parts, then considers:

*   all the elements that could go wrong;
*   all the incidents that could possibly happen in each of those component parts;
*   the likelihood of those incidents; and
*   the consequences of the incidents.

The risk assessment then defines the mitigating actions that will reduce the likelihood of these incidents occurring. A competent adventure learning provider will have a set of generic risk assessments for every activity it provides; this means everything that could happen at every point of the participant's time on site, travelling to and from an offsite venue and during any non-activity time, as well as the activity itself. These generic risk assessments are likely to be drawn up and reviewed annually by the provider but do not take account of every detail; alongside the generic risk assessments, the instructor should undertake a running risk assessment on the day in light of current weather, the particular participants and any relevant circumstances, such as perhaps works around the activity site. If the activities are to be delivered locally, that is by a local group leader rather than an adventure provider, responsibility for risk assessment rests with the group leader.

The nature of adventure learning is such that incidents and accidents will occur; by virtue of being outside and undertaking challenging activities, it is absolutely impossible (and highly undesirable!) to remove all risk and provide complete safety. A useful abstract way of dealing with incidents is the *incident pit*, a conceptual pit with increasingly steeper sides that converge to a point of no return; a seemingly minor incident can deteriorate over time into a spiral of increasingly worse incidents that become harder and harder to resolve, making escape from the incident pit less and less possible. First presented by E. John Towse at a Diving Medical Conference in Stoke Mandeville Hospital in 1973, the incident pit is a term used by scuba divers, engineers, medical professionals and technology managers to describe how to avoid being caught in an increasingly threatening situation (Figure 19).

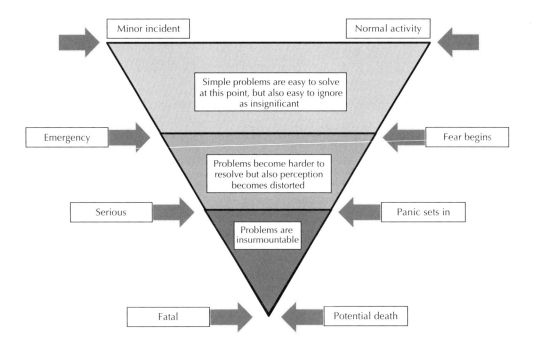

Figure 19 The incident pit

Imagine an adventure learning instructor with a group of participants at the start of a climbing session. The instructor has not set up the ropes beforehand or got the harnesses and helmets out ready for the group so they are trying to set up the ropes, get all the participants into the equipment and get the session started because the group is becoming restless at having to wait around. The instructor gets the participants peer belaying (belaying each other) to get everyone involved; because the group are peer belaying, the instructor saves time by not putting on their own harness or helmet. They notice that a couple of participants have long, loose hair, have loose sweatshirts over their harnesses and have not fastened up their helmets, but as most of the participants have climbed here before, the instructor assumes that they should be able to put the harnesses and helmets on correctly and will know to fasten their helmets before they climb. They also only do a short briefing because the group have done this before and everyone wants to get climbing. All of a sudden, a shout goes up, a belayer has their long, loose hair caught in the belay device. The instructor rushes to help, becoming engrossed in the situation. Then another shout is heard from the other side of the wall, a participant had their harness loose under the sweatshirt and has it caught on one of the holds because the belayer forgot to have them face the wall in an 'L' shape to walk down and they swung round. The climber is panicking, while swinging round trying to free themselves their unfastened helmet comes off and they bang their head, cutting themselves in the process.

The situation here may not lead to death (although potentially it could!), but the point is that it could have been so easily avoided. Setting up the ropes and equipment beforehand would have meant that the instructor was not feeling stressed; they could have got the participants into their harnesses and helmets straight away and got the session started. Checking harnesses beforehand, making sure long hair was tied back, allowing no loose clothing over the top of harnesses and insisting helmets are fasted would have prevented an escalating series of problems.

Adventure learning sessions are not always going to be able to be undertaken on site, at the provider venue, many of the more adventurous activities are undertaken in natural environments such as rock crags, open water lakes or moorland. Planning to go offsite entails more planning but is potentially far more effective in the learning process. The instructor has to be responsible for ensuring that the group gets to the venue safely, that all necessary equipment arrives at the venue and that the activity is set up while the participants are not endangered by the instructor being otherwise occupied. For any young person, parental consent must be obtained before they can be taken off site; the consent form must contain details of the young person and their parent/carer, including contact details, and any necessary medical information of which the instructor must be aware in order to safeguard the welfare of that young person while on the activity. The instructor must also have a safety mechanism in place for being offsite, for example, landline contacts in case of emergency (perhaps at the administration office) and contacts who know where the group are and what time they plan to return. It is always crucial after the offsite trip has ended to let the contacts know that the group has returned safely.

Inclusivity is another critical element of both group management and social education. Adventure learning engages all the senses, allowing young people of a more practical nature to work on a more equal basis to those with strong cognitive skills; the natural order of the classroom becomes disrupted and new leaders emerge. Inclusivity is about ensuring everyone has an equal quality of experience, which does not necessarily mean that everybody does exactly the same activity in exactly the same way or has exactly the same personal goals. While a group may be set a single overall task, individual members of the group may have their own challenges, their own hurdles to overcome and their own objectives to achieve. Quality of experience and thus inclusion is again the responsibility of the adventure learning instructor.

An adventure learning curriculum embodies cognitive development, skill development and social development, meaning classroom learning (or formal learning) is combined with personal development (or informal learning). While the ultimate goal of the curriculum may be the eventual achievement of good examination results for a school, there are intangible outcomes that should be evidenced in other ways, for example photographs, video, personal statements and peer reviews. The curriculum itself can be delivered in a number of ways and to be most effective should be delivered such that it progressively allows the participants to assume responsibility for planning how they will achieve their set task. In the beginning, the instructor will play a more directive role, known as behaviourist teaching, where they will essentially instruct the participants on what to do and how to undertake their task. As the participants gain in knowledge and confidence they enter a cognitive phase, increasingly willing and able to think for themselves, plan for themselves and make their own decisions; they begin to assume responsibility and lose their passiveness. Ultimately, the participants enter the experiential learning phase, where the instructor becomes merely the facilitator, the participants require almost no instructor intervention and are able to think, try and make decisions themselves. Through trial and error, through success and failure, learning becomes meaningful and achievement has a much greater positive effect. Experiential learning through adventure learning is more than simply undertaking adventurous activities; if simply presented as an activity, then the participants will learn how to do that activity and nothing more, they may enjoy themselves and they may become quite skilled in that activity. However, they would have learned nothing more than the skills of the activity. Experiential learning involves undertaking the activity and then being supported to reviewing it: what went right, or wrong, how decisions were made, whether people listen to one another and whether the group made any positive progression throughout the session. Moving from a recreational adventurous activity to an experiential learning session relies on the instructor's ability to see the activity not as the end in itself but as the means to a *learning* end.

19 Being an adventure learning instructor

Anyone who takes a group of people out of their traditional learning environment and provides them with an activity-based learning experience is an adventure learning instructor. If the activity is of a more adventurous nature, the instructor should be appropriately and adequately qualified, but beyond that, all adventure learning instructors should also have a range of personal skills, standards and strategies when dealing with participants because the instructor is pivotal to the success of the adventure learning session. The instructor is the personification of the activity and the participants will take their lead from the instructor; the way in which the instructor behaves, the way in which they care for their kit and the way in which they deal with issues will all present a particular image to participants that they will copy. As social beings, humans learn from one another, the commonest form of which is mimicry. The instructor must also have a particular personal code in their relationship with the participants. In adventure learning, the instructor is often faced with participants who lack strong positive role models and the intense emotions inspired by participation in adventurous activities may create the illusion of a close relationship that could become or be considered inappropriate. Adventure learning involves emotional as well as cognitive and skill development, therefore, relationships are a very important aspect of adventure learning but the boundary of the instructor/participant relationship is critical and the instructor must be clear with participants as to the nature of their relationship. The instructor can be *like* a friend but they cannot *be* a friend; friends share a closeness and an intimacy, they have personal lives that are closely entwined whereas the instructor is a professional with a duty of care. Instructors can offer moral support and even a degree of emotional support but they must be careful not to allow this to be translated into a deeper personal relationship with the participant.

Being an adventure learning instructor can seem to place a lot of pressure on the instructor at the start of the session, but some simple pointers can help alleviate that pressure and make the session more enjoyable for you, as instructor, as well as a positive experience for the participants:

1   The essence of experiential learning is action; participants want to get moving and do something, so if the group is expected to stand around and wait for instructions they will get bored, mess around and lose interest in what is to come before it has even started. They can be kept interested simply by getting them moving, which also gets their muscles warmed up for the activity to come; have a box full of beanbags or small rings to hand and get them playing a simple ice-breaker, or delegate some simple activities to the group to get them involved. If possible, don't have round balls anywhere in sight, they become a target for group members who then just want to play football or catch!

2   As you're getting the group sorted and organising them for the activity, talk with them, not at them; appearing as an equal is important in setting the scene for the group and establishing a solid basis for them to take responsibility. Almost all group participants are used to the formality of the teacher/pupil relationship, so they will tend to defer to the adventure learning instructor in the same way, expecting to be told how to do the activity, and ideally you want them to take the responsibility off you and plan their own strategy.

3   You may want to take part in the activity as well, which is fine if you are to become a participant and take your lead from the group. Taking part is a fantastic way of helping to make you an 'equal' and removes the barrier of participants seeing you as the leader, but it will only work if you do not assume the mantle and become directive.

4   If you're going to tell stories to make a point or set the scene, try to make them realistic and relevant to the group. The activity and the learning is about the group of participants, not about you, so stories of how fantastic you are at the activity (or even stories of you wrestling bears, scaling distant peaks and saving the world) are not going to endear you to the group or engender a positive propensity to achieve in participants!

As the adventure learning instructor, you are ultimately responsible for the safety and behaviour of the participants while out on an activity, irrespective of whether pastoral or other staff are with you. That responsibility starts right at the beginning of the engagement, which may be a while before the activity actually starts and may include the time spent travelling to the venue where the activity is to take place. Group management is a very important responsibility of the adventure learning instructor because it encompasses not only safety and behaviour but also participant interaction, presentation of the participants in public, the environmental impact of the group on the venue and the way in which members of the public will perceive a group and the adventure provider in the future. Whether in an urban or rural setting, sites where adventure learning activities take place may be very popular and frequently used. The impact on land of many groups attending the site and frequent use of natural features may ultimately be detrimental, particularly if instructors and groups are not careful about the after-effects of their attendance, for example leaving litter or damaging the ground. While delivering the activity, an activity instructor has to be mindful of the fact that the natural environment is publicly accessible and there will therefore be members of the public possibly around the group. The way in which the group behaves and the amount of noise they make will affect the enjoyment of the environment for other users and will influence the perception and reputation those people will build of the adventure provider, that instructor and the group. Being respectful and considering the experience of other users, whether alongside the group at the time or future users, is an important social education activity for young group participants, particularly ones with no positive role models or a poor understanding of environmental inheritance.

Adventure learning instructors are as fallible as anyone else; they are human and they have the capacity to get bored, over-confident, complacent or lazy. If you are working as a dedicated adventure learning instructor in a centre, you may find that you are required to run the same activities day after day, particularly where the group activities entail low levels of challenge; this means that boredom can be a dangerous issue, psychologically and physically to you and to others. Repetition can also bring you to become lazy and complacent, making assumptions rather than following process. Equally dangerous is the instructor who becomes over-confident or complacent, causing them to overestimate their skills and knowledge, underestimate the risks of what they are doing and hold an exaggerated belief in their ability to control the participants and events around them. Boredom or confidence bring you to lose focus, which heightens the potential for something to go wrong when you have the participants with you and are undertaking the activity. It is critical that you learn to recognise these traits in yourself and take steps to prevent them happening, otherwise the consequences may be serious, if not fatal.

Despite the best preparation and careful laying of ground rules with a group, there will still always be those participants who, for whatever reason, will behave wilfully and prove to be a sustained distraction to you as the leader and to other participants. How you handle this is crucial to the way the rest of the session will succeed; you have to deal with the situation but if you come down hard on the individual(s) immediately, you may lose group empathy and the rest of the session will be a disaster. There is no easy advice that can be given, other than to say that the harshness with which you deal with the situation depends on the circumstances and the group. Sometimes escalating the degree of strictness if insubordination continues after warnings may be appropriate, but sometimes starting out with strict enforcement and relaxing as the participants prove themselves is a more fitting approach.

Similarly, there will always be participants who decline even to attempt an activity or for some other reason cannot participate in the same way as the rest of the group. Again, there is no easy advice to be offered. The essence of adventure learning, as has already been mentioned, is challenge by choice, so theoretically a participant is entitled to decline joining in. However, it is important that you establish why they are standing back and try to find a way for them to participate with which they are comfortable; this may be for them to help timekeeping or scorekeeping, they may act as a 'spotter' if the activity is off the ground, or there may be another way they can participate alongside but not directly involved in the activity. The individual will learn from this and, if necessary, gain confidence such that later in the activity or at another time, they will feel able to participate.

20 | Icebreakers and energisers

Icebreakers are short, simple, structured activities that are designed to relax people, introduce them to each other or to energise them in what is normally a formal or unfamiliar atmosphere or situation.

The term 'icebreaker' comes from special ships called 'icebreakers', designed to break up ice in the arctic regions. Just as these ships make it easier for other ships to travel, an icebreaker helps to clear the way for learning to occur by making the learners more comfortable, clearing their minds, getting them moving and helping to bring about conversation.

Energisers are used to get a group moving, create a break from long periods of sitting down and excite a group about the next section of a programme. They are often useful at the start of the day or after a break to get people focused for the coming session.

Icebreakers are often not related to the subject matter and so are not activities that are generally reviewed. However, icebreakers and energisers are a good way of bringing group members to interact, they help to break up cliques and invite people to form random groupings in a non-threatening and fun way. When group members are completely unknown to each other or when a group is comprised of members from a number of pre-existing groups, history and established cultures need to be overcome, or else they will influence the culture and performance of *this* group, which can then hinder group performance, progress or success.

1   A great pair

Equipment: slips of paper
A slip of paper with the name of a 'famous' person is given to each person in the group. Each name must have a partner (for example, Adam and Eve). The participants must find their 'partner', by only asking closed questions (can only be answered 'yes' or 'no').

2   Alphabet letters

Equipment: none
Split the group into teams of three or four, with the whole group intermingling around the game area. The larger the game area, the better and a few strategically placed obstacles can increase the challenge. When the leader calls out a letter, each group must make the shape of that letter as quickly as possible.

3   Animal circle

Equipment: none
Get the group into a circle with one person in the middle. The middle person points to anyone in the circle, who must 'make' an animal with the person on each side of them. If the middle person counts to five before the animal is 'made', the chosen person comes into the middle to replace them. For example, an alligator could mean the middle person makes the jaws with their arms and the two side people make the body and tail by making a line.

4   Barnyard

Equipment: none
Each person is given the name of an animal, with three people having the same animal. No one is allowed to say which animal they are. At the signal, each person makes the noise of the animal they have been given. The first group of three animals to find each other and sit down are the winners.

5   Bean game

Equipment: none
Get the group to stand in a circle and explain the actions:

- French bean – do the cancan and sing it.
- Runner bean – run on the spot, knees up.
- Broad bean – stand on the spot with arms out.
- Baked bean – crouched down, hugging their legs.
- Jelly bean – wobble body like a jelly.
- (Add any other you think of!)

The group members jog around the circle and must do the actions when you call them out. You can call them individually or together.

The game finishes when group members have warmed up or are too out of breath to continue; alternatively, the game can be made faster by making people 'out' when they are the last to do the action.

6   British bulldog (bull rush)

Equipment: none
The players are split into two groups and take position at each end of the playing area, with three 'bulldogs' in the middle. Whenever they are ready, the 'bulldogs' call 'British bulldog' and all the players must run to the opposite side of the playing area without being caught. As players are caught, they join the 'bulldogs' in the middle.

7   Cat, mouse and dog

Equipment: none
Arrange the group into a square or circle, with their arms outstretched; outside three members are the dog, the cat and the mouse. The dog chases the cat and the cat chases the mouse through the alleyways formed by the outstretched arms. When the facilitator shouts 'change', the people making up the shape turn at right angles and break up the chase. The dog, cat or mouse caught exchanges places with that member of the shape; the facilitator shouts 'change' for the shape to reform and the chase begins again.

8   Catching the dragon's tail

Equipment: none
A dragon is formed by the players making a line, each with their hands on the shoulders of the person in front of them. The first in the row is the dragon's head; the last is the dragon's tail. The facilitator counts 'one, two, three, go' On the signal 'go', the head runs around toward the tail and tries to catch it. The whole body must move with the head and remain unbroken. If the head succeeds in touching the tail, the person continues as the head. If the body breaks before the tail is caught, the head becomes the tail and the next in line is the head, and so on until each has a chance to be the head and the tail.

9   Changing seats

Equipment: none
Half the group sits in a circle, the other half stands behind a seated person. One person has an empty chair in front of them. This person winks at someone, who has then to try to stand up and get to the empty chair before the person standing behind them can hold them down.

10   Clothes peg samurai

Equipment: clothes pegs
The group stands in a circle; one blindfolded person stands in the middle with a 'sword' and several clothes pegs attached to their clothing and shoes. Group members must remove the pegs without being 'stabbed' by the sword.

11   Dodge ball

Equipment: soft ball(s)
Divide the group into teams A and B. Team A forms a circle around team B and team A has the ball(s). Team A players throw the ball(s) at team B, attempting to hit them below the waist. Team B players may avoid being hit by moving or running aside or ducking. Players must leave the circle when they are hit or join team A.

12   Donkey dodgeball

Equipment: ball
The players form a circle with four people in the middle. The middle four people form a line by holding onto each other at the waist. The front and middle protect the back of the donkey by using their bodies as a block. The players who form the circle try to hit the back end of the donkey, below the waist with the ball. If someone does hit the last person of the donkey, then the thrower will join the front of the donkey and the person who was hit, joins the circle.

13   Dragon

Equipment: none
One person starts as the head of a dragon, with no body; the head chases the other group members until someone is caught. The 'dragon' then devours that person (as dramatically as they like!) and that person becomes a part of the dragon body, holding onto the waist of the original dragon. The dragon thus gets bigger and bigger, as more and more people are caught, until almost the entire group is the dragon and only one person is being chased. The last person caught becomes the head of the next dragon.

14   Duck, duck, goose

Equipment: none
The group all sit in a circle, facing inwards. One person is 'it'; they run around the outside of the circle, tapping people (gently!) on the head, saying 'duck' as they go. Then they tap someone on the head and say 'goose'. That person has to stand up and chase them, trying to catch them before they reach their space and sit down.

15   Electricity

Equipment: none
The players stand in a circle and face the centre. One player begins the game by doing an action and 'sending it' around the circle. After each person in the circle has done the action, the next person sends another action around. You can send different actions in opposite directions.

This also works with the group in rows, making it more competitive with the first row to copy the action down the line winning.

16   Everyone on!

Equipment: anything on which the group can stand/balance
Identify an object on which the entire group has to balance. Repeat the exercise with a range of (successively smaller) objects and see how small they can go.

17   Eye contact samurai

Equipment: none
The group forms a circle, with one person in the middle. The person in the centre says 'heads down' and everyone bows their head. When the person in the centre says, 'heads up', everyone looks up and at anyone else in the circle. If any pair makes direct eye contact, they must swap places, but the middle person must try to get into one of the places first. The person not able to get to a space becomes the middle person.

18   Find someone who ...

Equipment: none
Ask the group to find someone else in the group who has a particular characteristic; for example: find someone who:

- Has the same colour eyes as you.
- Has the same colour hair as you.
- Has the same shoe size as you.

19   Fizz buzz

Equipment: none
All participants sit in a circle; the facilitator starts to count '1', the next person says '2' and so on round the circle. Any number with 3 in it, or divisible by 3, must be said as 'buzz'. For example: 1, 2, buzz, 4, 5, buzz, 7, 8, buzz, 10. Once everyone has this, bring in the instruction that 3 remains as buzz, but that now 5 is fizz.

20   Friend and enemy

Equipment: none
Get everyone in the group to identify one person as a friend and one person as an enemy, without telling anyone (even their friend and enemy). Everyone must get as close to their friend as possible while staying as far away from their enemy.

Periodically stop the group and get them to identify their friend and enemy, to see how successful they have been.

21   Grandmother's keys

Equipment: keys (or other noisy object)

One person is the grandmother, standing at one end of the playing area, facing the wall with their back to the others. Near their feet is a large bunch of keys (or other noisy object). The rest of the group begin at the far side of the playing area and move slowly towards 'grandmother'. Every time grandmother turns around, they have to freeze and if she catches them moving, they have to go back to the start. The aim is for someone to retrieve the keys and get back to the start without being caught. Once someone grabs the keys, every group member has to handle them on the way back to the start. If anyone is caught moving with the keys, the keys are returned to grandmother and that person has to go back to the start.

22   Group juggle

Equipment: a number of balls

The group members stand in a circle; the facilitator tosses a ball across the circle, calling out the name of the player to whom they toss it. That player tosses it to a different player and so on until everyone has caught the ball and thrown it once, so it ends up back with the facilitator.

The sequence can be repeated a couple of times so that everyone gets used to it; the facilitator then adds a second ball, then a third, and so on. Every time the ball is dropped or the sequence is forgotten, the process starts again with one ball.

Players can call out the name of the person to whom they are throwing the ball as they throw it, making this an excellent way of learning each other's names!

23   Helium stick

Equipment: a long, thin stick/cane/rod

The group lines up in two rows facing each other, so that when they stretch out their arms, their hands meet in the middle. The group members point their index fingers and hold their arms out. The facilitator lays the 'helium stick' down on their fingers and gets the group to adjust their finger heights until the helium stick is horizontal and everyone's index finger is touching the stick.

The challenge is to lower the helium stick to the ground. Each person's fingers must be in contact with the helium stick at all times. Pinching or grabbing the stick is not allowed, it must rest on top of fingers.

The helium stick has a habit of mysteriously 'floating' up rather than coming down, causing much laughter. A bit of clever humour from the facilitator can help, for example acting surprised.

The secret (and keep it to yourself) is that the collective upwards pressure created by everyone's fingers tends to be greater than the weight of the stick, as a result, the more a group tries, the more the stick tends to 'float' upwards.

24 Human bingo

Equipment: a set of bingo cards and questions
This is much like a human treasure hunt. Develop a set of bingo questions and some bingo cards. The group has to see who can get a line or a full house by finding people who meet the criteria on the bingo card. It is up to you whether they are allowed to use the same person more than once for answering a question.

25 I went to market

Equipment: none
One person starts by saying 'I went to market and I bought a …'. Each person repeats that line, what the others have bought and then adds what they bought. Keep going until the group can no longer remember all the items.

26 Knights, horses and cavaliers

Equipment: none
Two equal circles are formed, with one inside the other; the people on the inside circle pair up with someone on the outside circle and remain with that partner for the rest of the game. The inside circle walks clockwise, clapping their hands and the outside circle, also clapping, walk in the opposite direction. When the leader calls out 'Horses!' everyone stops clapping and runs to find their partner. Once together, one partner goes on all fours, like a horse, and the other straddles their back. The last pair to get into position acts out a simple situation that makes use of a rider and a horse.

If 'Knights!' is called, one partner will sit on the other's knee. The partner therefore has one knee up to sit on and the other on the ground for support.

If 'Cavaliers!' is called, one partner lifts the other up into their arms (or just hold one leg up in the air, to avoid possible injury).

27 Mexican wave

Equipment: none
The group makes two rows, facing each other with one person outside the line; everyone holds their arms out straight in front of them almost touching the hands of the person opposite. One member of the group runs towards the line and the rest of the group do a Mexican wave as the person approaches, but as late as possible (without hitting the person).

28   Name arrange

Equipment: none
Once everyone has been introduced, get the group to arrange themselves alphabetically by first name *without talking*! When they think they are done, check by calling out names. This also works with all kinds of other information, such as birthdays, ages, home town …

29   Newspaper tower/spaghetti tower

Equipment: tape, scissors, newspaper/spaghetti, paper plate
Split the group into equally sized teams; each has a set amount of tape, scissors, newspapers, (or spaghetti) and a paper plate. The challenge is to build the tallest, self-supporting tower in a given time to balance the plate.

30   People to people

Equipment: none
This is a form of human twister. The group members form pairs and then get into a circle with one person in the middle. The middle person calls commands, such as 'left hand to left hand' or 'elbow to shoulder' to twist up pairs. At intervals, the middle person calls 'people to people' and everyone raises their arms (with optional yelling) and runs across the circle. Each group member must then find a new partner, including the middle person, so that there will be a new middle person.

31   Pulse race

Equipment: beach ball
The group forms two lines, holding hands. Everyone has their eyes closed, except for the leader of each line. A beach ball (or other object) is placed at opposite end of the lines from the leaders. When the facilitator calls 'Go!' the leaders start a pulse race by squeezing the hand of person next to them, which sets off a chain reaction. When last person in line feels their hand squeezed, they open their eyes and grab for the ball. Whichever team gets the ball first gets a point/prize.

 After each round, the leader goes to the end of the line.

32   Red blood, green blood

Equipment: none
Everyone moves about the playing area freely. The facilitator shouts 'Red blood!' and the group moves (flows/shakes) as many parts of their body as they can. The facilitator then introduces 'Green blood!' which freezes whichever part it enters, so the facilitator has to shout 'Green blood hands!' and the group has to freeze these, but continue moving all

other parts of the body. Gradually green blood freezes all the parts and the group is frozen, until the facilitator begins to thaw body parts with red blood.

33 Sharks

Equipment: none

An area is designated as the life raft and the group members move about around the raft, freely 'swimming', until the facilitator shouts 'Sharks!' and everyone has to jump onto the raft.

When the facilitator says it is safe, everyone has to leave the raft and begin swimming again, only the raft becomes successively slightly smaller. Anyone who cannot get on when the facilitator shouts 'Sharks!' is eaten.

34 Shoe game

Equipment: none

Everyone takes off their left shoe and throws it into a pile in the middle of the circle. Everyone selects a shoe other than theirs and finds the owner. They then exchange information about themselves, such as name, job, reason for being there, what they hope to get out of the day.

35 Shooting rabbits

Equipment: none

Everyone sits in a circle, with one person (the hunter) in the middle. The hunter points to a person and shouts 'Bang!'; that person raises their hands and waggles them by their ears (like a rabbit!), the players on either side must waggle the hand nearest the shot rabbit by their ears, thus there should a line of four hands waggling. Anyone who gets the wrong hand is out. As gaps open up, the players will find themselves next to a player some distance away but the game continues in the same way. The last 'rabbit' becomes the hunter.

36 Skinning the snake

Equipment: none

The group stands in a line, one behind the other; everybody puts their right hand through their legs and, with their left hand, grabs the hand of the person in front of them. Starting with the back person and without letting go, the group crawls through each other's legs. This works well with two or more groups to increase competition.

37 Skinned snake

Equipment: none

The group forms two lines, one behind the other; everybody puts their right hand through their legs and, with their left hand, grabs the hand of the person in front of them. Only the first and last person in the line will have a free hand. At a signal from the facilitator, the last person in the line will lie down on their back and the person in front of them backs up by straddling and 'walking' over this person's body, and then lies down on their back. The feet of this person will be next to the shoulders of the person lying down. This goes on while the entire team is still holding hands. When the last person has lain down and touched their head to the group, they get up, 'walk' forwards and 'pull' the other members up. This is skinning the snake. The first team up without unclasping hands is the winner.

38 Stand up

Equipment: none
The group members all sit on the ground in pairs, back-to-back, knees bent and elbows locked. They then try to stand up without falling down.

This can also work with putting the group members into larger groups

39 Teacher's pencil

Equipment: none
The group sits in equal rows, all facing the same way, and each row is numbered, with row 1 being the front. The aim is to get your row to number 1 position. The facilitator says 'Teacher's lost his pencil. Has row x got it?'

All row x stands and the person on the end says 'No Sir, not I Sir, not row number x Sir.'

This continues until a row makes a mistake (calls the wrong number, fails to stand up) and that row must then go to the back and all row numbers change. The row caller moves to the opposite end of the line so everyone takes a turn as caller.

40 The trust fall

Equipment: strong chair or table
One person stands on the side of the 'bridge' (table/chair); the rest of the group pairs up behind, standing opposite each other, grabbing the wrists of the person opposite. The person on the 'bridge' stands on the edge, with their back to the group. At a signal from the facilitator, the person falls backwards, being caught by the group.

(Group members may wish to fall facing forwards but this can lead to complaints of group members touching sensitive areas of the body).

41 The yes/no game

Equipment: none

Group members move around one another, trying to catch each other out by asking closed questions, for example:

- Were you born in a hospital?
- Were you born in this country?
- Do you like chocolate?
- Do you like vegetables?

There are so many questions that can be used, it is impossible to list them. The facilitator can provide the questions (which works well if the questions are built around the objective of the programme) or participants may be left to make up their own questions.

42   True and false

Equipment: pens and Post-It notes
Each member of the group writes two lies and one truth on a 'Post-It' stuck to their forehead; they walk around the rest of the group talking to as many people as possible. The object is to identify each person's lie. This can also work with a less mobile group by everyone sitting down.

43   Trust walk

Equipment: none
The group members form a line and hold hands, with all except the first and last person in the line having their eyes closed. It is the job of these people to keep the entire group 'safe' while on the walk. The person at the front (the leader) takes the group on a walk; the leader may pass instructions down the line and the last person may call out feedback on what is happening at the end of the line.

44   Vegetable cart

Equipment: chairs may be provided for the group members to sit on
Everyone sits in a circle, with one person (the greengrocer) in the middle. Each person is paired with another in the circle and each pair chooses a vegetable. When the greengrocer calls out one or more vegetable, the pair has to change seats. If the greengrocer shouts 'Vegetable cart!' everyone changes seats.

45   Wind in the willows

Equipment: none
The group forms a tight circle standing shoulder to shoulder with one member in the centre. This person clasps their hands to their chest to make themselves as streamlined

as possible. They lean forward, allowing the members of the circle gently to break their fall and pass them around the circle, off the floor.

46 Wink murder

Equipment: none
All except one group member forms a circle, eyes closed; this person picks the murderer and the detective.

This 'non-player' walks around the circle and taps someone once discreetly to indicate they are the murderer and someone twice to indicate they are the detective.

The players can open their eyes. The detective moves to the middle of the circle and has three chances to guess the murderer by asking closed questions. Meanwhile the murderer 'kills' people by winking at them, without the detective noticing. If a player is killed, they die as dramatically as they wish.

You can say if they fail, they must remain detective for the next round and if they guess correctly, the murderer is the detective for the next round.

47 Yurt circle

Equipment: none
Everyone joins hands in a circle and they are numbered 'one' and 'two' around the circle. All the 'ones' lean inwards and all the 'twos' lean outwards as the group tries to reach a point of balance.

21 | Teambuilding games

Teambuilding games are exercises designed for groups to work through together, for the purpose of building cohesiveness, raising issues in the group, and posing challenges to the team. They generally take longer than icebreakers and energisers, because more group planning, preparation and execution time are needed.

Teambuilding games encourage people to communicate, strategise and co-operate in order to achieve their goal(s); by encouraging learners to see and think differently, their brains are stimulated, improving the retention of learning.

While the games are under way, watch the participants; see how they interact and who takes on what role. Very quickly, it becomes apparent who likes to jump into an activity and learn by doing, who likes to think through each step before trying and who likes to talk through as many approaches as possible before acting. Inherent characteristics also come to the fore during the games: who takes the lead, who has the ideas, who supports everyone and ensures the group stays task focused. The established roles that learners may hold in the classroom or because of their position in a hierarchy can become challenged in a new environment as the individuals deploy different skills, confidences, knowledge and abilities.

If the individuals are not familiar with one another, for example the school transition years, the group process is fundamental. In the beginning, the group is not generally successful, as the members learn about one another and what they have to achieve; they generally listen little to one another as they all try to establish their identity within the group. There may be a period where the group members argue, still failing as they try to establish a common way forward. From this, the culture of the group develops and the members accept one another as they settle into working together and developing their strategy. As the activity concludes, the group will experience either the joy of success or the misery of failure. It is at this point that the facilitator has to make sure that they do not become overly confident or lose heart altogether. No matter how the group performs overall, the way they worked together and what they did can be analysed in a positive and constructive manner in order that members learn and develop.

1   Aliens attack

Equipment: none
Set up a base where people will go if caught. The group is organised into two teams, with two aliens and two people allocated as 'ray guns'. Give the 'ray guns' 1 minute to hide and then send the aliens off. After another minute, the whole group goes looking for the ray guns.

The point of the game is not to be caught by the aliens while looking for the ray guns (the only way to get the aliens out is to be holding onto the ray gun while touching the alien). The aliens chase everyone around while they are on the lookout for the ray guns.

2   Ball run

Equipment: small items such as small balls or wrapped sweets
Designate an area where the items are placed at one end of the playing area. The facilitator calls out questions, such as 'If you are wearing something red' or 'If you have a birthday in May'. If the question called out applies to any players, they have to run up and collect an object. The first to reach a specified number wins or whoever collects the most by the time the players are tired.

3   Balloon blow

Equipment: balloons
Divide the group into teams. Each team stands in a small circle and compete to see which team can keep a balloon aloft the longest using only breath.

Caution: watch out for hyperventilation.

4   Balloon bop

Equipment: balloons
A balloon is kept in the air, initially using breath. The facilitator calls out someone's name and a body part; that person has to use that body part to keep the balloon in the air with that body part until another person's name and body part are called.

5   Balloon frantic

Equipment: two to three inflated balloons per person, a stopwatch
Each person has a balloon and bounces it in the air. Every five seconds, the facilitator adds another balloon. A penalty is given when a balloon hits the floor or if not brought back into play within five seconds if hitting the floor.

6   Balloon game

Equipment: balloons, string
Tie a balloon on a long string to each person's ankle. The group can move around the playing space freely but the objective of the game is to be the last person with an unpopped balloon and to pop each other's balloon.

7   Blind partner tag

Equipment: blindfolds
Participants are in pairs, with one partner of each pair blindfolded. One pair is 'it'. Only the blind partner may tag someone (who also must be blind). Sighted partners may only guide by talking and may not hold onto their partner. When someone is tagged, that pair becomes 'it'.

After a while, switch roles so that everyone experiences being both blind and sighted.

8   Blindfolded shape

Equipment: rope
The aim is to make a length of rope into a given shape, while all of the group members are blindfolded.

Rules:

- There is no planning time.
- No-one is allowed to touch the rope until all group members are blindfolded.
- There is a limited time allowed for completion.
- Everyone must be involved.

9 Broom handle

Equipment: broom handle
A person holds a broom handle in both hands; they must pass the handle around their body, without letting go of either end and finish in the same position as they started.

10 Canyon bridge

Equipment: none
Designate a bench or log as the bridge. The groups line up at each end and need to pass each other to get to the other side of the 'canyon'. Anyone who falls off goes to the back of their group.

11 Cardboard box

Equipment: a cardboard box
The group members take it in turns to pick up a box from the floor. Only the soles of the feet may touch the floor and the person must stand at least a metre from the box. Every time it is picked up, a piece is torn from the box. See how small the cardboard can become before it can no longer be picked up!

12 Chair lift

Equipment: chair
The person stands two of their feet lengths away from the wall and put their head on the wall. They must pick up a chair that has its back on the wall.

13 Concentration

Equipment: none
The group members form two lines, facing each other. One group has 30 seconds to study the opposite line and then turns around. The second group changes ten things about themselves (swap jewellery, untie shoelaces, move a watch or bracelet to the other arm); nothing must be hidden. The first group turns back around and must identify the 10 changes.

14 Elf defence

Equipment: two sets of different coloured balloons
The group forms two teams of elves. Each team must defend its treasure (a set of coloured balloons) while attempting to steal or destroy the other team's treasure. When the designated playing time ends, the teams are given 1 point for their number of unpopped balloons and 2 points for any stolen, unpopped balloons.

15   Empires

Equipment: paper and pens

The facilitator hands each person a piece of paper and a pen; then the group picks a topic and each person writes the name of something associated with that topic. The paper is folded over and handed to the facilitator, without letting other group members know what they wrote.

The facilitator reads out what is on the papers, reminding everyone they need to remember as many as possible. One person starts and can ask anyone in the room if they are x (something from the list). If they are not, then they ask someone if they are y (from the list). If the person guesses right, then the person who has been 'guessed' moves to sit with the person who guessed and becomes part of their 'empire'. That person asks again. The members of the 'empire' can consult with each other, but the leader of the empire remains the spokesperson.

Small empires build around the room but if the leader of an empire is 'guessed', their empire is won. The winner is the person who ends up with everyone!

16   Fill the bottle

Equipment: a bottle per team, paper cups, bucket of water

One person of each team lies on the ground while holding a plastic pop bottle on their forehead. Their teammates take it in turns to run to the bucket, which is a few metres away at the finish line, to fill up their paper cup and then attempt to pour it into the pop bottle while standing over the person.

Once the bottle is filled, the bottle person should run to the finish line without spilling any of the water from the bottle.

17   Find the leader

Equipment: none

Players sit down in a circle. One player leaves the room while a leader is chosen from the remaining players. The leader starts to carry out actions which the others follow, during this the one that has left the room comes in and standing in the middle of the circle is given 3 tries to guess who the leader is.

18   Frozen pictures

Equipment: none

Split the participants into small groups, giving each group a common saying or expression (e.g. 'too many cooks spoil the broth'). Ask the group to come up with a frozen picture for the others to guess the saying.

This may be played using expressions, but works well in group training with real situations, such as 'you're coming home late' or 'you hear footsteps following you down the street'. Significant discussion can be created from this game, exploring the various suggestions provided.

19   Giants, wizards and elves

Equipment: none
The characters:

- *Giants:* Hands raised above head and 'growl'.
- *Wizards:* Hands in front as a wand, shouting 'Shazam'.
- *Elves:* Hands on head as ears and say 'nee nee nee' in a high pitch voice.

The hierarchy:

- Giants beat wizards.
- Wizards beat elves.
- Elves beat giants.

Split the group into two teams, facing each other. Designate a 'home' for each team. Each team needs to decide which character they are going to be (they can only be one) and when the facilitator shouts 'go', they act out their character using the guide above. See who wins and the winning team tries to catch the losing team as they run home.

   The game continues as above until all of one team is gone.

20   Great egg drop

Equipment: eggs, paper, sticky tape, bin bag, rubber bands, cardboard
The task is to build a single egg package that can sustain a substantial fall (2 to 3 metres at least).

21   Group knot

Equipment: none
The group stands in a tight circle, with their hands in the centre. Everyone reaches their *right* hand into the circle and takes the right hand of someone roughly opposite. They then take the *left* hand of someone different. The puzzle is formed and the game is for the whole group to work together to get themselves untangled without letting go of hands.

   It may get frustrating if they've formed a troublesome knot, but let them keep trying.

   There are three possible solutions: a circle facing inwards, a circle where people are alternatively facing inwards and outwards and smaller circles.

22   Hole in the bucket

Equipment: cans, water container, bucket
Punch several holes into the bottom and the sides of the cans. Fill up a large container of water at the start point and at the other end have a receiving bucket for each team.

This works as a relay race. The teams stand at the opposite end of the water container, with their receiving bucket. One person from each team goes to the large container, fills their can, puts it on their head and returns down the playing area to their teams and then pour what water is left into the team's receiving bucket. The next person takes the can and goes to fetch the water.

The first team to fill their receiving bucket is the winner.

23   Hug-a-tree

Equipment: blindfolds
The group is split into pairs, with one partner blindfolded. The sighted partner leads their blind partner to a tree. The blindfolded partner touches and feels the tree before being led away. After removing the blindfold, the tree hugger tries to locate their tree.

24   Ladders

Equipment: none
Players sit in pairs, facing each other with legs outstretched and feet touching to form the rungs of a ladder. Each pair is given a number. When their number is called out, each pair has to get up, run up the ladder *without* treading on any legs, down the outside and then back up the ladder to their original position.

The player who gets back first and sitting in position wins.

25   Loop-de-loop

Equipment: hula-hoop or tyre inner tube
The group stands in a circle and holds hands with one tube hanging over one pair of joined hands. Each person in the circle must pass the tube over themself and on to the next person without letting go of hands.

More tubes can be added as the game progresses.

26   N.E.W.S.

Equipment: none
Each side of the playing area is delegated a cardinal point (north, south, east, west). Players stand in the middle and when a compass direction is given, they run to that point, with those getting it wrong or last to get there being out.

This can be made more complex by including the intercardinal points (southeast, etc.).

Special commands can be given, such as:

- Dive-bomb = lie down on your front, hands on heads, as if being attacked from the air
- Tornado = spin around on the spot until told to stop or next command given

Instead of, or as well as, using compass points, the parts of a ship can be used.

- Bow = front
- Starboard = right
- Port = left
- Stern = back
- Captains coming = stand to attention with a salute
- Climb the rigging = mime the actions of climbing a rope ladder
- Pirates = everybody has to hide

27 Number circle

Equipment: none
The group stands in a circle and each player is given a number. When a number is called, those players have to run once around the outside of the circle back to their own place. The last one back is out. Multiple numbers can be shouted at the same time.

To add a little education to the game, rather than just calling out numbers try using maths questions.

28 The over and under game

Equipment: bucket, sponge, jug
Divide the group into two teams; each team forms a single file line, facing the same way. At the head of each line is a bucket of water and at the other end is a jug.

The person at the head of the line has a sponge and the water bucket. That person has to dip the sponge in the water to soak up as much water as they can. They then have to pass the soaking wet sponge over their head to the person behind, who passes the sponge to the person behind them through their legs. The sponge makes its way back over the head of one person and between the legs of the next until it gets to the person standing next to the jug. That person must squeeze whatever water is left into the pitcher and run the sponge back up to the head of the line. When this occurs, everybody moves back one position and the person who was at the back of the line now is at the head of the line. Continue the process until the jug is full or there is no water left.

29 Romeo and Juliet

Equipment: blindfold, belt

The group sits in a circle on the floor, ideally leaving no gaps but a large space in the middle. The facilitator picks two people. Using the belt, one person's ankles are fastened so they can only jump and using the blindfold, the eyes of the other are covered.

These two are 'Romeo' and 'Juliet'; Juliet has to try to catch Romeo and Romeo must try to avoid Juliet for as long as possible.

When Juliet calls out 'Romeo, Romeo', Romeo must reply 'Juliet, Juliet'.

30 Round the word

Equipment: pieces of card or paper

Write the names of various countries down, one on each card and have a list of well-known or not so well known attractions that can be found in each country, such as the White House (USA) or Big Ben (UK) and stick up the cards at various points around the playing area.

When the facilitator calls out a place to visit, players have to run to the card with the country where they think the place can be found. Those who are wrong are knocked out of the game.

This game has a superb educational value with almost unlimited number of variations using different categories for the cards, such as:

- Animal, vegetable or mineral.
- Mammal, reptile or amphibian.
- Fruit or vegetable.

31 Scavenger hunt

Equipment: none

The challenge is to complete the four stages within the given time; time is a crucial factor in completing the tasks successfully. Groups will need to work with others, be resourceful, imaginative, considerate and entertaining.

Rules:

- Do not damage the environment (plants, trees, wildlife).
- Keep away from any water's edge.
- Remain as a team.
- Be considerate towards other people around the site.
- At least one watch per group is needed
- Points will be deducted for lateness.

Stages:

- Teams have 30 minutes to collect as many items as possible (1 point per item).
- For each object, the teams must give at least one interesting fact (2 points per fact).
- Each group has to make a scavenger sculpture from their collected items (up to 30 points available). Points are given for imagination, teamwork, style and so on.
- Make up a poem, story or song about one or more items (up to 30 points available).

Things that may be collected: leaves, stones, unusual branch (dead branches), cans, sweet wrappers, plastic bottles, metal objects other than cans, pine cone, duck feather, swan feather, something to carry everything in …

32   Shaving cream shoot off

Equipment: water pistol, shaving foam
Divide the group into teams; each team has a large water pistol filled with water. On one team member, squirt shaving cream on the front of their shirt, the same amount for all teams. Each member of the team gets one squirt from the water pistol to try to remove the shaving cream.

33   Sheep and shepherds

Equipment: whistle, blindfolds
Designate an area of the playing area a pen. The group is allowed five minutes to plan. One person is designated the shepherd and remaining group members are blindfolded and spread out across the playing area. The aim is for the shepherd to get all the group members into the pen, without talking.

34   Star game

Equipment: small object (ball, wrapped sweet)
Divide the group into any number of equal teams with each team standing in a line as a star shape with their legs apart and facing the middle, where the small object is placed.

   Each member of the team from the middle outwards is numbered (so that all the 'ones' are nearest the centre). When a persons' number is called out, they have to leave their position, run around the outside of the star to the back of their team and crawl through their team members legs to reach the object first.

35   Survival

Equipment: none
Split the group into teams; their objective is to reach a group decision for survival (see

Appendix 2 scenarios). This is a discussion activity, with no winners or losers, that works well for all ages and purposes, indoors or outdoors; consensus can be hard to reach, however, set the aim for all participants to at least partially agree to each ranking on their final list.

Encourage groups to complete the task without the use of tactics such as voting, trading or averaging, but by discussion and reason. Watch for participants avoiding conflict or changing their minds simply to come to agreement (these behaviours can be highlighted at review points). The most important outcome is probably understanding that sometimes compromise is necessary to move towards a solution.

It is important that the activity is accompanied by some basic survival facts, such as the role of water, shelter, warmth and food in increasing a person's chances for survival. This can come before, during or after; the scenarios are rich material for a whole range of subject learning if used appropriately. For example, there is no substitute for fresh water; people can survive only days or even less without it. It is also important to note that drinking ocean water will only hasten illness because the salt in ocean water increases dehydration.

Shelter and warmth are also essential basics for survival. Prolonged exposure to sun, rain, or cold can lead to a person developing either hypothermia (the body becomes too cold) or hyperthermia (the body becomes too hot), both of which can cause severe illness or even death. The risk of hypothermia is present even in tropical climates, as it can occur *any time* a person's body temperature is less than 37 degrees Celsius (normal temperature) for an extended period of time.

Food is another key element in survival, as it directly relates to a person's state of health and energy. Without health or energy, it is near impossible for a person to survive in an extreme situation and, ultimately, to escape.

Some variations include:

- Appoint a timekeeper in each group and encourage them to keep the group task focused.
- To emphasise individual versus group decision making, split the session into three parts:
- Individuals make their own selections first, on paper and not shared.
- Groups discuss and reach a group decision.
- Compare individual and group decisions.

36   Team ski

Equipment: two equally sized planks of wood

To prepare for this game, put a piece of rope around each end of each plank and tie the ends together to form a loop handle (you may want to put holes through the wood to make it easier for the rope to stay in place.

The group members stand with one foot on each plank; the members at the front and back of each plank must hold onto the handle. The aim is for the group to walk from one place to another or to negotiate a course.

37   Team skipping

Equipment: a length of rope (suitable for skipping)
Split the group into teams and issue each team with a length of rope. The task for the teams is to perform a routine or series of skipping exercises as a whole team.

38   Thar' be dragons

Equipment: scarf (or similar)
The group can work as one or more teams. The team members stand in a line and the back member of each team has the scarf as a tail. The head of the dragon has to catch the tail of the other dragon or catch its own tail; the chain of people cannot be broken.

39   The water tube

Equipment: piece of drainpipe, bucket of water, plastic cups, ball
A drainpipe with any number of holes of various sizes is placed on either a base or hanging. The ball is placed inside the tube. The group is given a bucket of water and a few plastic cups. The challenge is for the group to recover the ball without inverting, or touching, the tube.

40   Train wreck

Equipment: chairs
Set up one fewer chair than there are players, so somebody is left standing. The facilitator calls out a category, such as 'If you're wearing green, go!' All those who fit that description run and the person who is standing also runs until the facilitator shouts 'Stop!' Everybody running has to find a seat and sit down. The player who is left standing is out of the game. The facilitator calls another category and while everybody is moving, removes one or two chairs. When the facilitator calls 'stop', all those left standing are out of the game.

If the facilitator calls 'Train wreck' at any time, everybody has to move!
Rules:

- You have to move if your category is called.
- You can't move between a few seats repeatedly.
- You can't switch with someone repeatedly.
- You have to move around the whole area.

41   Undo the knot

Equipment: rope
A knot is tied in a rope. The group must all hold onto the rope with at least one hand and untie the knot without letting go of the rope.

42   Water balloon dodgeball

Equipment: water balloons
Have at least five water balloons per player. Divide into two groups on opposite sides of a line with each side having their balloons in a plastic tub. If you are hit with a water balloon, you are out (like dodgeball). The last person 'standing' wins.

22 | **Wide games**

'Wide games' are any game requiring or making use of any large area of land. Provided you stick to a few simple rules, they are very easy to set up, very popular and can take advantage of almost any space. Particularly good areas are those where it is easy to hide, such as woodland or heath, but they can be played in fields and parks too!

The importance of risk assessment is increased because of the nature of the space. All wide games need you and all players to be aware of the size and type of playing area. This is mainly from the point of view of safety, particularly if you are playing in areas open to the public. It helps when setting boundaries to take advantage of natural barriers like paths, streams, edges of woods or fields. If necessary walk everybody around the boundary and/or spend a little time placing boundary markers that are within sight of each other (strips of bright cloth tied to a tree); boundary markers are only really necessary if is difficult to determine a boundary. The facilitator should complete a full risk assessment ahead of the day, thinking through every conceivable risk associated with the activity and the weather, the likelihood of the risk happening and how they will alleviate the risk. Some degree of risk will inevitably remain, but if the facilitators are aware of it, they can be ready to act promptly should it occur.

Depending on the age of the players and the size and openness of the playing area it may be worthwhile having 'marshals' patrolling the area and you may even want to consider using mobile telephones or short-range radios if the area is very large or quite hilly.

Wide games often take longer to set up than indoor games, but they also last longer for the participants. The space brings an added dimension as the group members are further distanced from one another and so communication is more complex, emphasising planning and co-operation.

1 Bigfoot

Equipment: life bands, energy tokens (cards)

Bigfoot is based on the legend of the 'sasquatch'. 'Bigfoot', a large hairy manlike creature is loose and said to have been recently discovered in this area. It has never been captured and only spotted a few times. Your mission is to capture it. However, Bigfoot is notoriously hard to find because it can take the form of any animal at will and when cornered it has the ability to paralyse others by freezing them. In order to trap it, you not only have to find Bigfoot but you will need to have life bands and enough energy tokens to protect you from being frozen by its power.

Give everybody a life band (coloured cotton to go around the wrist or other method) and energy tokens (the cards can have different energy amounts on them). Before they go out, warn them that not only will failure to capture Bigfoot result in loss of their life bands, requiring them to return to base for a new one, but Bigfoot will also steal all their energy and have its power increased by that amount.

What the young people don't know is that one of the facilitators with them at that moment is playing Bigfoot. It would be useful for one or two facilitators who are known to the young people to be mysteriously absent (and in the woods) so the young people immediately suspect them.

Bigfoot is given a high energy rating to start with, so the young people have to discover not only who Bigfoot is, but to capture them they have to work together to have enough energy tokens between them to win.

When the groups disperse into the woods, the facilitator playing Bigfoot sets the game in motion, waiting for an opportune moment to freeze the members of a small group.

Bigfoot has one other trick: on meeting another facilitator, they can make the other facilitator become Bigfoot (and hand over the power tokens) so that young people don't always know who Bigfoot is.

If challenged, Bigfoot must confess who they are and find out the collective power rating of the hunters; for example, if Bigfoot has a 15 energy rating and a group of players challenges with a collective energy between them of 12, the 12 is lower than the 15 so the group all lose their life bands *and* power cards. Bigfoot keeps these and now has an energy rating of 27!

In the event of a power-rating tie, players lose their life bands (forcing them to return to base and get new ones) but not their power rating cards

2   Bulldog

Equipment: none

One or two players take position in the centre of the room, facing the group. At 'go', the entire group charges and tries to reach the other side of the area, without being caught. To catch someone, the 'bulldogs' in the centre must hold the player long enough to yell '1, 2, 3, bulldog!'. When a player is caught, they become a 'bulldog' for the next charge. Not more than three 'bulldogs' can tackle a single player; if a struggling player is not held while the group slowly counts to ten, they are declared free for another charge.

The game is run until everyone has been caught. The last person charging the line without being caught is the winner.

For safety, have players take off watches, glasses and other breakables.

3   Capture the flag

Equipment: two flags on staffs and two different coloured sets of arm or headbands

Divide the group into two teams. Identify each by a set of arm or headbands. Set up a gaol area and a separate hiding spot for each flag. Gaols are set up at opposite ends of the playing area. The object of the game is to penetrate the other team's area and capture their flag. A flag is 'captured' after it has been returned to the captor's gaol area.

Prisoners are taken by having their arm or headbands removed by an opponent. Prisoners are taken to the gaol of their captors, where they wait quietly until released; prisoners can only be released when a member of their team (with arm or headband intact) runs through the gaol in which they are being held captive. After their release, prisoners are given free escort back to a central spot near their end of the area. Here, they are issued a new arm or headband.

The game continues until a flag is captured, or the allotted time is up.

4   Catch the snake

Equipment: a piece of rope

The snake is the piece of rope. One player is 'it', holds an end and drags the rope about, so that the snake writhes over the ground. The other players give chase and whoever succeeds in catching the snake becomes 'it.'

5 Coastguards and smugglers

Equipment: none

Players are divided into two teams, a small team of 'coastguards' and everybody else becoming 'smugglers'. The number of coastguards depends on the terrain; in open spaces, smugglers need the advantage of people, while in woodland where there are many places to hide, coastguards need people!

Coastguards establish a base, which becomes the 'gaol'. Smugglers are given time to get away and hide.

Coastguards have to catch all the smugglers and the game ends when this is done. In the event of this not occurring in a reasonable time (as it does frequently!), points are made on the number of smugglers remaining in gaol at the end of a time limit.

Smugglers must remain free; once captured they can only be released from gaol by being touched by a smuggler who is still free.

Coastguards can use whatever technique they want to try to capture smugglers, (hunting as a pack, in pairs or singularly). Capture is by touch; once a coastguard has caught a smuggler, the smuggler must go back to gaol (players showing any resistance or cheating can be expelled from the game for not playing fair!).

Only a limited number of coastguards can protect the gaol.

6 Collecting cattle

Equipment: potatoes, ink pad and face paint, cardboard 'cattle' concealed around the field

Divide the group into a tribe and wardens. Each tribe believes all the cattle on earth belong to them. Cattle are valuable as a source of food, clothing and warmth, and all cattle found are immediately claimed and branded.

Groups make brands from potatoes and mark their faces with the same sign. Groups travel in tribes, find cattle and brand them. Wardens will arrest any tribes caught branding and imprison for ten minutes. Points are awarded for the number of cattle branded and for the number of prisoners taken.

7 Compass relay

Equipment: none

Line up teams in relay formation, parallel to each other. Opposite each team, a compass is drawn on the floor, the cardinal (and maybe inter-cardinal) points are indicated but only the north is lettered. The facilitator calls out a direction; the first person of each line steps out and places a pencil on the compass, pointing in the given direction, before the facilitator has counted to six. If correct, the player falls in line behind the compass; if incorrect, they go to the back of their team line. Another point is called and the second member steps out. The first complete team to fall in behind the compass wins. There should be a referee for each team to avoid time waste in verifying the compass directions shown.

8   Dispatch running

Equipment: long coloured ribbon, a headquarters and perimeter boundary

A team member is chosen to carry a dispatch to the designated headquarters. The dispatch runner must wear a coloured tag pinned to their shoulder; they must reach their goal with this in its proper place.

The besieging enemy must prevent them reaching the headquarters, but cannot go within the perimeter. To catch them, the enemy must take the tag from their shoulder. They know the despatcher starts from a certain place at a certain time (as far from the headquarters as the facilitator likes) and they may take any steps to capture him, except they may not actually witness the departure.

The game may be played in any space, the larger and with the more obstacles, the better and the dispatch runner can adopt any disguise, so long as they wear the rag pinned to their shoulder.

9   Fool's gold

Equipment: bands (a different colour for each team), and 'gold ingots' (15 potatoes per team)

Split the group into teams and establish a base for each team. Each base should be an equal distance from all others. Place the team's 'gold' (the 15 potatoes) in a pile at the base. Only a limited number of the team can hover round the base as defenders. Tie a band to the wrist of each player and blow a whistle to allow combat to commence.

Players must infiltrate the other team's base to steal their 'gold', but players may only take one potato at once. Once out of the opposing base, they may pass it to another player or can take it back to their base themselves.

Everyone must keep their team band on show while in the game and only players with a band may remove another player's band. To remove their life, simply take it off their arm but the other player may resist.

Rules for safety:

- No punching.
- No scratching.
- No gouging.
- No kicking or tripping using the legs.
- Do not play near cliffs.

10 Fox and hounds

Equipment: a whistle or flour

Divide into two teams, approximately a quarter being 'foxes' and the rest 'hounds'.

Foxes are given either a whistle or a packet of flour and a time limit is set. Foxes are given a minute's head start and must either lay flour every 20 seconds of their journey or blow the whistle every 20–30 seconds.

After the initial minute is over, the hounds are let out to chase the foxes following their path and every fox tagged is out.

The foxes win if any of them are still active after the time and the hounds win if all foxes have been caught.

11 Lighthouse

Equipment: none

One of the players is the lighthouse, parked at one end of the area. Half the group are rocks and they are spaced around the area, with a gap between each of them. The rest of the group are ships who have to make their way, blindfolded, through the rock to the lighthouse.

On 'go', the lighthouse goes 'woo-woo' to guide the ships. The rocks go 'swish-swish', very gently, to warn the approaching ships of danger, and the ships are supposed to sail between the rocks to the lighthouse beyond. If a ship hits a rock it sinks and stays where it is. When all the ships arrive at the lighthouse, the two halves of the group swap sides: the rocks become ships and the ships become rocks.

12 Meet my friend

Equipment: none

The object of this game is to discover a friend in nature, without harming any living thing that might be found outdoors. Players are taken on a short walk during which time each player collects something from the natural environment (nothing may be broken or picked from any living thing, the item has to be either lying on the ground or resting on another object like a tree stump). Everyone keeps their object hidden from all players.

Following the walk, each player is given the opportunity to build a small home for his 'friend'. He is also asked to give his friend a name, and to think of one way in which they could take care of their friend out of its natural environment.

When all in the group is ready, everyone tours the small homes that have been created, and meets each special friend.

13 Silly symphony

Equipment: none

The purpose of this game is to discover the beautiful sounds that can be created by the natural objects in our environment. Each player is given time to find objects in nature that make a noise when banged, blown or rubbed. Players bring back their 'instruments' and a conductor is chosen to organise the group into an orchestra.

Each musician is allowed to 'tune' their instrument, so all the group can hear the different sounds.

The conductor chooses a familiar tune that all can play and leads the orchestra. Players can make requests for songs to play and the musicians can work on 'solos' to perform for everyone.

14 Smugglers and spies

Equipment: armbands, pieces of paper with the smuggled items, (with point values written on each):

- 10 × chocolate (50 points)
- 8 × sugar (75 points)
- 8 × animal pelts (100 points)
- 6 × gunpowder (150 points)
- 3 × designs for new secret weapon (300 points)
- 1 × map to buried treasure (500 points)

Divide the group into two teams. Each team member puts on an armband; one team becomes the smugglers, the other the spies. Each team retreats to separate ends of the playing area.

The smugglers each receive the pieces of paper, which they are going to try to carry into enemy (spy) headquarters. The spies set up their headquarters inside an area that has a definite perimeter. The scorekeeper sits inside spy headquarters.

After each team has been given time to develop their strategy, play begins. The spies move away from their headquarters and try to intercept smugglers as they attempt to take their goods inside.

When a smuggler is caught, they must stand still and permit a one-minute search of their person by the spy who caught them. If the spy cannot find the piece of paper within one minute (the paper has to be hidden in external clothing layers), the smuggler is free to try to advance again into the headquarters. If the spy does find the 'loot', they take the piece of paper into spy headquarters and give it to the scorekeeper, while the smuggler returns to their headquarters to receive another piece of paper.

If a smuggler penetrates spy headquarters, they give their goods to the scorekeeper, and are escorted back to their own headquarters by the facilitator supervising the game. The winner is the team with the most points at the end.

15 Squat tag

Equipment: none

One person is chosen to become 'it'. The players scatter around the area and 'it' tries to tag them. The players may become safe from being tagged by assuming a squatting position. When 'it' is not close by, they can stand up and run again.

Each player may only use this method of escape three times and then they can only escape by running. If 'it' retreats five steps from a player who has escaped by assuming the squatting position, and then returns, the player must run or they will be caught. Anyone who is tagged becomes 'it' and the game continues.

16 The stalker

Equipment: blindfolds and stones

Half the group is given blindfolds to wear. These players are scattered around the playing area. A stone is placed between their feet, but not touching them.

The other half of the group (the ones who can see) begin to stalk the blindfolded players, trying to obtain the stone from between their feet. To stop a stalker, the blindfolded players may point to any sound they (think they can) hear. If a stalker is there, the two players switch positions.

Stalkers try to collect as many stones as possible without being caught.

17 Traitor's letter

Equipment: a small ball for each player

The idea is that the group is divided into two halves: the French and the Prussians. The French camp on one side of the wood and the Prussians camp on the other. In the Prussian camp is a traitor, who has made an agreement with the French to place a letter containing important information about Prussian plans in a tree, which they will mark in a certain way. This tree should be near the centre of the area. The 'traitor' heads out to place the letter in the tree and retires again to their own camp. Their treachery has been discovered and they are arrested on their return to camp (a member of staff could undertake this role as the traitor refuses to divulge the hiding-place of the letter and is therefore sentenced to be shot, so takes on the part of onlooker or assistant facilitator).

At a given signal from the facilitator, the Prussians set out to recover their letter and try to prevent the French from obtaining it; meanwhile the French simultaneously leave their camp intent on obtaining the letter, and watching out for the Prussians. Each young person is armed with a tennis ball for if they are found. The Prussians must look for signs of the traitor being there and the French must look for a tree marked a particular way. When two opponents meet, the first one hit by a ball will be 'out of action' and that young person takes no further part in the game (or whichever part of the body is hit cannot be used again for the remainder of the game). One mark is awarded to the French or Prussians for every person they put out of action and four marks are awarded to the side that finds and takes possession of the letter. The side with the most marks are the winners.

18 Troglodytes

Equipment: a candle, a box of matches, some torches

One or two group members are designated troglodytes, the remainder are defenders of earth. The premise behind the game is that troglodytes have landed on our planet from another galaxy and are preparing to take over the world. The troglodytes have a faulty spaceship, which will explode if it is set on fire. The team has to try to sneak up to the troglodyte ship and blow it up. However, the troglodytes are more advanced than humans are and have laser blasters (torches) that can kill the team members. The candle and some matches are placed at the location of the spaceship. The team must navigate to the area, sneak up and try to light the candle. If a troglodyte hears them, they turn on their flashlight and blast the defender (but warn them not to shine torches into people's eyes). If a defender is 'hit' with the laser, they are out. The game continues until the candle is lit or until all defenders are dead.

19 Witch in the woods

Equipment: none

Establish a base and select one person to be the witch, who goes off and hides. After a short while, the other players disperse out from the base to seek out the witch. Once the witch is discovered, players run back to base. The object is for the witch to catch as many team members as possible, even if they 'surprise' them from their hiding place(s) before they can get back to base.

20 You can't see me!

Equipment: none

The object of this game is to allow the players the opportunity to pretend they are animals, trying to hide from man. Each player is given time to hide along the trail.

They may travel no more than a set distance from either side of the trail, and may use anything in the natural environment to provide camouflage. The seeker waits about five minutes until all players are hidden. They walk the distance of the trail *once only*, and try to find as many players as possible. After the walk, they call out, and watch to see where all the successful 'animals' hid.

23 | **Problem-solving games**

The following games and puzzles are 'active' games that often involve activities that may feel 'adventurous' but can be carried out in centres, in playgrounds, in parks or on playing fields without specialist staff. Many of them need considerable preparation, including collecting necessary resources and equipment, but this shouldn't deter you. The outcome is worth the effort!

Problem-solving games are fun, cooperative, challenging games in which the group is confronted with a specific problem to solve. The activities bring out young people's communication skills, as well as encouraging leadership, teamwork, decision making and initiative, which help to promote emotional and psychological growth, and they demonstrate a process of thinking about actions and consequences that helps participants learn how to reflect on an experience and learn from it. Problem-solving is an absolutely crucial life skill for everyone, whatever their age, status, position or background. Fortunately, it is a skill that can be learned over time and with practice; these activities allow individuals to learn, practice and make mistakes in an environment that is safe for them physically, emotionally and psychologically, helping them to develop their identity, capacity and character with which they will manage their life.

Reviewing the activity and the way that it was executed is a crucial stage of the learning process, as individuals need to recognise the approaches that do and do not work. For example:

- Don't panic.
- Don't rush into the first solution that comes to mind.
- Take emotional responses away from the process.
- Gather as much data as possible about the issue.
- Generate possible alternatives, think laterally about whether there are innovative solutions to the issue.
- Consider the consequences to each approach.

All of these activities should be reviewed properly and debriefed to attain the maximum learning from them. As with all activities, review points should be embedded in the course of the activity, not left to the end as an 'add-on' before going home.

1 Acid river

Equipment: tape or rope to mark the ends of the 'river' and some mats, cardboard or other material to create 'islands'
The whole group must get from one end of the 'river' to the other. The group gets half as many 'islands' as there are people in the group. The whole group must be off one shore and onto the 'islands' before anyone moves onto the other shore. There are penalties for anyone who 'dips' into the river (such as going back to the beginning, the whole group starts over, that person must be silent, etc.).

2 Blind tent pitch

Equipment: blindfold and tent
The goal is to pitch a tent with every member bar one blindfolded. The person without the blindfold calls out direction to the others. Alternatively, every team member can be blindfolded, but beware of damage to the tent!

3 Diminishing resources

Equipment: newspaper squares large enough for one person to stand on, with five more newspaper squares than the number of people (vibrant music can add a touch of drama!)
Rules:

- Communicating the first instruction is important for the facilitator; hold one of the newspaper squares, but don't say 'newspaper square', only say: 'square'.
- Everyone must have both feet in a square
- When the facilitator says 'switch', everyone must move to a new square immediately.
- The game cannot continue unless everyone has both feet in a square.

Put all the newspaper squares on the floor, spaced randomly. Ask all the participants to stand with both feet in a square. The 'switching' and 'moving' to new squares shouldn't be a problem at this stage, because there are more than enough newspaper squares for everyone. After about three 'switches', begin to remove squares as you walk around the room; keep on taking newspaper squares away until there are not enough squares for everyone.

Leave the group for a while to see if they can work out that there may be more than one person per square.

4   Minefield

Equipment: three mats per three participants in the group and rope to mark off the ends of the 'minefield'
Split the participants into groups of three. Each group has to work together to cross the minefield as quickly as possible without touching the ground. If any of the team touches the ground, they must start again. The winning team is the one that reaches the finish and clears all their mats from the minefield the quickest.

Once the group has the idea of the activity, they can work in larger groups. It adds an interesting challenge to give out fewer squares than there are people in the group.

Note: this may be played with upturned crates/boxes.

5   Multi-way tug-of-war

Equipment: ropes tied to a central ring
Several teams pull against each other, requiring communication and tactics as well as strength to outmanoeuvre the opposition and win.

Lay out the ropes in a spider shape, with the ropes stretched out from the central ring. Divide the participants into groups of similar strength.

Safety rules:

- No wrapping or tying rope around anyone or anything; only hold rope with hands.
- Watch out for rope burn, tell participants to let go if the rope is moving through their hands or if they lose their footing.

The first command from the facilitator is 'take the strain'. This is only to take up the slack. The leader makes sure the centre ring is stable and centred.

The second command is 'Go!'

The teams attempt to pull the centre ring or knot over their finish line. This can rarely be achieved by strength alone but requires cunning and strategy.

6 Name in the pocket

Equipment: a piece of paper and a pen for each person

The entire group sit on chairs in a circle, with nothing inside the circle. Each person writes down the name of another person in the group – they can only write down one name. Everyone folds their piece of paper and puts it in their pockets.

On the word 'go', each person has two minutes to persuade that person to make that person their partner. When everyone has their partner, they sit next to one another in the circle.

Only pairs are allowed.

7 Nightline

Equipment: a length of rope and a blindfold for each member of the group

The blindfolded group follows the line, which has been laid out in advance around, through, under and over various objects.

The first person relays a description of the terrain and obstacles to the person behind, who passes it to the person behind, and so on down the line. It is always interesting at the end to compare what was said at the start of the line and what was heard at the end!

8 Red–blue teambuilding activity

Equipment: flipchart paper, pens, a stopwatch, copies of the score clarifying sheet and the score sheet

The game is that each team must pick red or blue. The significance of each choice is in the way the points are scored. The objective for each team is to finish with a *positive* score. The game is played over 10 rounds of 2 minutes.

Divide the group into two teams. Each team needs to be out of sight and hearing of the other (preferably in separate rooms or out of sight of each other outdoors). Give each team a score clarifying sheet and a score sheet.

Score clarifying sheet

If team A play	And Team B play	Team A scores	And Team B scores
Red	Red	+ 3	+ 3
Red	Blue	− 6	+ 6
Blue	Red	+ 6	−6
Blue	Blue	−3	−3

- Each team scores points according to the relationship of the choices of both groups.
- During each round, neither team knows what the other group has chosen until both made their choices.
- After both teams have made their choice, the facilitator tells each group the choices and the scores.
- Two 3-minute inter-group conferences are allowed, involving one or two representatives from each group. However, a conference can only take place at the request of both teams and must take place out of sight and hearing of other team members.
- Rounds 9 and 10 will score double.

Score sheet

The only way to finish with a positive score is if both groups choose red every time. The aim of the game is to demonstrate the importance of trust: choosing red runs the risk that the other team will choose blue, in which case the team ends up with −6 and the other team with +6. The perceived safe option is to choose blue, so as not to be 'beaten' by the other team.

	Team A Played	Team A Scored	Team B Played	Team B Scored
Round 1				
Round 2				
Round 3				
Round 4				
Round 5				
Round 6				
Round 7				
Round 8				
Round 9				
Round 10				
Total				

9 *Rollerball*

Equipment: a piece of drainpipe or guttering for each person in the group, a ball, a post, a bucket

This game is best played in an open space where the bucket and post can be placed a good distance apart. The players must move the ball from the post to the bucket without carrying or touching it.

Rules:

- Nobody is allowed to touch the ball directly, only by using the pipe sections.
- Nobody is allowed to walk with a pipe if it is touching the ball
- If the ball touches the ground, it must be returned to the start.

Additional challenges may be added, for example:

- The ball must change direction through 180 degrees on its journey.
- All pieces of drainpipe must be used more than once.
- The ball must drop vertically at least x cm on its journey.
- Complete the task without anyone talking.

10 Rope circle

Equipment: a length of rope, knotted or fastened securely at the ends to form a circle
All the group except one takes hold of the rope, holds it about waist height and leans backwards, so that the rope makes a taut circle. The remaining group member climbs onto the rope and walks around the whole circle on it.

11 Spider's web

Equipment: several ropes, two trees or substantial posts spaced a couple of metres apart (and helmets if the web is to be above shoulder height)
With the ropes, form a web with varying sized holes. All group members must pass through the web from one side to the other without touching the ropes forming the web.
   Rules:

- Nothing must touch the web, or the spider will get you!
- Once through the web, you cannot return.
- Each hole in the web can only be used once.

Facilitator note: you will need enough time to prepare and test the web before using it!

12 The acid marsh

Equipment: planks of various sizes (for a group of 8 people, one long plank and two short planks are adequate), several mats or tyres and a rope to outline the marsh
The group must work as a team and cross the acid marsh taking all the equipment with them.
   Rules:

- Only the equipment provided can be used.
- If anyone falls in the acid, they must go back to the beginning; this includes standing in the middle of the tyres.
- The planks are not acid resistant and must not touch the ground.

- Only the tyres are acid proof, these are permanent and must not be moved.
- The group must *not* throw the planks or jump from tyre to tyre.

Additional challenges may be added:

- Provide an object to carry (e.g. bucket of water).
- Blindfold one member of the team.
- Eliminate some of the tyres to make the crossing more challenging.

13 The maze

Equipment: masking tape and a replica of your maze design on paper (for the facilitator!) Mark the maze out on the floor with the masking tape; the blocks should be around 30cm × 30cm (big enough for one person to step into).

The paper maze replica will have 'hot spots' marked out, which should form a route through the maze; there may be two 'entrances', but one should be a dead end and the other should lead through to the other side. One side of the maze should be the start and the other side the end, such as in the sample maze below.

Sample maze

START					
X		X			
	X		X		
X				X	
	X				X
					X
X			X	X	
		X			
	X			X	
		X	X		X
					X
FINISH					

- The facilitator should stand at the end of the maze to monitor progress.
- Number the participants so that they have an order in which to proceed through the maze.
- The objective is for the team to navigate through the maze, getting all the team members through in numerical order but individually.

Ground rules:

- Some squares are 'hot' and some are not.
- The players have to find the route through the maze by trial and error.
- Person number one starts by stepping on one of the squares at the entrance of the maze. There can be a bell or other noise if a square is not 'hot'.
- Team members may take it in turns to choose the next square of their route, or it can be a collective decision.
- If someone steps on a square that is not 'hot', they have to retrace their steps exactly as they came in, not just step off the maze on the side.
- There can only be one person on the maze at any given time.
- Movement is only from one adjacent square to another (forward, backward and sideways).
- The team can talk while they strategise, but after person number 1 has put their feet in the maze, there can be no talking until they finish, except to give the next direction. They can still communicate, just not verbally (funny sounds and 'hmms' count as talking as well!).
- No squares or routes can be marked with physical objects (pens, scarves).
- Everyone needs to take accountability for remembering the route, no one can write it down.

14 The Zin Obelisk

Equipment: a copy of the 'Zin Obelisk instruction sheet' for each participant, a set of 'Zin Obelisk information cards' for the group (thirty-three cards per set)
After the members have had time to read the instruction sheet, distribute the Zin Obelisk Information Cards randomly so that each participant gets an equal number of cards. Nobody is allowed to gather the cards in front of them, everyone should keep their cards but they can only share what is written on the card verbally. *The answer is Neptiminus.*
   Rationale:

- The dimensions of the Zin indicate that it contains 50,000 cubic metres of stone blocks.
- The blocks are 1 cubic metre each; therefore, 50,000 blocks are required.

- Each worker works 7 schlibs in a day (2 schlibs are devoted to rest).
- Each worker lays 150 blocks per schlib; therefore, each worker lays 1050 blocks per day.
- There are 8 workers per day; therefore, 8,400 blocks are laid per working day.
- The 50,000th block, therefore, is laid on the sixth working day.
- Since work does not take place on Daydoldrum, the sixth working day is Neptiminus.

The Zin Obelisk instruction sheet

In the ancient city of Atlantis, a solid, rectangular obelisk, called a Zin, was built in honour of the goddess Tina. The structure took less than two weeks to complete.

The task of the team is to determine on which day of the week the obelisk was completed.

You have twenty-five minutes for this task

Do not choose a formal leader.

You will be given cards containing information related to the task. You may share this information orally, but you may not show your cards to other participants.

The Zin Obelisk information cards

1. The basic measurement of time in Atlantis is a day.

2. An Atlantian day is divided into schlibs and ponks.

3. The length of the zin is 50 metres.

4. The height of the zin is 100 metres.

5. The width of the zin is 10 metres

6. The zin is built of stone blocks.

7. Each block is 1 cubic foot.

8. Day 1 in the Atlantian week is called Aquaday.

9. Day 2 in the Atlantian week is called Neptiminus.

10. Day 3 in the Atlantian week is called Sharkday.

11. Day 4 in the Atlantian week is called Mermaidday.

12. Day 5 in the Atlantian week is called Daydoldrum.

13. There are five days in an Atlantian week.

14. The working day has 9 schlibs.

15. Each worker takes rest periods during the working day totalling 16 ponks.

16. There are 8 ponks in a schlib.

17. Workers each lay 150 blocks per schlib.

18. At any time when work is taking place, there is a gang of 9 people on site.

19. One member of each gang has religious duties and does not lay blocks.

20. No work takes place on Daydoldrum.

21. What is a cubit?

22. A cubit is a cube, all sides of which measure 1 megalithic yard.

23. There are 3 and a half metres in a megalithic yard.

24. Does work take place on Sunday?

25. What is a zin?

26. Which way up does the zin stand?

27. The zin is made up of green blocks.

28. Green has special religious significance on Mermaidday.

29. Each gang includes two women.

30. Work starts at daybreak on Aquaday.

31. Only one gang is working on the construction of the zin.

32. There are eight gold scales in a gold fin.

15   Toxic waste

Equipment: a small bucket, a large bucket, a rope to mark out the radiation zone and a range of planks, ropes and bungees

The challenge is to move the toxic waste contents to the neutralisation container using minimal equipment and maintaining a safe distance within a time limit.

The challenge is for the group to work out how to transfer the toxic waste from the small bucket into the large bucket where it will be 'neutralised', using only the equipment provided and within a set time. The waste will blow up and destroy the world after 20 minutes if it is not neutralised.

Anyone who ventures into the radiation zone will suffer injury and possibly even death, and spillage will create partial death and destruction. Therefore, the group should aim to save the world and do so without injury to any group members.

The rope circle represents the radiation zone emanating from the toxic waste in the bucket. Emphasise that everyone must maintain a distance from the toxic waste wherever it goes, otherwise they will suffer severe injury, such as loss of a limb or even death.

Setting up:

- Use the rope to create a big circle on the ground to represent the toxic waste radiation zone. The larger the radiation zone, the more difficult the activity.
- Place the small bucket in the centre of the radiation zone and fill it with water or balls to represent the toxic waste.
- Place the neutralisation bucket a good distance away. The greater the distance, the more difficult the activity.
- Put all other equipment (i.e., bungee, cords and red herring objects) in a pile near the rope circle.

16   Traffic jam

Equipment: one mat per person, plus one extra for the centre

The aim is for two equal teams to exchange places on a line of shapes that has one more place than the number of people in both groups.

Rules:

- Divide the group into 2 equally sized teams.
- One team stands on the places left of the middle square and the other team stands to the right. Both teams face the middle unoccupied square.
- Using the following moves, people on the left side must end up in the places to the right and vice versa.

Legal moves:

- A person may move one place into an empty space in front of them.
- A person may move around one person who is facing them into an empty space.

Illegal moves:

- Any move backwards.
- Any move around someone facing the same way.
- Any move which involves two people moving at once.

17 Tyre pyramid

Equipment: tyres (decreasing in size or the same size but numbered sequentially), arranged in a pyramid, and three flat wooden posts
The group must re-build the pyramid, moving it one tyre at a time from one side to the other (either in decreasing size order or number order).
Rules:

- Only one tyre may be moved at a time, a second tyre can only be moved after the first one is in place.
- A smaller tyre can only go on top of a larger one; a large one cannot go on top of a smaller one.

Additional challenge: encourage the group to lift the tyres as a team without touching the post.

24 | Parachute games

The parachute is a useful way of involving a large group in an activity. Because of its novelty, even those who would normally opt out tend to get involved. Between 20 and 50 group members can be directly involved around the perimeter of a parachute. The majority of games are cooperative rather than competitive and so good for generating cohesion and team spirit.

Parachute games can help to mould a group into a working unit before progressing onto other projects, but are also a wonderfully motivational resource for exercise, movement and social interaction when a group is less mobile.

Some of the benefits of parachute games are:

- they overcome language barriers;
- they overcome shyness or reticence;

- they encourage cooperation;
- they are non-competitive, so varying levels of ability are not an issue;
- they refine perceptual skills;
- they reinforce sharing;
- they reinforce the following of directions; and
- they promote social interaction.

A close group environment can be created by sitting on or under the parachute, when post-activity reflection requires quiet and concentration.

1 Air condition

Hold the parachute stretched out, with approximately a third of the people laid on the ground under it (facing upwards, heads pointing towards the centre). The rest mushroom the parachute up and quickly pull it down again repeatedly. Air rushing in and out cools those underneath like a giant fan, and the sensation of watching the parachute rise up and then come down on top of you is very strange.

2 Bouncing balls

The canopy is held taut at chest height with two or three foam footballs on the surface. Three or four young people underneath the canopy have to try to knock the balls off while those around the canopy try to keep them on.

3 Cat and mouse

Everybody sits down with their legs crossed. Pick two people to crawl as low as they can underneath the parachute (the mice); then pick a cat to crawl on their hands and knees on top of the parachute (eyes closed or blindfolded) to try to catch the mice. Everybody else shakes the parachute to hide the mice.

4 Colours

Everybody stands holding on to a colour on the parachute. Start lifting the parachute up and down; the leader then shouts a colour and the person holding that colour runs underneath the parachute to the same colour somewhere else on the parachute.

5 Mexican wave

The idea is to get a ball travelling around the outside of the parachute in a circle. To do this, the players hold onto the parachute, bend their knees and hold the parachute down until the ball passes them. They then lift the parachute up.

6 Para-ball

Place a lightweight football on the parachute surface and experiment with moving it. What happens when you shake the parachute? Can you flip the ball off over people's head? Can you develop a wave technique that will cause the ball to move in a circle? Using a small ball (like a tennis ball), can you drop the ball through the hole in the middle? Can you stop the ball disappearing down the hole?

7 Para-shuffle

Simply pass the parachute round in a circle, rather like hauling in a rope, as fast as possible.

8 Para-sight

After lofting the parachute several times, everyone steps inside, bringing the fabric taut behind their body, either to shoulder height or to ground level with each person sitting on the edge of the parachute, thus creating a tent with everybody underneath the canopy. Once practised, this is a useful technique for getting everybody's attention (such as for storytelling, instruction giving, reviewing).

9 Para-swap

Number the young people 1 to 5 around the circle. Lift the parachute and after a few times, shout a number. The young people with that number then have to swap places under the canopy before it falls to earth. Make sure that those who remain around the edge allow the canopy to fall rather than pulling it down hard.

10 Popcorn

Number all members of the group 1 or 2. The number 1s stand back from the parachute and place a number of soft balls in the centre. The number 2s shake the balls off the parachute while the number ones throw the balls back onto the parachute. See who can react faster, the 1s or the 2s!

11 Rocket

Everyone stands holding the parachute, with a ball in the middle. Everyone bends their knees, counts to three, lifts the parachute above their head and throws the ball into the air. Try to use the parachute to catch it when it comes back down. Use as many balls as you can.

12   Round the plughole

If the canopy has a hole in the centre, place 3 or 4 light small balls (like tennis balls) on the surface and keep them moving around the canopy, avoiding dropping them through the holes.

13   Scoring game

Everyone stands holding on to the parachute. Divide the parachute in half, one team playing against the other. Fling the ball on top and to score a goal one team has to fling or shake the ball off the other team's side of the parachute.

14   Sharks

Everybody sits down with their legs straight out in front of them underneath the parachute. Pick a shark to go underneath and catch the fish by grabbing their legs. Once caught, the fish lie still with their eyes closed underneath the parachute.

15   Shoe shuffle

Number around the circle one to five or six. All of one number remove a shoe and throw it under the canopy. On a count of three, the canopy is lifted, mushroomed up and all those missing a shoe go into the middle, retrieve their shoe put it on and get back to their place as fast as possible, before the parachute comes down.

16   The Grand Old Duke of York

Everyone stands holding on to the parachute and starts singing 'The Grand Old Duke of York'. Every time they sing 'up', lift the parachute up and every time they sing 'down', pull the parachute down.

17   Washing machine

Half of the group of the young people are the machine; the others are the washing. Just like a washing routine, in goes the washing (young people sit under the parachute); in goes the powder and mix (give the parachute a good shake). The washing turns one way (the remainder of the group runs around in a circle turning the parachute) and then the other. The washing is rinsed (shake the parachute), spun (run in a circle), shaken and then dried (up and down in big movements).

25 | Musical games

Music is very important in many people's lives and using music to direct games is a good way of getting people enthusiastic about moving. Music and rhythm have been used to energise, uplift and get people working together for thousands of years. Music is an international language that can be used by people of all abilities, ages, levels of understanding and temperaments; the focus, listening, co-operation and joint achievement of making or moving to music helps people to develop team working and communication. Music can set the mood, pace and energy of a session, as different music provides different volumes, tempos and atmospheres.

Musical games can involve making music or playing games to music; it is the collaborative creativity that brings about the results. Games to music do not rely on having a sense of rhythm, so no one need feel embarrassed at participating! It can be as educational as it is fun to provide the group with a range of musical instruments and then encourage them to play together, bringing people together in a shared experience.

Often, the less structured and the louder the session, the more successful the outcomes! However, as a facilitator, you do need to have the session carefully planned so that you build in the learning element and make sure the participants understand what has been achieved, or else all you will have from the activity is a headache!

1   Bumps music

On the blow of the whistle or stopping of music, the last person to sit on the floor is out.

2   Crash music

Players mingle, constantly moving until the leader shouts out a number. All players must then try to get into groups of that number; any group that doesn't succeed is out. Players can also find others who have things in common, such as the same shoe size.

3   Dancing feet music

Participants change at a signal from the facilitator from running around to running on the spot (or some other shape or movement).

4   Figure-of-eight musical chairs

Arrange the chairs so they are facing outward in two circles, about a metre from one another. Play as normal musical chairs, but players walk around the circles in a figure-of-eight pattern.

5   Musical chairs

Have one or less chairs than players. Chairs can be in any arrangement, a pattern or randomly scattered. While the music is playing, players walk around the arrangement of chairs, waiting for the music to stop. When the music stops, players have to find a chair to sit on. The player(s) who don't get a chair have to stand out of the game. At each round, another chair is removed until only two players are left vying for the last chair.

6   Musical statues

Participants move around the playing area, as directed by the facilitator (such as running, hopping, skipping, bunny hops). Players continue to move in this way until either told to change or the signal is given to stop. When this is given, all players have to freeze in the position they were in when told to stop. The last player to 'freeze' and/or anybody caught moving is out.

7 Partners music

Players pair up and create two concentric circles, with one partner in the inner circle facing clockwise and the other one in the outer circle facing anti-clockwise. On command, each circle runs in opposite directions until the leader calls out 'partners'. Players then have to find their partner and sit on the floor. The last pair to sit down is out, but remains in the circle to keep it large.

8 Shipwreck music

Place a number of hoops around the floor. Players are told that these are islands and they have to be standing in them to be safe from the sharks when the signal is given (either when the music stops or the leader shouts 'sharks'). At any other time, they may not stand or step inside the hoops. When the signal to stop is given, players have to find a hoop in which to stand. Those who didn't find a hoop to stand in are out.

9 Surge

Arrange the chairs in a big circle facing inwards; everyone apart from one player has a chair to sit on in a circle. The remaining player starts the game by standing in the middle and calls out a theme when the music stops (such as month of birthday, colour of hair, colour of clothes). Everyone to whom it applies has to get up and switch places with another player to whom it applies. The person in the middle also tries to get in a seat.

26 | Card games

Card games are excellent for helping with number skills and memory, or are simply a way to encourage a group to communicate and work together when they can't be outside. A deck of cards has easily as much developmental potential for group work as outdoor and higher risk, more adventurous activities; physical ability is irrelevant when playing card games, so groups with a wide range of abilities can work together. Card games refine mental skills like logic, observation and memory, as well as encouraging players to communicate, strategise and make decisions.

If the group has visual issues (or just because you can!), you can get decks of large playing cards, which can make it easier for the group.

Card games represent psychological adventure, a different way of working with numbers and visual acuity, still involving decision-making and strategising.

1   *Five-card game*

Deal five cards to each player, then place the remainder of the cards face down in the middle. The players may look at their cards.

    The dealer starts by putting down a card as a starting suit. Going clockwise, the next player has to follow suit, put down a card of the same denomination or put down one of the special cards in the list below, which affects the next person. If a person is unable to put any card down they must pick a card up from the remaining pile and play goes onto the next player:

- 2 = pick up two cards.
- 3 = pick up three cards.
- 7 = reverse go.
- 8 = next person miss a go.
- Ace = pick up the pile.

2   *Eights*

Deal eight cards or less to each player, then place the remainder of the cards face down in the middle. The players may look at their cards.

    The dealer starts by putting down a card as a starting suit. Going clockwise, the next player has to follow suit, put down a card of the same denomination or put down one of the special cards (below) which affects the next person. If a person is unable to put any card down they must pick a card up from the remaining pile and play goes onto the next player:

- 8 = miss a go.
- 2 = pick up two cards from the remaining pile.
- Jack = pick up one card from the remaining pile.
- Queen = reverse order of play.
- King = change suit to one of the players choosing.

The object of the game is for a player to get rid of all the cards in their hand. Anyone with only one card left has to knock on the table or face a forfeit.

3   *Cheat*

If a large number is playing, you may want to combine two or more packs of cards.

    Deal out all the cards in the pack. The object of the game is for a player to get rid of all their cards, but in order to do so they have to discard cards face down into a central pile, in multiples of the same rank (that is two kings, four 10s, three 4s). However, each player chooses whether to be truthful or whether to cheat when they put their cards down (for example, they could say they are putting down three aces when they are putting down a random combination of cards, like a 2, a 3 and a 9). The other players must decide if they're telling the truth or not and can call 'cheat' if they think that they are not putting down the cards they say.

If a player is caught cheating, they have to pick up the cards they have just put down and the rest of the pile. If someone calls 'cheat' and they were not cheating, they turn over the cards they just put down to prove it and the person who accused them of cheating has to pick up the pile of cards.

Play continues until one player gets rid of all their cards.

4   Chicken feed

Spread a pack of cards face up on the floor or a table. One person is the caller and sits with their back to the cards and players. The caller, working through a separate pack, shouts out a card. The players scan the cards on the floor or table for it. The first player to spot it places a forefinger on it and begins dragging it back to their place. Of course, as soon as their finger lands on the card, many will join it, all determined to get it to their place.

The winner is the one who captures the most cards. Anyone using more than one finger or using elbows to defend their claim is instantly disqualified.

5   Eleusis

A more complex game, calling for inductive, rather than deductive, reasoning.

The dealer shuffles one or more packs of cards and deals them all out to the players. The last card dealt is placed face up in the middle of the table as the beginning of the starter pile.

The players pick up their cards and organise them into any order they choose.

The dealer invents a secret rule that determines which cards can be placed on the starter pile; they write the rule down in secret on a piece of paper and hide it until the game is over.

Players take turns to choose a card from their hand and place it face up on the middle pile. If the card complies with the dealer's secret rule, the dealer says so and the card remains on the pile. If the card does not comply with the rule, the player places the card face up in a 'mistake' pile in front of them (each player creates their own mistake pile). Play continues until players have used all the cards in their hands, when they move on to use the cards from their 'mistake' pile. Play continues in the same way.

The game ends when a player has no cards left or when the dealer declares that it is impossible for anyone to play a card that conforms to the secret rule.

It is best for the dealer to keep the secret rule simple (for example, 'alternate black and red cards').

6 Pontoon

This game is complex to explain, but easy once you get the idea! Pontoon can be played by two or more players with a supply of betting tools (money, chips, matchsticks, marbles).

The cards have the following values:

- Ace is worth one or eleven (the holder's choice).
- Kings, queens, jacks and tens are worth ten.
- Remaining cards are worth their face value.

The aim is to build a hand with a total value as near as possible to 21, without going above it.

One player is designated as the banker, and each of the other players bets on having a better hand than the banker has.

- The best hand of all is a pontoon, which is 21 points in two cards (this can only be an ace and a picture card or a 10).
- Second best is a five-card trick (five cards totalling 21 or less).
- Third best is a hand of three or four cards totalling 21 points.
- Hands with 20 or fewer points and fewer than five cards rank in order of their point value (the nearer to 21 the better).
- Hands with more than 21 points lose.
- If the banker and a player have equal value hands, the banker wins.

The banker deals one card face down to each player, starting with the player to dealer's left, going round the table and ending with the dealer. All the players except the banker may look at their card.

Starting again with the player to dealer's left and working clockwise, the players other than the banker place their initial bet (matchsticks or sweets are easier to use than money!).

The dealer deals a second card face down to each player and all the players (including the banker) look at their two cards. If the banker has a pontoon, they show it immediately and collect double the bet from each player.

If the banker does not have a pontoon, the players work clockwise from the dealer's left to try to improve their hand with extra cards.

The possible options:

- Pontoon: if a player has an ace and a ten-point card, they place them on the table with the ten-point card face down and the ace face up on top of it.

- Split the cards: if a player has two cards of equal value, they may split them into two hands, putting them face up apart on the table and placing another bet equal to their initial bet. The banker deals another card face down to each of the hands and the two hands are played separately. If either of the new cards is equal to the first, the player may choose to split again, creating three or even (theoretically) four separate hands, each played individually with its own stake (ten-point cards cannot be split unless they are the same, for example two queens can be split but a queen and a jack cannot).

- Buy a card: if the total value of the cards is less than 21, the player may buy another one. They must increase the bet by adding at least the initial amount, but not more than double (for example, an initial bet of six may be increased to between six and twelve). The dealer hands out another card face down. If the total is still less than 21, the player may buy a fourth card, increasing the bet by any amount between the initial amount and the previous increase. If the four cards still total less than 21, a fifth may be bought.

- Twist: if the total value of the cards is less than 21, a player may twist. The bet is unaffected and the dealer hands out one card face up. If the total remains below 21, a fourth (and even a fifth) may be twisted. Once a player has twisted, they cannot buy cards in following rounds.

- Stick: if the total value of the cards is at least 15, a player may stick, staying with the cards and bet they have.

Whenever the total of a hand adds to more than 21, the player is out, loses their bet and the banker adds their cards to the bottom of the pack.

No player is allowed more than five cards.

The banker's turn: when all the players except the banker have finished, the banker's two cards are turned face up (the cards of the other players are still face down unless they have split, twisted, declared pontoons or gone bust). The banker may add more cards to the initial two by dealing them face up one at a time. At any point, the banker can stop dealing and play the cards.

The possible outcomes:

- The dealer goes bust: if a card dealt takes the dealer's hand over 21, the dealer loses.

- The dealer gets 21 or less, with four cards or less: the dealer pays an amount equal to their stake to any player who has a higher value hand than the dealer, and collects from those who have equal or less.

- The new deal: if no one had a pontoon, the dealer adds all the used cards to the bottom of the pack and without shuffling deals a new hand. This makes it possible to improve one's chances by remembering which cards are out of play. If there was a pontoon, the cards are shuffled and cut before the next deal.

7   Slap jack

Deal out all the cards between the players, face down. Keeping their cards face down in front of them on the table, players take it in turn to turn over their top card and then place it in the middle onto a discard pile. Whenever a jack is turned up, the first player to slap it wins.

In the traditional way the game was played, players have to slap the jack card, but it may be more even if players only have to slap the discard pile on seeing the jack, otherwise the player holding it may have the advantage.

8   Three-card brag

Three cards are dealt to each player. A player who holds any of these cards wins:

* Three 3s or an ace.
* Two or three of the same number or suit.
* King, queen or jack.

But if two players both have winning hands, three 3s or an ace beat the two or three cards of same suit or number, which in turn beat a king, queen or jack. If there is a tie between players, three cards are dealt again, but only to those who tied. The first person to win 20 times is the winner.

27 | **Just being outdoors**

Sometimes the benefit to a group of participants comes from simply being in the outdoor environment, rather than undertaking elaborately planned activities. Groups with limited resources do not need to venture far offsite or those operating in a restricted area, such as in a crowded city environment, may gain as much from simply being outside and seeing their environment in a different way as they would from travelling far afield.

Walking

Taking a group for a walk allows the leader to involve all the group participants in some way, from initial route planning to navigation while outdoors. A 'walk' may be a short excursion or a multi-day expedition. The art of good leadership rests on the ability to delegate and co-ordinate, rather than *doing*; this applies as much to adventure learning instructors entrusting tasks and responsibilities to participants as it does to leaders of a team of workers. This allows the leader to retain oversight of what is happening and to ensure that every task is completed, rather than becoming locked into one element and distracted from their overall responsibilities.

There are different types of land where groups may walk:

- Urban streets and parks, with clearly defined features and facilities close by.
- Lowland territory, with well-defined tracks and easily identifiable features, relatively close to public services (roads, telephones).
- Moorland, heath and hills, which are more remote, carrying therefore greater risks because of the greater inaccessibility, fewer features and distant access to services and facilities.

Problems can occur even when in the middle of a city; in fact, the risks are arguably greater here because the instructor can be fooled into assuming that the close proximity to facilities and services equates to a relatively safer environment. The essential criteria when out walking are founded on common sense:

- Check frequently that the group is together; with less challenging terrain come greater distractions and more areas where participants may be inclined to walk away on their own.

- Be aware of individual problems, such as blisters, tiredness, cold and hunger; these can develop into bigger problems if unattended. Participants not used to walking far may not realise they are becoming fatigued or a sore 'hot spot' is becoming a blister.

- Details should be left with someone at a 'base' with a landline telephone and they should be informed when the group has returned. It should not be assumed that mobile telephones would work, even in an urban environment, so the safety contact should have an estimated time of return and there should be an agreed process of what to do if they have not heard from the instructor by this time.

- Be mindful of the environment and property. This applies to the manner in which the participants behave in respect of the members of the public and the environment in which they are out walking but also the potential interaction of members of the public with the group. In the modern world, the threat that unknown strangers can pose to children, young people and vulnerable adults cannot be underestimated and the activity briefing should cover a process for unsolicited encounters, as well as warning participants of the need to keep their possessions safe.

The Countryside Code is a set of rules that apply to all regions of the United Kingdom, although aimed specifically at rural, particularly agricultural, areas. Whatever the environment, the rules can be presented and discussed with participants as a part of heading outdoors; put simply, they are 'respect, protect and enjoy':

- *Respect* other people: consider how actions affect others, such as the entire group spreading across a footpath so others cannot get by, leave gates and property as they are and follow footpaths.

- *Protect* the natural environment: 'leave nothing but footprints, take nothing but photographs'; once the participants have left there should be no trace of them left behind.

- *Enjoy* the outdoors: plan and be prepared for weather changes, follow local signs.

A part of planning is to plan the route that will be followed, which is something that can involve all participants. The first step is to work out the route the group will follow. All areas in which an adventure learning instructor will be operating will be covered by a map, the commonest being an Ordnance Survey map, making route planning an valuable exercise in geography and mathematics as participants work out distance, pacing, timing and direction, as well as the description of the route they will follow.

Scale

A map is a drawing of an area of land to a pre-determined scale, which is the amount by which you would have to enlarge the map to get it as big as the ground it is demonstrating. Every map has a scale printed on the front and you should always check this figure before you start. Although maps may be drawn to any scale, the most commonly operated two scales are known as 'one to twenty-five thousand' and 'one to fifty thousand':

- 1:25,000 means 1 centimetre = 250 metres on the ground (or 4 centimetres = 1 kilometre)
- 1:50,000 means 1 centimetre = 500 metres on the ground (or 2 centimetres = 1 kilometre)

The grid lines on an Ordnance Survey map are called eastings (those going east to west, with the scale along the bottom) and northings (those going north to south with the scale up the side), which are used to locate a place within the square. Each square represents a kilometre and has *grid reference*, which is found by putting together the numbers of the easting and northing that cross in its bottom left hand corner (four-figure grid reference); the saying to remember it is 'go along the passage, then up the stairs'. Each square is sub-divided into tenths and a place can be more accurately identified by adding the tenth to the grid reference and pinpointing a location within the square (a six-figure grid reference); further accuracy can be achieved by sub-dividing the tenths further into tenths again (an eight-figure grid reference).

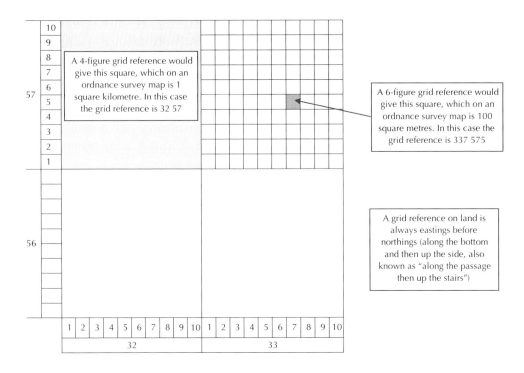

A 4-figure grid reference would give this square, which on an ordnance survey map is 1 square kilometre. In this case the grid reference is 32 57

A 6-figure grid reference would give this square, which on an ordnance survey map is 100 square metres. In this case the grid reference is 337 575

A grid reference on land is always eastings before northings (along the bottom and then up the side, also known as "along the passage then up the stairs")

Figure 20 Four- and six-figure grid references

Contour lines

Down the side of a map are the symbols and other useful information to aid in route planning and interpreting the map to the ground. There are lines on a map that show the height of the land, called *contour lines*; they join together places of the same height and form patterns to show valleys, hills and flat land. The closer together the contour lines appear, the steeper the land on the ground. The numbers that appear on the contour lines show the height above sea level and face uphill (the top of the number is the uphill side). Similarly, the writing on a map is always to the north (the top of the writing is the north side).

Direction

When in the outdoors, direction is found using a map and compass. People happily say that a compass points north but there are in fact three 'norths': grid north, true north and magnetic north! Grid north refers to the direction northwards along the grid lines of a map projection and is related to the way in which the spherical earth is represented on a flat piece of paper. True north is the North Pole, the axis on which the earth rotates.

Magnetic north is the place where the earth's magnetic field points directly downwards. Maps are oriented to grid north, whereas a compass will point to magnetic north. The magnetised needle on the compass aligns with the earth's magnetic field and is drawn to magnetic north; this north moves very slowly and continually because of the movement of the earth's magnetic core, so the variation between grid and magnetic north is shown on the side of the map.

When converting from the map to a bearing, the variation is added ('grid to mag: add') and when taking a bearing and putting this onto the map, it is subtracted ('mag to grid: get rid').

A bearing is simply the angle calculated from one point to another, relative to north. Imagine a circle, with north at the top; there are 360 degrees in a circle, so north would be at zero or 360 degrees. From this point, the *cardinal points* indicate east (90 degrees), south (180 degrees) and west (270 degrees) and the *intercardinal points* are the intermediate points that show northeast (45 degrees), southeast (135 degrees), southwest (225 degrees) and northwest (315 degrees).

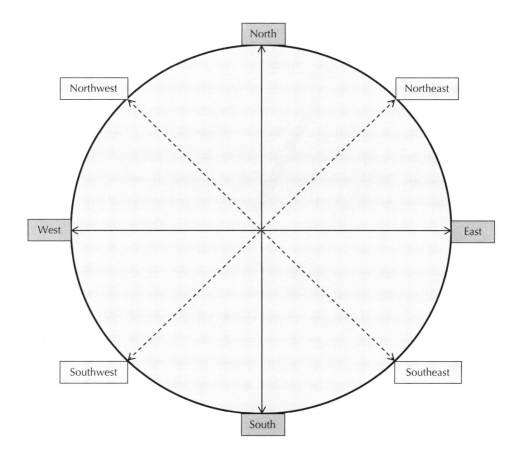

Figure 21 The cardinal and intercardinal points of a compass

There are three arrows on a land compass:

- The big arrow on the top is known as the direction-of-travel arrow.
- The arrow in the middle of the compass with a red end that points north; never follow this arrow, because it only points north!
- The arrow marked on the dial that matches up with the red and white arrow (the orienting arrow); where this touches the dial indicates the number of degrees (the bearing).

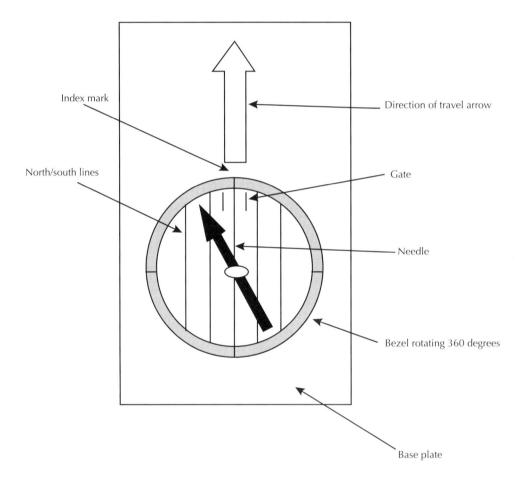

Figure 22 Basic land compass components

When using a compass, make sure it is away from metal or magnetic objects, as this will attract the arrow and distort the reading.

To take a bearing from the map, line up the long edge of the compass between the two points, with the direction-of-travel arrow pointing to the destination. Turn the dial in the middle of the compass so that the parallel north/south orienting lines in the centre are lined up parallel to the grid lines. Finally, read the number of degrees (the bearing) and adjust for magnetic variation. In order to move in the right direction, hold the compass and turn until the magnetic north needle points in the same direction as the orienting arrow; the direction-of-travel arrow is now pointing in the direction to walk.

The compass must be used continually throughout the walk to stay on track; to make navigation easier divide the route into short sections and use landmarks and features as a 'tick list' that you can use to confirm you are on route.

To convert a bearing from the ground to the map, point the direction-of-travel arrow at a feature on the ground (a hill, a church spire), line up the orienting arrow with the north arrow and read off the bearing from the direction-of-travel arrow, make the adjustment for magnetic variation and then place the compass on the map with the direction-of-travel arrow pointing at the feature. Line up the parallel orienting lines with the grid lines on the map and your position is somewhere on that line along the side of the compass. By doing this for two or more features, you can *triangulate* where you are.

Distance

It's very rare that a route will follow a straight line between two points on the map; roads, rivers and footpaths all have curves and bend around features like woodland, so it can appear tricky to measure the distance travelled. Commercial map measurers are available to buy, but two simple ways of measuring distance are with string or with a piece of paper and the scale marker down the side of the map.

- Place one end of a length of string on the starting point and carefully follow the route on the map, laying the string along the footpaths and following curves as closely as possible. If the string is longer than the route, the end point can be marked on the string with a pen; if the route is longer than the string, the exercise can be undertaken as many times as necessary and the distances added together to find the total. The straightened piece of string is laid along the scale bar to measure the distance of the route.

- Using a piece of paper and starting at one corner, pivot the paper so that the edge follows the route, marking every bend and turn on the paper until the end of the route. The piece of paper can be laid against the scale bar to measure the distance of the route.

Timing

Once the participants know the route they intend to follow, they need to work out the time that they expect it to take them. This is obviously not going to be accurate to the minute, but will provide a guide both for the participants and for the safety person, who will contact the emergency services if the group is not back at the time expected. The average walking speed is estimated at 5 kilometres per hour (12 minutes per kilometre), although this will vary according to the group ability, what they are carrying and what they are doing along the way. It takes longer to walk uphill and therefore it is usual to add one minute for every ten metres of height climbed (known as 'Naismith's rule'). Contour lines appear at 5-metre intervals on a 1:25,000 scale map and at 10 metres intervals on a 1:50,000 scale map.

Another way of calculating distance travelled is to count paces; mark out a one hundred metre line and have the participants work out their average pace per 100 metres (how many double paces they take to one hundred metres). Then while out on the walk, the young people can see how their pacing compares to the terrain they are traversing.

When transferring the planned route and timings, it is essential to add in any time for rest stops and activities along the way so that a reasonable estimation of the duration for the walk can be calculated and provided to the safety person, as well as to the parents or carers who may be collecting the participants at the end.

While out walking, participants can collect and record a set list of items, they can undertake a survey (for example of people they meet, of flora and fauna) or they can take pictures and make up a photomosaic of an area (which works really well with macrophotography).

Orienteering

Orienteering is a navigating challenge, where participants may undertake a walk that requires them to navigate around set features or they may have to navigate a sequence of 'control points' around a course, both demand the use of a map and a compass. The course may be a permanently fixed one or one specifically set up for the group and may be anywhere from a park, heathland, over hilly terrain or even around an urban landscape. The start, finish and interim control points are set, but the participants select their own route to navigate between them. Although orienteering maps are available for permanent courses, bespoke maps and courses can easily be developed according to the abilities and learning experience of the group and the terrain available.

On a standard orienteering course, the control points are marked on the map by circles, connected by lines and numbered in the order they are to be visited and on the ground the control point has a square 'flag' with a diagonal line forming two triangles, one white and one orange. The map is accompanied by control point descriptions (clues) and to prove they have found the control point, the orienteer marks their scorecard with a punch attached to the control point (each control point has a punch with a unique patterns of holes).

A bespoke course can be set up in a relatively small area, and may even include some indoor control point locations if there are not enough control point locations outdoors. In setting up a bespoke course, the challenge is to make sure that the course is interesting for the participants but not beyond their ability. It is critical that the course setter select control point locations that are easily identifiable on a map and on the ground, but which are also accessible from different directions; the activity will not work if the participants are all following each other.

Photo orienteering

This is ideal for an urban environment or for a group not familiar with rural features; it uses pictures to supplement navigational, visual and logical thinking skills. The participants are provided with a map showing specific locations or features and a set of photographs; they must navigate their way to each in turn and mark which location or feature they think they have found. An added challenge can be to ask the participants to work out from which direction each photograph was taken.

Spell a word

More along the lines of traditional orienteering, the control points have letters rather than a punch. The letters may spell out a word when the course is followed sequentially, or the letters may form an anagram.

Map windows

If a group of participants knows the terrain well or are skilled in navigation, this adds more of a challenge. The map with which they are provided shows only a small area around each control point, adding a greater cognitive challenge in that the participants have less visual data with which to work.

Measure it

The participants are provided with a map, control point descriptions and compass, as usual, but also they have a metre length of string, marked off at centimetre intervals and a set of control point instructions. At each control point, the participants must provide the measurement of the control point instructions (for example, the circumference of the post or the height to the top of the tenth brick).

Beeline hike

The group are provided with a map, compass and a route. The route has a start point but only a hint as to the final destination. The participants must trek the route to find the final destination. Usually the participants are told to follow the direct route as given, no matter what obstacles lay in their path (rivers, walls), so the terrain must be carefully risk assessed and any land owners notified.

Treasure hunt

The participants are provided with a map, compass and a navigational clue to the second point, where they will find the navigational clue to the third point, and so on until they reach the final point, which is either the treasure itself or a further clue or riddle to be solved to find the final prize.

Blind direction

Participants are spread around the playing area, orient themselves to 'north' (the real north or a convenient visible location) and then are blindfolded. The facilitator calls out a compass direction and the participants point in the direction they think this is. Anyone pointing in the wrong direction is out. The game can be made more challenging by calling out bearings as well as compass points.

Egg box course

Participants are provided with a number of egg boxes, coloured marker pens, glue, a large sheet of board and a set of minimum requirements (for example, three rivers, four bridges). Using the materials provided, they must build a model terrain on the large sheet of board and then develop an orienteering course within it, setting the control points and writing the descriptions that accompany them. It is the decision of the leader whether they may add in more features or use additional materials.

Strip maps

Participants are provided with vertical or horizontal strips of the terrain map and clues as to the location of control points. They must complete the blank sections while navigating to the control points.

Route choice

The facilitator prepares a map on a large piece of paper, with grid squares just like an Ordnance Survey map. Each square has a score attached. The participants must take it in turns to make a route from a given start to a given finish point, one square at a time, and record their score. The aim is to have the lowest score on completion of the route.

No participants may be on the same square at the same time.

O cards

The facilitator prepares 30 cards in advance, with 16 penalty cards, 8 bonus cards and 6 blank cards. Minutes are added for penalty cards (given on the card) and subtracted for bonus cards (given on the card); nothing is added or subtracted for blank cards.

The cards are shuffled and laid out, face down, at random around a start card bearing a triangle symbol: ▲ (the starting symbol in orienteering; this exists simply to indicate a starting point, in the same way that a starting point exists in orienteering). Players take it in turns to select a card at random and read it out. The game is given a playing time of 120 minutes (as if you are giving them a time to complete an orienteering course) and each player's time is altered according to the bonus or penalty they receive from the cards they pick up. This activity enables younger, less physically able participants or participants who struggle with verbal descriptions to understand orienteering in an interactive and visual way.

28 More adventurous activities

Some activities require qualified and professional instruction because of the level of risk involved. These may be at a residential centre or as part of an organised day's programme, delivered by an external provider or, if facilities allow, by the organisation's own staff.

While it may seem unnecessary and somewhat intrusive to the educator to involve themselves in the programme of an external provider, in reality it enhances the programme immeasurably. Many external providers offer a 'menu' of programmes that they deliver routinely, but by working with them to develop a more bespoke programme, the educator can develop and strengthen the learning objectives of programmes to which they have been working at the home base. Having an understanding of the games and activities that can be provided, the educator has a greater understanding of the potential and can embed them into their core programme, rather than having an externalised and often discrete set of outcomes from a programme not associated to that with which the participants may have been working for some time.

Using an external provider is a costly alternative to developing a provision in-house. All of the activities in this section can be conducted by a member of staff, as teaching staff leading their own pupils in adventure activities and assuming responsibility for their safety do not have to be licensed. There is a natural duty of care that remains with the governing body of the establishment to ensure that the member of staff is appropriately skilled, qualified and experienced to undertake the proposed activity. The advantage of retaining responsibility for activities in-house is that the school team can work together to develop a programme that encapsulates the ethos of the establishment and builds directly on the objectives of the particular subject fields of learning. In addition, of course, using an in-house provision allows valuable and stretched resources to deliver the maximum provision. The disadvantage of in-house provision is that the alien territory of an external provider and a 'new face' in the shape of the instructor can bring an added dimension to the learning.

Canoe and kayak games

1   *All in one*

All the group get into one boat and try to get it back to the jetty.

2   *Ball into boat*

Each boat has a ball and all the other boats are goals. Working as teams or individual boats, each team/boat must score as many goals as possible.

3   *Ball juggle*

Use small balls to juggle, the same as on land, to learn names. You could have boats paddling a spin if they succeed and a penalty roll if they don't (or individuals, if they catch or miss the ball).

4   *Basketball*

Basketball using hoops and buoys can be played the same in boats as on land.

5   *Beach ball football*

Using the boats to 'kick' the ball, participants must score as many goals as they can on a pre-set 'pitch' of water.

6 Blindfold pairs

In twos, with one of the pair blindfolded and with the only paddle. The sighted person gives directions around a course.

7 Boat orienteering

An orienteering course is set up around the water, with control points at various locations (under buoys, on trees, on bridges).

8 Fill the other boat with water

Within a given time limit, teams try to get the most water into other boats as they can, while avoiding others putting water into their boat.

9 Gunnel bobbing

One person stands on either gunnel to bob the boat (nervous participants can stand on the seats).

10 Pirates/captains coming

When the facilitator shouts 'Pirates', everyone has to lay down in their boat, or 'Captain on deck' means everyone must stand up in their boat and salute.

11 Randomator

With boats rafted up, participants change places, first in pairs and then increasing in number until everyone is up and swapping places.

12 Rock the boat

In pairs, each person stands on the gunnel; when the facilitator shouts 'go', both start bouncing and rocking the boat to try to make the other person fall in the water, while maintaining their own balance.

13 Submarine hunt

Flip the boats so that there is an air pocket underneath them. One boat is the hunter, the others the prey, the players have to go into the air pocket under their boats so they can't see where they are going or where the other players are. The person in the hunter shouts 'Echo!' and the prey return the shout. The hunter has to swim the boat about and try and bump into the prey to catch them and win, the prey have to avoid the hunter. With this game, it's best to have a small playing area and set a time limit so that the air in the boats doesn't run out.

14 Death match

Tie three balloons to the end of a length of rope, about two metres long. Hang these from the back of each boat (or just one if playing tag); each person gets a plastic fork as well as their paddle. The teams chase each other and try to burst the other boat's balloons with the plastic forks. When all your balloons have been burst, you are out.

15 Greased melon hunt

Grease a melon with margarine or lard and place it in the playing area while the players aren't looking. The teams then start at the bank and have to search out the watermelon and get it into their boat to win. For rougher games, you can play the winner is the team who gets the melon back to base first and allow boarding and/or tipping.

You need still water for this one or the melon will probably be a couple of miles away before you give up trying to find it!

16 Tag

With a ball, participants try to hit one of the people in a different boat. If you hit the person, then it is their turn to throw the ball. If you miss, than you will need to retrieve the ball and try again.

To play tag without a ball, players will need to actually chase another boat, and touch the back of the boat with a paddle. This version of the game is particularly useful when participants are learning to manoeuvre a boat.

17 Follow the leader

Play a game of follow the leader. To play follow the leader in a boat, the boats simply take turns being the leader. The leader can move fast or slow. The leader can paddle in a zigzag formation, turn around, paddle down the middle of the river, or close to the edge. Wherever and however the leader paddles, the rest have to follow.

18 Bingo

Before leaving, make up cards with pictures of things you may see while travelling. For example, you may include a pine tree, geese, a deer, a fallen tree or a large rock sticking out of the water. Then have the cards laminated, so they won't be ruined if they get wet. Give the participants the cards and a dry erase marker at the start of the trip, and help them spot items on the cards as they travel.

This can help to occupy participants not paddling and it can be played from just one boat. It keeps participants attentive and watching the area around them.

Another way to make this even more involving is to bring binoculars and/or a camera; binoculars add another dimension of participation and being able to take pictures with the camera allows participants to share with others everything they saw.

19 The boat star

The objective of the game is to have all the players stand up in their boats at the same time. All players get into their boats and steer them until they are in a circle formation. Each player removes their spray deck, moves to the back of their boat and places their feet firmly in the seat. Each player must then use their arms to encircle the players on each side. Once everyone is attached, the players try to stand up at the same time without falling in the water.

20 Boat polo

It is best to play this game on flat water such as in a lake or swimming pool until players are better able to gain control of their boat. There are two teams of players, and all that is needed is a net for each team, one placed at each end of the play area. Players cannot hold other players' boats, the ball must be in the water while they are moving, and they must help other players who have fallen out of or tipped over their boat. After a ball is thrown into the middle of the play area, teams must use their paddles to try to get the ball into the opposing team's net. Each time the ball goes into the net, one point is earned. The winning team is the one to reach five points first.

21 Sharks and minnows

Sharks and minnows is a game of tag that teaches paddling, aim and speed. The game begins with one player becoming the shark and the other players becoming the minnows. The shark must paddle around the play area trying to tag the other players. When a player is tagged, they become a shark as well. Play continues until only one minnow is left. The last minnow is the winner and becomes the new shark for the next round. This game prompts boating participants to use different manoeuvres to accomplish their goals.

22 Eskimo kiss game

This is a great game to do to introduce the history of kayaks and canoes. What you do first is explain some of the history of boating, for example, you talk about how the boats were made from seal and other animal skins and then the Inuit's would stitch them around a framework of whalebone or driftwood. Once they have done that, they would perform this ritual of kissing the nose of their boat with their nose. Therefore, that is what you have to do today. One by one the group stand up, shout the name of their boat and Eskimo kiss their boat. There are different variations you can do such as doing it in pairs, doing it in a long line or doing it individually.

23 Tap tap tag

All you do is set the perimeters and one person is the tagger. The aim is to tap the nose of everyone's boat. Once you have been tagged, you have to put your paddle down and put your arms in the buoyancy aid.

Raft games

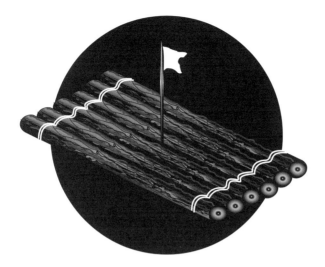

1   Heads, shoulders, knees and toes

Label the players 1 or 2. Number 1s stand up and sing 'heads, shoulders, knees and toes' while the number 2s remain seated, trying to rock the number 1s out of the raft.

2   Cat and mouse

One person is the cat, one is the mouse. The cat has to chase the mouse around the raft before the mouse can get back into their original boat.

3   Evolution

Explain that evolution is going from lower life to a higher form of life and then define what the levels of life will be. All the group starts as the lowest life (they can make the noise(s) they think this lowest form of life (primordial ooze?) might make), and paddles towards evolution. As each paddler encounters another of the same evolutionary stage, they play 'Rock, paper, scissors' to see who evolves to the next level of life (rock beats scissors, paper beats rock, and scissors beats paper). The aim is to see if every member of the group can evolve.

4   Randomation

Boats are rafted up and paddlers change places across the whole raft, first singly, then in pairs and finally to everyone moving around the raft and back to their original place.

5   Floating raft

Boats are rafted together upside down. Divide the group into 2 on opposite sides of the raft, with each side having water-filled balloons. Dodgeball begins! If players are hit with a water balloon, they are out

6   Push me pull you

Two canoes or kayaks are rafted lengthways, paddlers face opposite directions and each tries to paddle forwards.

Archery games

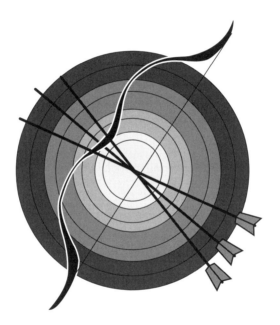

1   Scores (archer darts)

Using targets as a dartboard, with different colours scoring different points (the same as a dartboard and awarding more points towards the centre). The rules are the same as normal darts.

2   Soccer

Each team member has two arrows; the firing archers (one team) stand along a firing line, with the other team behind them, and the ball in the middle of the playing area. The idea is to hit the ball with the arrows and nudge it across the other team's goal line. After the first team shoots, the opposition takes up position on its firing line, with the first team now standing behind them.

Blunt or wooden arrows are best so the ball is not destroyed.

3 Flight

All the group members stand in a line and fire at the same time to see who can launch their arrow the furthest.

4 Clout

A wooden pole is sunk about 75 to 100 metres out. A rope is tied to the base of the pole, marked at one-metre intervals for each colour (white, black, blue, red, yellow). The idea is to get as close to the pole as possible.

5 Pin-up target shooting

Put some sweets into balloons, blow them up and hang them onto targets. If an archer pops one, they get the sweet. Alternatively, have the participants make balloon animals, hang them on targets and shoot them.

6 Instinct shoot (Robin Hood)

There's a big difference between target shooting and 'Robin Hood' style shooting. Robin Hood and his merry men never really knew how far away the targets were, so they couldn't aim very well and had to rely on instinct. The two types of shooting require very different skills and sometimes a participant who is poor at target aiming is better at instinct shooting. Remove all the targets and any clues to distance before placing objects around the range, including target mats on the ground, at strange angles, in odd positions and at different distances.

Walk around the area and, when the facilitator shouts 'fire', the participants shoot at a set target instinctively (i.e. without stopping and aiming).

7 Field course

Hay bales are placed along a path so that they are visible only from a certain point or perspective and pictures of animals of different sizes are attached to them. Participants march through in single file and from a predetermined spot take it in turns to fire at the target.

8 Marbles

Place tennis balls in a small pyramid surrounded by a rope circle with a two-metre radius. Using blunted arrows, the participants have to try to knock as many of the balls out of the ring as possible in a certain number of shots.

9   V-shoot

A large masking tape 'V' is placed on the target. Two archers then compete in trying to hit lower on the 'V' than the other.

10   Archery golf

Archery golf can be played on a normal golf course or on one set up by the facilitator. Each 'shot' consists of firing an arrow down the fairway towards the hole, with the first one being fired from the tee and subsequent shots being taken from where the previous arrow landed (just as in golf). To finish a hole, the arrow should be fired into a hoop placed on the green.

11   Archery pitch and putt

The rules are the same as for archery golf, but the playing area has obstacles and a smaller course.

12   Archery noughts and crosses

Draw a noughts and crosses grid on the back of an archery face. Participants take turns to fire. An arrow doesn't count if it lands in a square where there's already another arrow, but the player does get another shot. The winner is the first person to get arrows in three boxes in a row.

13   Archery pin the tail on the donkey

Draw a picture of a donkey on the back of an old target face, blindfold the participant, spin them around a few times about 50 to 100 metres from the target, and point them in vaguely the right direction. Each archer gets three arrows and the one with the arrow nearest the donkey's tail is the winner.

14   Archery blind man's buff

The 'blind man' is blindfolded and spun round several times. They fire arrows wherever they think they hear someone, while the other players move out of the way. The first person to hit becomes the next blind man.

   Use indoor arrows only (the ones with suckers and not points on the end)!

15   Archery water polo

Played according to normal water polo rules, with goals at either end of the water, but using an arrow instead of a ball. All passes and shots must be made underwater (to take the speed out of the arrow); no player may have their feet touching the bottom.

16 Archery relays

Four archers are spread around a square of roughly 100 metres on each side. Each archer has six arrows to fire at a target set up beside the next archer in the team. As soon as an arrow hits the target, the next archer may start firing at their target. The relay is finished when the last archer hits their target.

The facilitator can decide whether archers may move along the line of their side of the square, closer to the target if they miss (but the target must move with them!).

Climbing games

Some of these work equally well as traversing or bouldering games.

1 Add-on

Players begin by agreeing on the first sequence of three to five moves. The first climber gets on the wall and makes the sequence of moves. The moves can be marked by chalk, tape or memorised. When the first climber finishes, they add the next move and the next climber gets on the wall. Each time a climber completes the sequence, they add another move. To make it easier, 'hands only' can be played (where any foot-hold can be used), or both hand-holds and foot-holds can be selected as part of the sequence.

2 Pointer

The person designated as the pointer simply points out the next hold to the climber. This should be timed so that the next hold is tapped just ahead of the person climbing, rather than them holding on and waiting.

3 Memory

The first person points out a sequence of four to ten moves, with no markings placed on the wall. The second person has to climb the route, remembering each hold. On successful completion of the moves, the second person adds on another move, which the first person has to memorise and complete.

4 Take away

A route of about 20 holds is agreed and the holds marked with chalk or tags. Each climber climbs the route and after each successful climb, the finishing climber rubs out a chalk mark. If the next climber cannot climb it without falling, the turn is passed to the next person. If no one can do it, the original climber must prove it can be done. If they cannot make the move, the mark is put back on.

5 Tag

The first person is 'it' and tries to climb to another person and touch them. The person being 'tagged' then must tag someone else, excluding the person just touched. The previous tagger climbs down until the next person is tagged.

6 Dyno

Agree one or two foot-holds and one or two hand-holds, with a large hold higher above the hand-holds. Each person takes turns 'dynoing' (making a dynamic move) to the hold. The dyno can be vertical, off vertical or even horizontal.

7 One arm/one foot

Two or more climbers decide on a sequence and attempt it using one arm and/or one foot only. This can be done as an add-on or take-away game.

8 Quickdraw climbing game

Designate eight to ten 'goals' (such as holes in the wall, big holds) and place the same number of quickdraws in a location near them (hanging on another hold). The climber must climb back and forth from the pile of quickdraws, taking one at a time to each goal. (A quickdraw consists of two karabiners connected by a textile sling, as used by climbers to attach their rope to pieces of protection when lead climbing.)

9 Round-about

One person is 'in'. They select a place with quite a few good holds. Their partner has to try to climb around them in a circle, while the person 'in' has to try to stop them by getting to the holds before they do. When the circler goes for more than 10 seconds without changing a hand or foot, they swap places.

10   Blind climb

Blindfold one climber; they start to climb by feeling with their hands and feet. The spotter may support by calling out directions.

11   Amputee

Other people from a set distance throw a small hoop or beanbag (gently!) at the climber as they climb. If a limb of the climber is hit, the climber can no longer use that limb. If the climber's head is hit, they lose. If the climber is hit on the back three times, they lose. If the climber falls, they lose. If the climber gets to the end of the climb, they win.

12   Twister

Set out a section of the wall as the 'twister' area and play with the same rules as normal twister.

13   Spiderman

One person climbs about a quarter of the way up the wall and selects a hold about two metres away in any direction; they name it and the belayer locks off the rope, telling the climber when they are safe to proceed. The climber yells 'I'm Spiderman!' and dynos (jumps) for the hold. If they make it and hold onto it, they go again, if they don't, they swap with the belayer.

14   Hoarse

The first person chooses a point to begin and a point to end, then they roll a dice to see how many holds they can use (it is the facilitator's choice whether this includes the starting and ending holds or not). If the first person completes their route then the rest of the players must complete it.

15   Lapping

The first climber climbs the wall to make the most laps of a route that they can; the second climber tries to beat the time of the first climber.

16   Time's up

Starting with a ten-second time limit, the first climber gets to as many holds as they can before the time is over. The second climber tries to beat that number in the same sequence.

17 Lucky draw

Climbers write down all the climbing moves they can think of (such as lay-back, drop-knee, pinch, dyno) on slips of paper, then put the slips into a hat/chalk-bag. Three slips of paper are drawn out and the climber must make a route using only those movements.

Alternatively, the climber can draw out the slip of paper in secret, make the move and the others in the group have to guess what it is.

18 Add-on choice

Climbers are paired; they devise a route, one climber choosing the first two or three moves and their partner choosing the next two or three.

19 Gladiator

The climbers number themselves 1 and 2. Number 1 ties a short sling around their harness (loosely enough to be pulled off but not too loose, as it will fall off). Number 1 climbs about a quarter of the way up the wall and number 2 chases them. If climber 1 gets to the top without losing their sling, they win.

20 Simon says

'Simon' gives the group 15 seconds to get off the ground before calling out various commands (for example, 'Simon says move your left foot'); everyone must make the move, unless the command is not prefixed with 'Simon says'. Players are out if they fall or do not obey the command.

21 Wimbledon

On a slab or corner, the climber holds a tennis ball in each hand and climbs the route. The game allows some use of hands for balance and a little pulling on massive holds, but teaches that power comes from the thighs.

22 Tag team

Two people start at the bottom, race up to the top of the wall and back down, 'tag' the next person in line, who races up to the top and back down.

23 Taps

Climbers climb as usual but every time they use a hand, they have to first tap their head and then count aloud the number of times they have used it, starting at one (it makes it more fun to have them do it in a foreign language!). The goal is to have the climber try to beat their personal best by trying to lessen the number of times they use their hands.

24   Arch runner

A climber climbs all the way up, across and down the wall, then goes back to the starting point and repeats without re-using moves or holds from before.

25   Tap its

One person chooses a hold for each hand and one foot. With the other foot, they see how many holds they can touch while their partner counts. They then swap places using the same holds, the person that touches the most wins.

Bouldering games

1   Flag tag

Take two pieces of webbing, cloth or flags approximately a metre in length and have the two players tuck them into their pockets or waistbands. The climbers start at opposite sides and begin to climb towards each other. The object is to steal the flag of the opponent.

2   Follow the leader

Played just as it sounds, a participant begins climbing and once they reach a certain point the next participant in the line begins traversing the wall, using the same holds as the first participant used. If a participant falls, they join the back of the line. If the leader falls, the second climber becomes the leader.

3 Horse

Just as in follow the leader, the first participant to step onto the wall chooses holds that the others must use. Each turn consists of a player following the route that the previous turns have created and then adding on a hold or two of their own. Participants must be able to complete the sequence they choose. If a participant falls during any part of the turn, a letter (H, O, R, S or E) is given to them and once 'horse' is spelled out, that climber is out.

4 Mountaineering

When mountaineering, crossing glaciers and on some types of rock climbing, it is common practice to link the team together by a rope, which prevents the team from losing a member if an accident occurs or someone falls. Tie several knots in the rope (one for each participant) about 1.5 metres apart, with one at the beginning and one at the end of the rope, clip the karabiners onto the knots and then clip a karabiner into each climber's harness. The climbers must negotiate the wall together, making their way from start to finish without the whole group falling.

5 Routes

Choose a sequence of moves and mark all of the holds to be used. Participants climb the routes as set. The routes can have a theme (such as all rounded holds, all crimps, all one colour).

6 Tag

Line participants up as in 'follow the leader', and have the first climber start negotiating the wall. Once they reach a designated spot, the second participant starts climbing, chasing the first. Once the second climber reaches the designated spot, start the third, and so on. The object is to tag the climber in front, but participants may only tag those in front of them. If a participant is tagged or falls off the wall, they go to the back of the line.

7 Get dressed!

Hang different items on the wall (such as hats, gloves, trousers, shorts, jackets, shoes). The climber must climb around the wall and whenever they find something, they must put it on, without coming off the wall. The same can then be tried as they undress.

8 Shark attack

The climbers start in a circle in the middle of the floor facing inwards. When the facilitator shouts 'Shark attack!', they must get onto the wall as quickly as they can. The last person on the wall is the loser. The loser either is out of the game altogether or 'loses' an arm or leg.

9 Pirates of the karabiner

Give the climbers a foam sword each and, as they boulder around the wall, they chase and fight one another.

10 I went to the wall and used ...

One person starts at one end of the wall. Their spotter calls out 'I went to the wall and used a ...', and the climber has to make that move (such as crimp, undercut, smear). After the move has been completed, the climber steps off and the partner repeats the move. The new spotter calls out the next move to be used, such as 'I went to the wall and used a crimp and a smear.' The list gets longer, the climbers have to memorise the moves and the route gets longer.

Traversing games

1 Addition

The climbers agree the first few moves on the wall; the first climber traverses this sequence and then adds the next (a hold or a particular move). Every time a climber completes the sequence, they add on another move.

2   Blind climb

A blindfolded climber is directed around the wall by the directions of the other group members.

3   Lapping

The first climber traverses across the walls and makes the most laps they can. Then the second climber tries to beat the number of laps the first climber performed.

4   Over and under

One person climbs on to the wall, traverses several moves along, the next person traverses to them and has to go over them. The next person traverses along and goes over the first person and under the second person (between their feet and hands). Once everyone is on the wall, the first person goes over and under everyone and it starts again if you have enough wall! This can be played with as many people as you want and the more people, the longer they have to stay on.

5   Leap frog

The first climber gets onto the wall, the second person must climb past the first, the first climbs past the second, and so on. The leaper cannot use the hand or foot-holds that the person they leap is using.

6   Freeze

All participants traverse at the same time anywhere on the wall, while the facilitator stays on the floor and randomly calls out 'freeze.' When that command is given, the climbers must cease all movement, even if in the middle of moving from one hold to the next, while the facilitator counts to 10 (or 20, or 30!). Climbers may not move until the facilitator says 'go'. If a climber moves while in a 'freeze' or falls, they are out until the next round.

7   Limbo

Participants must traverse the wall and make their way under a limbo pole. A broomstick or even a person with long arms will suffice for the limbo pole. Each time participants finish making their way under the pole, move it down and have them try their luck, making their way under the pole again. Since indoor walls have bolt-holes, resting one side of the pole on a hold and moving the pole down one hold (or bolt-hole) every time is easy enough.

29 Why review activities and games?

Learning is most effective when you take time to think through the process and impact of your experiences and attempt to make sense of your thoughts, feelings and reactions; alternatively, you can support others to undergo that process. Such reflection can help to identify patterns of behaviour, resolve issues and make decisions for tackling similar or new situations in the future. This is the reviewing process.

Reviewing is simply learning from experience, or enabling others to do so, by revisiting the event and by working through the way in which it was tackled and the outcome that was achieved. This is a valuable process that helps to make use of personal experience and setting it in the context of what you already know and understand, so that you can learn and develop by it.

These reviewing processes can include:

- Carrying out the activity, through visualisation and verbalisation.
- Reflecting on the experience, emotionally and psychologically as well as physically.
- Analysing and making sense of experience, looking at how it affected participants and why.
- Communicating experience, verbalising thoughts to others and expressing oneself.
- Reframing experience, relating experiences to different contexts.
- Learning from experience, realising how experiences correlate to 'normal' life.

Alternative terms for reviewing are 'processing', 'debriefing' and 'reflection'. Reviewing is also:

- *Learning* – the process of learning from experience itself (e.g. by keeping a diary, confiding in a friend, or talking with your mentor). This is about what the individual does themselves.

- *Helping others to learn* – the process of facilitating learning from experience for others (e.g. by asking questions, giving feedback, or exploring alternative explanations). This is about what the facilitator does.

Other aspects of reviewing include:

- *Adding value to the experience* – the value gained from experiences depends very much on how experiences are reviewed. Reviewing is an opportunity to add value and meaning to experiences however 'small' or 'large', 'negative' or 'positive' they may be.
- *Getting unstuck* – without reviewing, groups and individuals can be stuck at a particular stage of development. Reviewing provides a range of strategies for moving beyond this stage and for getting the cycles of learning and development turning again.
- *Achieving objectives* – reviewing can help to clarify, achieve, measure and celebrate objectives.
- *Opening new perspectives* – people generally review experiences from their 'normal' perspective. By also 'seeing' an experience from the perspectives of others and by 're-viewing' an experience through a variety of 'windows' (reviewing techniques), people can escape from tunnel (or normal) vision and learn from the 'bigger picture'.
- *Developing observation and awareness* – the more involving an experience, the harder it is to observe what is happening. Reviewing can encourage observation, perception and realisation both during and after experiences.
- *Caring* – by reviewing activities, we show that we care about what people experience, that we value what they have to say, and that we are interested in the progress of each individual's learning and development. When people feel cared for, valued, and respected as individuals they will be better learners!
- *Encouraging self-expression* – it is not always easy to talk about experiences. An imaginative and sensitive approach to reviewing can help people to find the medium, situation, symbol or question through which they can most readily express themselves. This is where the expressive and creative arts can be particularly helpful.
- *Using success* – focusing on success may be a strange experience if it is usually problems that are the focus of attention in reviews. Reviewing can help people to enjoy success, to understand how it happened and to get accustomed to the idea that they can be successful.
- *Providing support* – reviewing can be a valuable safety net. The reassurance that support will be available in the event of failure encourages people to take risks (of the kind that will be supported). Whether people experience failure or success, the causes can be analysed so that they learn how to avoid failure (or win from failure) and how to achieve success.

- *Empowerment* – reviewing enhances people's ability to learn from individual or group experiences. Improved learning ability, together with increased confidence, allows people to become more independent and more capable of self-development, and even of self-actualisation! ('Self-and-others actualisation' may be a more suitable aspiration for those who acknowledge the mutually supportive nature of reviewing).

EXPERIENCE + REVIEWING = LEARNING + DEVELOPMENT

1 *How to review?* Thinking ahead obviously increases the chances of successful reviewing, but it is always better to have an unplanned or improvised review than to have no review at all.

2 *Purpose*: When and how are group aims and objectives decided? When and how are individual aims and objectives decided?

3 *Timing*: Immediately after the event? After a short break? Next week? A quick on-the-spot review, followed by a longer one later? After another activity, and review both together? Same duration as the activity? Or shorter? Or longer?

4 *Place*: Where the activity took place (while experiences are fresh and are the natural topic of conversation, and while it is easier to demonstrate a point or repeat parts of the activity)? While walking, travelling or eating (providing a chance for informal reviewing, especially with 'loud' or 'quiet' individuals who find it difficult to participate in a group setting)? The review room (ideal surroundings, comfortable air-conditioned, quiet, no interruption or distraction, plenty of space and resources)?

5 *Climate*: How structured? How informal? Easy-going? Business-like? Free-flowing discussion? Open forum? Challenging? Fun? Covering lots of ground quickly or one aspect in depth? Using several reviewing methods or just one?

6 *Ground rules*: No contract or agreement unless problems arise? Can rules be expressed positively? Agreeing principles rather than rules? What is negotiable? What is not negotiable?

7 *Participation*: How will you maintain high levels of involvement for each individual? How will you help those who cannot express themselves readily (especially as they may have the greatest need to do so)

8 *Ending*: How will you decide when to finish? Will this be agreed in advance? Will important points be summarised? How? How will you gauge and attend to emotional needs at the end? How will you help learners to work out realistic follow up action? How will learners be supported in carrying out follow-up action? There are often unplanned and unexpected outcomes and learning that derive from activities – space and time must be made to identify and celebrate these with a group.

It is critical to remember that a review is not just an evaluation of the activities and how well the group members could do them! The sleepiest and least productive reviews are those where the leader is exclusively concerned with evaluation. Starting a review by asking 'What did you learn?' is not likely to turn into a memorable review session, yet at the end of a good review, participants might be expected to respond more intelligently and enthusiastically to the question 'What did you learn?' At the very least, a good review will have stimulated reflective processes that might otherwise have been brushed aside by the next activity.

Holistic learning is about personal development, social development, team development, leadership development and decision-making, as well as social education, life skills, basic skills, lifelong learning and curriculum education. Much advice about reviewing (or debriefing) assumes that the main purpose is to facilitate *learning* and holistic learning is also about *development* rather than simply educative progression. So what should you, as a competent facilitative reviewer, do differently? One (partly right) answer is that *development* arises as a direct result of what is experienced during the 'activity' and that *learning* mostly happens after the activity when reviewing that experience. For example, the sense of achievement on completing a rock climb happens as the climber completes the final move; such achievements have an impact on development, whether or not much learning arises directly from the achievement. It is during reflection and review *after* the climb that the climber can learn more from the experience than was possible while engrossed in the climbing. The climber may learn through feedback during a review that their communication was poor or that their recklessness was endangering others or during a review they may learn how they can also control other fears in other situations. A review can take learning in many directions that were not fully apparent at the time of the developmental experience.

I said that the answer is 'partly right' because it is by no means always true that development happens during 'the experience' and learning happens during 'the review'. Many exceptions spring to mind. However, more important than recognising exceptions, is to recognise the flaw in the original proposition.

What flaw? The flaw is thinking of a review as a period during which *experiencing* is switched off. The experience of a review is at least as important as the experience of the event being reviewed. (How can you advocate learning through experience without paying attention to the experience of learning?) It is easy to see how this flaw has come about. When reviews are designed for learning from an experience that has just happened, the experience of the reviewing process is given little (if any) attention. However, if you want to use both the activity *and* the review for development, it is important to consider the quality of experience throughout the whole process.

A second flaw is that generally reviewing is considered as something that takes place *at the end* of the activity only, as a kind of 'round up' to the session as a whole, but this is not only wrong, it can also reduce the overall level and impact of learning. At any point during the execution of the activity, there can be some form of review to assess what the group has achieved and help them to refocus on what to do next.

Does that mean putting learning objectives on one side while you attend to developmental aims? Probably not. Many reviewing techniques can work well at both levels simultaneously, especially if your own mind is working at both of these levels and is in touch with what people are *experiencing* during the review as well as with what they are *learning* during the review.

Reviewing a learning process is important and needs to be as carefully planned as the learning activity itself. There are a number of ways in which the facilitator unintentionally puts up barriers to the learning potential with subliminal messages to the group members that suggest the review process is nothing more than a 'wind down' after the core activity:

- Never apologise for a review session taking place or promise that it won't take very long. This implies the review is an inconvenience that must be endured for as short a period as possible. It is important to be as positive and enthusiastic about the review session and to raise all the positive achievements of the group members, before looking at what could have been done better. Focus on success, not failure, even with the most ineffective group performance, a good facilitator can find something positive to say!

- Never start the review session by asking 'What did you learn?' This suggests that the review is pointless as the learning has already taken place and the group will gain nothing from the review session. You can start the review with other questions, such as who took what role or who did what; some pictures or re-enacting may help things along or you can focus on particular aspects that support the learning message. Remember to explore emotional development and how the activity may have been affected by feelings, motives and intentions, as well as exploring the physical and practical elements.

- Never expect the responses to be immediate; the first thing that comes into a participant's head or out of their mouths is not necessarily the most accurate reflection on their experience. People need to be brought to their learning and so need time to think through what they really felt or how to express themselves; it may be that vocalisation is not the best method, so a range of review tools may be better than just one (visualisation, demonstration, writing, drawing, activities). Just as people learn in different ways through different platforms, so too do they express themselves differently.

- Never make the session appear simple by asking for 'one picture/one word to sum up the day/what you learned/how you feel today went'. The learning process is a significant aspect to a participant's life and should not be trivialised; a participant will experience a range of emotions, thoughts, realisations, interactions and achievements and there should be the capacity for them to express all of these as fully as possible.

- Never appear as if only you are in control the review; if you have planned the session appropriately, you have spent a good deal of time and effort encouraging the group members to think and act independently, so it is essential not to undermine that work by implying the group members have no responsibility for themselves when it comes to the review. Certain things will have to be in the control of the facilitator, such as the time allotted to the review or ensuring that everyone is involved, but the content and direction of the review must be a *joint* process. However, never allow one or two voices to dominate a review (including your own!), every member of the group must feel included.

- Never assume that everyone has had the same experience or will have achieved the same level (or type) of learning. This takes away individuality and undermines anyone with an experience or outcome that varies from the mainstream. Allow everyone to express themselves before drawing conclusions, acknowledging that diversity is positive and to be embraced. There may be a range of learning from an experience, that may or may not all be recognised by every member of the group; this is not a problem!

Review may be undertaken in a number of ways, including:

- *Visualisation:* imagining the steps undertaken that led to certain actions or consequences.
- *Demonstration:* providing a clear guide or benchmark of a standard or type of achievement.
- *Pantomime:* a dramatic and exaggerated representation of an action to emphasise a behaviour or performance.
- *Coaching:* building on success for enhanced future performance, providing the stimulus, environment and objective steps.
- *Verbalisation:* a running commentary to highlight particular aspects of behaviour or performance, communicating the thought processes.

These can be used singly or in combination, or specific review activities can be deployed.

30 | Tools for reviewing

1   Active reviewing cycle

Recommended uses: for enabling well-paced and well-sequenced reviewing and for developing learning skills. Create a huge circle with the longest rope that you can find or create four circles representing the four stages of the learning cycle (facts, feelings, findings, futures). If space allows create another circle at the centre for the joker or wild card, as a reminder that no model is perfect and that there are always exceptions.

Participants now find a partner and walk round the sequence and discuss experiences. One person acts as a facilitator while the other responds. After each circuit, partners swap roles and/or swap partners.

2   Activity map

Recommended use: to find out what makes people tick (or not). This is an active and game-like way of sharing likes and dislikes and getting to know each other's values. Mark the ends of one rope 'past' and 'future', and mark the ends of the other rope 'happy' and 'sad'. Use the ropes to create a quadrant in which the zones represent:

- *Past + sad:* activities I'll never do again.
- *Past + happy:* activities I like doing.
- *Future + sad:* activities I'll never try.
- *Future + happy:* activities I'd like to try.

Call out the name of an activity and ask everyone to go to the zone where that activity would belong on their own personal map. Keep calling out activities, pausing now and again for comments and questions. To make it more of a game, let participants call out names of activities. Define 'activities' as narrowly or broadly as you like, relative to the experience being reviewed.

3   Brief encounters

This is one of the most dependable methods of all, but it does itself depend on having a good set of question cards suited to your group and to the theme or purpose of the programme.

- Find a partner and stay on your feet.
- Ask one of the questions on the back of this card.
- Answer each other's question in less than 1 minute.
- Swap cards and find a new partner.

The purpose of this exercise is to meet everyone and to hear about their experiences of success.

4   Changing places

Recommended use: for developing empathy and providing feedback. 'Changing places' is a reviewing method that allows people to see how others see them. It is a combination of several techniques in one: a feedback exercise, a guessing game, an empathy exercise, fish bowl and a buddy system. The basic concept is quite simple but the method is only suitable for groups where trust is well established and where individuals are open to personal feedback.

First, set up a buddy system in which pairs (A and B) take it in turns to be doers and observers. If there is an uneven number, the person left on their own can get useful experience as co-facilitators. A task is set up. For the first few minutes, As are doers and Bs observers. After 5 or 10 minutes, call a review break. Those who have just been observers (the Bs) sit in a circle, facing inwards, with their friend (A) sat behind them in an outer circle. The inner circle (of Bs) can now talk while the outer circle (of As) remains silent. Bs pretend that they are the person they were observing. They participate in the review as if they are their partner.

5   Chuff line

You will need something like a piece of rope to delineate a line between two trees or posts, with numbers from one to 10 spread along the line.

Explain to the young people that they are going to award themselves a 'mark/score' to each question you ask by going and standing on that number on the line. The higher the score, the more positive the response. Illustrate how to do this, talking through your reasoning.

Ask such questions as:

- How much did you enjoy …

- How well did you work with other people when we …
- How well did you listen to what others had to say when we…
- How much did you help when …
- How happy did you feel when…?

6   *Magic spots*

You will need something to signal it is time to return (e.g. a bird caller, tin whistle and recorder).

Explain that the young people are going to make their way to a special spot in the woodland by themselves to close their eyes, sit down if they like, listen to the sounds of the wood and think about what they have done today.

Demonstrate the signal for their return. Tell them they are to take up to 20 steps to find their magic spot (this will help keep them reasonably close and can be increased or abandoned later when you are confident the young people can do this activity sensibly). All start counting together and moving off to find their place.

Enjoy some peace and quiet for a few minutes!

7   *Classroom baseball*

A list of questions is prepared by the leader and/or young people. The group is divided into two teams. Four positions are allocated – home plate, bases 1, 2 and 3. One team is up to bat. The first batter stands at home base as the facilitator reads a question. If the batter gives the correct answer, the batter goes to first base. The game continues with each batter moving one base as questions are answered correctly. When a participant reaches home base, a run is scored. If an answer is incorrect, the batter is out. When a team has three outs or has been given ten questions, the other team is up to bat.

8   *Force field*

Recommended use: For helping groups or individuals to get unstuck, ask the group (or an individual) to set up two (or more) tug of war teams. One team represents forces for change and the other team represents forces resisting change; alternatively, the teams could represent success/failure or a number of different options for tackling an issue. Each individual represents a force within their option. The core question to ask (if change is wanted) is how the forces can be changed to generate forwards momentum towards change. The advantage of having individuals representing each force is that they can each think about solutions from the perspective that they represent. Dialogue between forces is also possible.

9   Find a picture/object

If indoors, you need plenty of pictures or objects available. If outdoors, there should be a wide variety of objects people can pick up without damaging the environment. The structure is simple. You have one or two questions about which you want people to think. They then look for pictures or objects that in some way answer your question(s). You then meet in a circle and each person introduces their picture/object and explains why they chose it.

10   Goldfish bowl

Recommended use: for focusing attention on the reviewing process itself. Make a rope circle on the ground. Divide the group in two. One half sits inside the circle and may talk. The other half sits outside the circle and may only observe and listen.

People in the inner circle review the previous exercise. After a few minutes, the half groups change places and the new inner group continue with the review or comment on the review process they have just been observing.

11   Hokey-cokey

All sit or stand in a circle. Ask questions such as 'what did you do well as a team?' As each person gives an answer, they step into the circle. If anyone is left on the outside, others can suggest a new answer for that person to 'use' to step inside the circle. You now have a huddle of people in the middle. The next question is 'what did someone do well as a team member?' This is effectively an invitation to give positive feedback to others.

As each person is given (and accepts) one genuine positive comment they step back to the original circle. You reach a stage where two or three people are in the middle waiting for positive feedback. You may need to prompt, coax or give feedback yourself.

12   Horseshoe

Recommended use: for exposing and discussing different views

Simply define the two ends of the spectrum and ask everyone to stand at a point on the line that represents their point of view. The benefit of the horseshoe shape is that everyone is more likely to be in eye contact with each other, which makes facilitating whole group discussion much easier. For example: one end represents 'we were a good team during that exercise', the other end represents 'we were a hopeless team during that exercise'. Everyone chooses their point on the line and then talks to one or two neighbours to check whether they need to adjust their own position on the line. Once everyone is in position, encourage questions from participants to each other.

As a variation, it may be helpful to choose different points during the activity, such as:

- 'How would you each have rated this team before the exercise started?'
- 'What was the quality of teamwork like up to the end of the initial planning?'
- 'What is your personal prediction for the quality of teamwork in the next exercise?'

Another variation: arrange chairs in a horseshoe with the facilitator sat in the gap. Have about twice as many chairs as there are people to make movement easier and to allow for different patterns of clusters and spaces to develop.

13 Individual happy charts

Recommended uses: for discovering the diversity of experiences and for enabling the telling of experience-rich stories. People make a line graph on the ground showing their emotional highs and lows during the experience being reviewed. People now tell their story to a partner or to the whole group.

14 Missing person

Recommended use: for helping a group to assess its needs and priorities, create a rope outline of a body in the centre of the group circle. Explain that this represents a person who can join the group. Ask participants to think creatively about the kind of person they would like this to be. The person will probably share some of the characteristics already in the group (e.g. sense of humour, good looks, friendly and enthusiastic) and may represent some characteristics that are missing (e.g. time-keeping, leadership, telling decent jokes). Try to bring the person alive by asking for a name, their interests, their strengths and weaknesses. Now pull the rope away with a flourish and ask the group what they will do now that this person no longer exists. The response is not guaranteed, but this often provides a lively and creative way into developing action points.

15 Objective line

Recommended use: for reviewing progress against a goal.

Individuals lay their rope on the ground. The near end represents their starting point (now) and the far end represents their goal (for the next activity, for the programme or for the transfer of learning). Ask each person to walk slowly along their line into the future towards their goal, pausing for thought in a few places along the way. Ask them to think about what would be happening at each point and how they would be feeling. Once everyone has completed their journey to their goal on their own, ask them to find a partner and talk through their anticipated journey as they walk along the line. Partners then swap roles so that each can do their own 'walk 'n' talk' into the future.

So far, this exercise has been an 'active preview'. However, once there has been an opportunity for participants to make progress towards their goal, they return to their objective lines (with or without partners) and 'measure' their progress by choosing where to stand on their line. In just one move (to a point on a line), each person is making a self-assessment, and is doing so in a way that is instantly visible to others. Once everyone is in place you can ask questions to help people reflect on their own position, or to encourage them to notice the positions of others. In these scattered positions, it may be difficult to facilitate a group discussion, but talking to a partner can work well.

Variation: Encourage people to shape their lines to represent the journey being taken (direct or U-turn or meandering) and to add objects along the way to represent points in their journey.

16 Paper bag notes

Each group member puts their name on a paper bag. Each participant writes notes to any or all other participants expressing appreciation for something done or complimenting on something, to be placed in the bag.

There are also various charts and other ideas, such as 'Post-it' notes put onto flipchart or the 'jelly man' tree. There is a wealth of reviewing sheets downloadable from the internet.

17 Q-jumping

Recommended use: for encouraging more balanced participation. This is the rule: anyone who speaks for more than 10 seconds or for more than one sentence jumps to the head of the Q. Everyone sits in a circle as for a 'normal' group discussion. Mark a break in the Q by making a space in the circle. Place a rope (or similar object) across the space so that it looks like the squiggly bit of the capital letter Q. The rope signifies that the rule is in force. The person on the right of the rope is at the 'head' of the Q.

If a person sitting opposite the squiggle speaks for more than 10 seconds, they walk across to the head of the Q. The former head of the Q and everyone who was sitting between the speaker and the former head of the Q moves back (anticlockwise) one place so that the new head of the Q has a seat. Half the group are not affected and stay in their seats.

If a person sitting next to the head of the Q speaks for more than 10 seconds, they simply swap places with the head of the Q.

If the person at the back end of the Q speaks for more than 10 seconds, everyone moves one place in an anticlockwise direction.

Anything can happen. In essence, it is just a simple wordless way of reflecting back the pattern of contribution in a group discussion. It automatically brings the pattern to everyone's attention. If the amount of movement is disrupting the discussion you can extend the time that people can speak without moving to (say) 20 seconds, or suspend the rule. You can join in as a facilitator at the head of the Q, and perhaps have a secret goal of trying to get to the other end of the Q (if, for example, you happen to be trying to develop a less dominant facilitation style).

18   Replay

Recommended use: for easing conflict and for building trust and understanding. Using action replay is another way of making visible what was not noticed first time round. Critical moments during the activity are reconstructed and re-enacted (usually through mime rather than by doing the real activity again). People do not simply 'see' the activity again (or from a different angle), they also have the chance to stop the action and interview people to discover what was going on in their hearts or minds at the time. This brings out new information that was not apparent at the time. This new information can be critical, and really does result in a 'review' of the incident, and leads to people revising what they had originally learned.

19   Rounds

These are sentences started by the reviewer, which are finished by each person in turn. The sentences can be about facts or feelings, self or others, past, present or future. Rounds introduce some basic principles common to many reviewing methods, such as the right to be heard and the right to pass.

Examples:

- The high point for me was when … / The low point for me was when …
- The hardest thing for me was … / The easiest thing for me was …
- What surprised me was …
- Something I knew would happen was …
- Nobody listened when … / I'm really pleased that I …
- I wish I had …
- I felt like going home when …
- If I could do it again, I would …
- I wish I had been asked …
- I was annoyed when …
- My motivation went down when … / My motivation went up when …
- I was helped by … / I helped …
- I appreciated … / I was appreciated by …
- I'd like to complain to … / I'd like to congratulate …
- I'd like the group to tell me …
- One last thing I'd like to say is …

20   Simultaneous survey

In 'brief encounters' (above) the encounters are random and there is no collating of information. Simultaneous survey looks the same (from a distance) but everyone is carrying out a survey, making a note of the answers, and then summarising them to the whole group. Depending on numbers (of people and questions), surveys can be carried out by small teams rather than by individuals.

21   Sketch map

Recommended use: for reliving a journey and discovering issues that deserve review that is more detailed. After any event that has involved a journey, ask participants to illustrate their journey with the help of a rope (or ropes) to trace the route taken.

Add labels with words (e.g. tie-on luggage labels) or symbolic objects to mark out different parts of the journey. This is best set up as a creative project in an area (indoors or outdoors) where suitable symbolic objects can readily be found. Much informal reviewing takes place during the making of the map. Once the map is complete, it can be used as a means of re-telling the story and/or identifying key moments on the journey for more detailed review.

Variation: Create a sketch map using more conventional materials, such as paper, pens, paints and materials for collage or a natural art sketch from materials around the reviewing area.

22   Spider's web

The group forms a circle. One person has a skein of yarn; they say why they enjoy the group (or answer a particular review question) and toss the skein to another person. This person responds to the same question and tosses the skein to another person. This continues until everyone in the group has caught the skein. The web formed between all of the members illustrates the individuality of the group and the ties that bind them into a group. This continues with as many rounds as you like, including rewinding the string.

23   Spokes

Recommended use: for reviewing progress against group-related goals.

This is a variation of 'objective line'. Each rope is laid on the ground to make the spokes of a wheel. The outer end of each spoke is the starting point and the centre is the goal. This can be used for individually different goals, but is particularly suitable when looking at goals that have a group dimension or goals that are shared by everyone in the group. For example, the spokes can all be 'listening' spokes. Each person assesses the quality of their own listening during the event being reviewed and then looks around at where others are standing. You could do the same for 'talking', 'supporting others', 'providing leadership', 'speaking up', 'clear thinking' and so on.

Variation: For the end of the course or the end of a group, reverse the polarity of the spokes, so that the inner end now represents the starting point and the outer end represents future goals. Each person walks into the future (simultaneously or one at a time). Whenever someone turns round to look at their starting point they are also looking back at the group, which may be slowly dispersing as others leave.

24 Talking knots

Recommended use: as a temporary gimmick for encouraging more equal participation in reviews.

- *Version 1*: Tie a knot in a rope to make a rope circle. Everyone holds on to the rope while standing or sitting in a circle. The circle should be a suitable size for group discussion. There is just one knot in the rope. The person with the knot in front of them may speak. When that person has finished speaking, they start moving the rope in a clockwise direction. The knot keeps moving round until someone with the knot in front of them wants to talk. That person calls 'stop' and holds the rope either side of the knot.

- *Version 2:* Each person ties (say) five simple knots in their rope. The ropes are arranged as spokes and everyone sits in a circle. Each time a person speaks, they pull their own rope towards them until their hand is on the next knot. When a person runs out of knots, they should continue to listen but may not speak. Interruptions are not allowed, unless you choose to establish and enforce a time limit on how long participants may speak.

And finally …

… a few brain teasers to use when you have a few minutes to fill with a group!

1   Coin and bottle

Put a coin in a bottle and then stop the opening with a cork. How can you get the coin out of the bottle without pulling out the cork or breaking the bottle?
Answer: Push the cork into the bottle, and shake the coin out.

2   One-way street

A girl who was just learning to drive went down a one-way street in the wrong direction, but didn't break the law. How come?
Answer: She was walking.

3   Mystery ball?

How can you throw a ball as hard as you can and have it come back to you, even if it doesn't hit anything, there is nothing attached to it, and no one else catches or throws it?
Answer: Throw the ball straight up in the air.

4   Shared desk

Two participants are sitting on opposite sides of the same desk. There is nothing in between them but the desk. Why can't they see each other?
Answer: The two participants have their backs to each other.

5   Trains

Train A and train B are crossing the country, from coast to coast, over 3,000 miles of railroad track. Train A is going from east to west at 80 miles per hour, and train B is going from west to east at 90 miles per hour. Which train will be closer to the west coast when they meet?

Answer: When the trains meet, they will be at exactly the same point. Therefore, they will each be the same distance from the west coast.

6   The river

Jake was standing on one side of the river, and his dog Scruffy was standing on the other side. "Come on Scruffy, come, boy!" shouted Jake. Scruffy crossed the river, ran to Jake and got a treat for being a good dog. The amazing thing was that Scruffy didn't even get wet! How did Scruffy do that?

There are two possible answers:

1   The river was frozen.
2   There was a bridge over the river, and Scruffy crossed the bridge.

7   Holes

How much dirt is in a round hole that is 9 feet deep with a diameter of 3 feet?
Answer: None. You make a hole by digging out the dirt, so the hole is empty.

8   The farmer's dogs

Once a dog named Nelly lived on a farm. There were three other dogs on the farm.
   Their names were Blackie, Whitey and Brownie. What do you think the fourth dog's name was?
Answer: Nelly. (If there are only four dogs on the farm, the fourth one must be Nelly!)

9   Shopping spree

One day, two mothers and two daughters went shopping for shoes. Their shopping spree was successful, each bought a pair of shoes, and all together, they had three pairs. How is this possible?
Answer: Only three people went shopping: a grandmother, a mother and a daughter – but remember that the mother was the grandmother's daughter!

10   Rope ladder

The rope ladder of a boat hangs over the side of the boat and just reaches the water.
   Its rungs are 8 inches apart. How many rungs will be under the water when the tide rises 4 feet?
Answer: When the tide rises 4 feet, the boat and its ladder will also rise. So, no rungs will be under the water.

11 Donkey's cargo

Amir tied two sacks of salt to the back of his donkey and headed for the market to sell the salt. On the way, Amir and the donkey passed a stream. The donkey jumped in to cool himself. As a result, much of the salt dissolved into the water, ruining the salt for Amir but improving matters for the donkey because his load became much lighter. Amir tried to get to the market on the following days, but the donkey always ruined the salt. Finally, Amir decided to teach the donkey a lesson. He once again set out with the donkey and the two sacks. What did Amir do differently this time so that after that day the donkey stopped taking a swim?

Answer: Amir loaded the sacks not with salt but with sand. When the donkey jumped in the stream and got the sacks wet, they became much heavier.

12 The traveller

A traveller arrives in a small town and decides he wants to get a haircut. According to the manager of the hotel where he's staying, there are only two barber's shops in town – one on East Street and one on West Street. The traveller goes to check out both shops. The East Street barber's shop is a mess, and the barber has the worst haircut the traveller has ever seen. The West Street barber's shop is neat and clean; its barber's hair looks as good as a movie star's does. Which barber's shop does the traveller go to for his haircut, and why?

Answer: The traveller goes to have his hair cut at the barber's shop on East Street. He figures that since there are only two barber's shops in town the East Street barber must have his hair cut by the West Street barber and vice versa. So if the traveller wants to look as good as the West Street barber (the one with the good haircut), he'd better go to the man who cuts the West Street barber's hair-the East Street barber.

By the way, the reason the West Street barber's shop is so clean and neat is that it seldom gets customers.

13 Cats and dogs

All of Jenny's pets are dogs except one, and all of her pets are cats except one. How many cats and dogs does Jenny have?

Answer: Jenny has one cat and one dog.

14 Shocking?

A man walks into a bar and asks for a drink of water. The bartender thinks for a minute, pulls out a gun and points it at him. The man says, 'Thank you', and walks out. Why?

Answer: The man has hiccups; the bartender scares them away by pulling a gun.

15   The recluse

There was once a recluse who never left his home. The only time anyone ever visited him was when his food and supplies were delivered, but they never came inside. Then, one stormy winter night when an icy gale was blowing, he had a nervous breakdown. He went upstairs, turned off all the lights and went to bed. Next morning, he had caused the deaths of several hundred people. How?
Answer: He was a lighthouse keeper who switched off the lighthouse.

16   Manhole covers

Why is it better to have round manhole covers than square ones?
Answer: Round covers cannot be dropped or slip down a manhole, unlike square ones.

17   The Coconut Grove

An American nightclub called The Coconut Grove had a terrible fire in which over 400 people died. A simple design flaw in the building led to the death toll being so high. Subsequently, regulations were changed to ensure that all public buildings throughout the country eliminated this one detail, which proved so deadly. What was it?
Answer: The doors at The Coconut Grove opened inward. In the mad panic to escape the fire, people were crushed against the doors and could not pull them open. After The Coconut Grove disaster in 1942, all public buildings had to have doors that opened outward.

18   Dead in the water?

A man holidaying abroad fell off a yacht into deep water. He could not swim and he was not wearing anything to keep him afloat. It took 30 minutes for the people on the yacht to realise someone was missing. The missing man was rescued two hours later. Why didn't he drown?
Answer: He fell into the Dead Sea, which lies between Israel and Jordan. The water is so salty and dense that anyone in it floats very easily.

19   Determined to die?

There is a room with no doors, no windows, nothing; a man is hanging from the ceiling, and a puddle of water is on the floor. How did he die?
Answer: He stood on a block of ice to commit suicide.

20   Inescapable

A man is trapped in a room. The room has only two possible exits: two doors.
   Through the first door there is a room constructed from magnifying glass. The blazing

hot sun instantly fries anything or anyone that enters. Through the second door, there is a fire-breathing dragon. How does the man escape?

Answer: He waits until night-time and then goes through the first door.

21   Supposing

Supposing three men were frozen and two died, how many were left?

Answer: None, you were only supposing.

22   Cliff bottom

A man is at the bottom of the cliff; he is dead and has half of a match in his hand. How did he die?

Answer: He was in a hot air balloon with friends, it started to go down so they decided to draw matches and the one with the shortest should jump off, he drew the shortest match.

23   Houses

There are three houses. One is red, one is blue, and one is white. If the red house is to the left of the house in the middle and the blue house is to the right of the house in the middle, where is the white house?

Answer: In Washington DC.

24   Hotel rooms

Three men walk into a hotel and rent a room for 30 pounds. But the hotel manager realised the room should have been only 25 pounds, so he sent for the dishonest bellboy and told him to give 5 pounds back to the men. The bellboy cheated and said to the three men the room was actually 27 pounds and gave them 3 pounds back, and donated the other to his favourite charity. Where is the missing pound, because 25 +4 =29?

Answer: There is no missing £1! There is £25 in the till, £2 in the messenger's pocket, £1 in each of the men's pocket and they paid £9 each, with £1 still in their pockets, which makes £30 in total. The messenger's £2 should be added to the manager's £25 or taken from the men's £27, not added to their £27.

25   The man in the small house

A man lives in a small house with a farm as his back garden and has a river beside his house. On the other side of the river is a shop. One day he visited the shop. He bought a chicken and a fox for his farm and bought a bag of corn to feed the chicken. The man can only take one thing and himself across in the boat. Without killing any animals or letting another animal eat an item or animal, how will the man get across?

Answer: Bring the chicken first, then the fox, take the chicken back, bring the corn across and finally go back for the chicken.

26   Telephone box

The police are called to the scene of a crime at a telephone box. The telephone is off the hook and dangling down; the man in the telephone box is dead; he has injuries on his wrists; there is no knife or other tool to slash them; he is covered in blood. How did he die?

Answer: He was a fisherman, on the telephone telling his friends about how big his catch was, his wrists smashed through the telephone box and he bled to death.

27   Seventh-floor flat

A person lives in a block of flats, lives on the seventh floor. Every day they come out of the flat, go down in the lift to the ground floor and then when they return they go up the stairs. Why is that? (And it's not because they are keeping fit!)

Answer: It is a child/small person and they can only reach the ground floor button, the seventh floor one is too high for them.

28   Johnny's mother

Johnny's mother had three children. The first child was named April, the second was named May. What was the third child's name?

Answer: Johnny, of course.

29   The butcher's clerk

There was a clerk in the butcher's shop; he was five feet ten inches tall and wears size 13 shoes. What does he weigh?

Answer: Meat, of course.

30   Mount Everest

Before Mount Everest was discovered, what was the highest mountain in the world?
Answer: Mount Everest, it just wasn't discovered yet.

31   The hole

How much dirt is there in a hole that measures two metres by three metres by four metres?

Answer: None, there is no dirt in a hole.

32   Spelling

What word in the English language is always spelt incorrectly?
Answer: 'Incorrectly', of course.

33   Billie's birthday

Billie was born on 28 December, yet her birthday is always in Summer; how is this possible?
Answer: She lives in the Southern Hemisphere.

34   Indian pictures

In India, you cannot take a picture of a man with a wooden leg. Why not?
Answer: You can't take pictures with a wooden leg, you need a camera.

35   US president

What was the name of the US president in 1975?
Answer: Same as it is now.

36   The running race

If you were running a race and passed the person in second place, what place would you be in?
Answer: Second, because you passed the person in that place.

37   Grammar

Which is correct: 'the yolk of the egg is white' or 'the yolk of the egg are white'?
Answer: Neither, the yolk of any egg is yellow.

38   The farmer's haystack

If a farmer has five haystacks in one field and four haystacks in another field, how many haystacks would he have if he combined them all in one field?
Answer: One haystack; if he combines them all then he builds one big haystack.

39   Christmas Day

When did Christmas Day fall on Boxing Day?
Answer: 1966, Christmas Day was a horse that fell while running in a race on Boxing Day.

Appendix 1
Sample lesson plans

Sample lesson plan 1

<table>
<tr><th colspan="2"></th><th>Subject</th><th>Objectives</th><th>Some ideas of the adventure learning potential</th></tr>
<tr><td rowspan="3">Core subjects</td><td></td><td>Science</td><td>Forces: the effect of friction and pressure
Gravity</td><td>In 'stand up' the pairs can vary how successful they are by changing how tightly they press their backs together or how hard they push against one another.
In 'toxic waste', the group learns how much pressure is needed to remove the container.
In 'egg drop', the group see gravity in action and how varying designs will affect the impact of the egg on the ground.
Changing the number of members on each part of the rope in 'force field', it emphasises how volume affects friction.</td></tr>
<tr><td></td><td>Mathematics</td><td>Problem solving
Angles</td><td>Thinking through how to move the container of waste to safety, considering the size, distance and resources available.
The position of each group member in relation to the others affects success.
Placing the ropes at different angles in 'force field' demonstrates angles and their relationship to one another.</td></tr>
<tr><td></td><td>English</td><td>Development of ideas
Planning
Communication
Vocalisation of ideas</td><td>As the group plan, execute and review their activities, they learn to express themselves.
The facilitator must ensure that every member of the group has the opportunity to participate.</td></tr>
<tr><td rowspan="5">Foundation subjects</td><td></td><td>Art and design</td><td>Use of shape, colour and textures</td><td>The group has access to a range of materials from nature to pictorialise their experience.</td></tr>
<tr><td></td><td>Citizenship</td><td>Discussion
Decision making
Compromise</td><td>If the group is given the responsibility of debating their ideas and deciding how to tackle the 'problems' presented to them, they have to negotiate, discuss and determine how to proceed.</td></tr>
<tr><td></td><td>Computing</td><td>Presentation
Use of different media</td><td>The group can be provided with the opportunity to describe and present their feedback in a number of ways.</td></tr>
<tr><td></td><td>Design and technology</td><td>Planning
Designing</td><td>Group members must decide how to tackle the 'problems' and so they can develop a number of different possible solutions to test in practice.</td></tr>
<tr><td></td><td>Languages</td><td>Communication</td><td>The group members can explore ways to communicate throughout the activity and the review.
The facilitator can present a number of foreign language words into the session.</td></tr>
</table>

Subject	Objectives	Some ideas of the adventure learning potential
Physical education	Planning Strategy Communication Collaboration	The group works together on active projects that require movement and exertion, as well as having to design and execute a plan of how to tackle the activities. The group members have the opportunity to review their performance and adapt their methodology according to their level of success as they proceed.

Energiser	Stand up	The group members all sit on the ground in pairs, back-to-back, knees bent and elbows locked. They then try to stand up without falling down.	
Activity 1	Toxic waste	The challenge is to move the toxic waste contents to the neutralisation container using minimal equipment and maintaining a safe distance within a time limit.	
Activity 2	Egg drop	The task is to build a single egg package that can sustain a substantial fall.	
Review 1	Force field	The teams attempt to pull the centre ring or knot over their finish line.	Use different lengths of rope, or change the position where one rope joins another to emphasise the different effects of the strength of feeling, as well as allowing the group participants to determine their positive, negative or neutral feelings freely.
Review 2	Nature art	Using whatever they can find in the environment, group members create an image that represents their experience.	This can be on paper or on the ground. Group members are encouraged to use their imagination and to be as creative as possible.
Review 3	Discussion	The discussion runs concurrent to the force field and art activities, as the group members review the activities, achievements and develop their learning.	

Success criteria	Opportunities for assessment
Group members can: • Vocalise their thoughts and ideas during the planning. • Demonstrate negotiation skills, compromise and decision-making on a rational, informed basis. • Describe gravity, forces and friction, demonstrating a basic understanding of each. • Explain the sequencing of their actions and the effect of different solutions tested on group success. • Can analyse group performance and recognise weaknesses in planning.	After each planning stage. Intermittently during the activities. At the end of each activity. At the end of the session overall.

Resources	Timing
Lengths of rope: to remove the 'waste', to fasten together for 'Force Field' Container of 'waste' Eggs: per pair/group String Sticky tape Newspaper Plastic bags.	Depends on how the staff decide to set up the event; this can be run on one day as a continuous sequence, or over a number of days as separate planning, activity & review sessions. • Stand up: 20 minutes • Toxic waste: 15 minutes planning + 30 minutes activity time • Egg drop: 15 minutes planning + 30 minutes activity time • Force Field: 30 minutes • Nature art: 40 minutes The timing can be stretched as desired and, for example, lesson content can be used as the basis for activities in computing and/or D&T.

Sample lesson plan 2

Subject	Objectives	Some ideas of the adventure learning potential
English	Communication, understanding each other and situations, responding to others	The 'trust fall' encourages group members to behave in a responsible manner; nearly always the 'faller' is reluctant and has a couple of hesitations before actually managing to do the fall. Usually this is because of their hesitation in trusting the members of the group to behave appropriately and not hurt them, reinforcing the noting of our impressions of people and how they will react. It leads well into 'Frozen Pictures', where any situation, phrase of image can be set up, creating a starting point for exploring interpretations, reactions and thoughts. It is always interesting to see what group members think is happening!
Citizenship	The self as an individual and as a member of a community Taking responsibility for personal behaviour and actions	
History	The effect of behaviour, relationships, expectations and perceptions on world events (for example, the alliances and perceptions that led to World War 1)	
Physical education	Trust and co-operation Activities are exerting energy and using muscles	

237

Energiser	The trust fall	One person at a time stands on the side of the 'bridge' (table/chair); the rest of the group pairs up behind the 'bridge', standing opposite each other, and grabs the wrists of the person opposite. The person on the 'bridge' stands on the edge, with their back to the group. At a signal from the facilitator, the person falls backwards, being caught by the group.	Group members may wish to fall facing forwards but this can lead to complaints as other group members may end up touching sensitive areas of the body.
Activity 1	Frozen pictures	Split the participants into small groups, giving each group a common saying or expression (e.g. 'too many cooks spoil the broth'). Ask the group to come up with a frozen picture and ask the group to guess what the saying is, alternatively create a scenario picture and ask the group to decide what is happening.	This may be played using expressions, but works well in group training with real situations, such as 'you're coming home late' or 'you hear footsteps following you down the street'. This can lead onto further work around 'put yourself into the picture with how you would react'.
Review 1	Discussion	The issues of trust, first impressions and confidence in people can be explored really well through these activities. In 'Frozen pictures' you can present a whole range of scenarios that open opportunities for discussing trust, behaviour, self-presentation and the effect of these on others.	These activities can both give rise to quite significant emotional responses, so it is essential that all group members have adequate opportunity to express their feelings and process what they experienced.

Success criteria	Opportunities for assessment
The group members take part and complete the activities in a sensible manner	Throughout the activity

Resources	Timing
Chair or table strong enough for someone to stand on	Trust fall = 30 minutes (may take longer if every member of the group is to have a go or if there are several interruptions or hesitations)Frozen pictures = about 60 minutes, but may be significantly longer if there are several to present and the discussions are to happen within the same session (which is most effective)

Sample lesson plan 3

This is designed to be run over a longer period, involving a significant amount of preparation over a number of subjects and a number of sessions; the learners will need to be given time to absorb their preparatory learning before launching into the main activity of survival.

	Subject	Briefing / preparation
		Objectives
Core subjects	Science	Depending on the scenario, a lot of science can be brought into this, such as magnetic forces, life processes, nutrition, circulation, insulation, condensing, filtering, earth, sun and moon cycles. The group members need to be able to understand what they need to do to survive and plan accordingly; building the theory around a particular scenario adds interest and meaning as the participants have a vested interest in learning and succeeding.
	Mathematics	Navigation introduces angles (links with magnetic forces in science), problem solving, division of resources, designing appropriate shelter (working out size, proportions, weight, transporting materials and resources).
	English	Group members develop their ideas; planning, talking, debating and discussing within their group(s) to work out their survival strategy.
Foundation subjects	Art and design	Participants can design clothing, shelter, materials to attract attention for rescue. They need to understand the properties of materials for keeping themselves warm or cool, how textiles/materials feel on the skin, whether they can work in their designed clothing.
	Citizenship	Participants start understanding how to exist within a community, how to negotiate and compromise, making informed choices, taking responsibility for their behaviour and contributing to group survival.
	Computing	Ideas and plans need to be collated and presented to instructors and teaching staff in an appropriate manner, explaining and justifying decisions
	Design and technology	Group members have to design shelters, collect resources, preserve materials
	Geography	Ideas can be introduced from other countries and time periods, contrasting environments and examining the outcomes achieved
	History	
	Languages	Ideas can be expressed and developed in a range of ways, linked to the people and times considered within Geography and History sessions

239

Subject	Objectives
Music	Again, the people and times considered in the Geography and History sessions can form the basis of exploring their music and instruments; group members can compose the theme music to represent their plans or form the backdrop of subsequent presentations
Physical education	These are very active sessions, where group members can begin to assess their resources available, work out how long they take to cover set distances, how much weight can they safely carry, how to transport materials and resources or mapping their terrain

Activity 1	Survival	Any of the survival scenarios can be used, or even a specific one created bespoke to the environment of the learning organisation.	The possibilities and learning from this activity are vast, but the group needs to be given significant time to work through their plans and then putting them into action.
		The beauty of writing a bespoke scenario is that something like an 'island survival' can be created, where the group have more physical involvement, such as to develop a map, locate resources and plan (and build) their escape mechanism, as well as having to work through the logic process of ranking scavenged items (which could be hidden for them to find, rather than just giving them a list).	Time may also be allowed to revisit their plans and amend them. If there are different groups, each could be presented with a different scenario, which adds interest and avoids opportunities for rivalry!

Debrief / Review:

There will need to be review points built in throughout all the stages of the briefing and the main activity, where the group members can reflect on their progress and amend their plans. Just as the preparation can cover sessions in every subject of the curriculum, so can the review. The planning that was undertaken by group members within each subject can then be reviewed, exploring what happened and why. The participants can deliver a presentation of their overall experience to people not involved (such as other teaching staff or parents), which enhances the quality needed of their presentations. As with the preparation session, having a specific activity in which the group members have participated adds interest and meaning, as they have concrete experiences on which to base their learning and transmitting their learning.

Success criteria	Opportunities for assessment
Many different criteria can be applied, as every subject is engaged. It depends on how strict the teaching staff wish to be in the application of their criteria! In essence, success is represented by group members emerging with plans that are basically workable and they execute them in a reasonable manner.	These are simple to build in within every subject, as participants demonstrate learning and understanding as they develop their plans and strategies.
Resources	**Timing**
Compass Items to be 'salvaged' from the survival site Additional items that may be secreted in the area for the group to find to facilitate their survival and escape.	This is intended to last a number of sessions across the whole curriculum, as the planning, execution and review take place.

Sample lesson plan 4

	Subject	Objectives	Some ideas of the adventure learning potential
Core subjects	Science	Forces, Gases	The 'Helium Stick' presents the notion of gravitational pull and the properties of gases; try sticks made of different materials to demonstrate the different effects they have on the 'pull'. The rope circle highlights the properties of materials and how they may change.
	English	Co-ordination, working together, describing what is happening	The activities create such an unusual effect that the group members have to work hard to express what they think is happening and why.
	Citizenship	Responsible behaviour	Each group member has to consider the effect of their behaviour on the safety of the person walking around the rope.
	Computing	Use of technology	The participants can present their understanding of what happened and why.
	Physical education	Active collaboration and interaction, communication	The group members must work together, else the stick will not move (or falls) and the individual cannot make it around the rope.

242

Energiser	Helium stick	The group lines up in two rows facing each other, so that when they stretch out their arms, their hands meet in the middle. The group members point their index fingers and hold their arms out. The facilitator lays the 'helium stick' down on their fingers and gets the group to adjust their finger heights until the Helium Stick is horizontal and everyone's index finger is touching the stick. The challenge is to lower the Helium Stick to the ground. Each person's fingers must be in contact with the Helium Stick at all times. Pinching or grabbing the stick is not allowed, it must rest on top of fingers.	The Helium Stick has a habit of mysteriously 'floating' up rather than coming down, causing much laughter. A bit of clever humour from the facilitator can help, for example acting surprised. The secret is that the collective upwards pressure created by everyone's fingers tends to be greater than the weight of the stick, as a result, the more a group tries, the more the stick tends to 'float' upwards.
Activity	Rope circle	All of the group except one takes hold of the rope, holds it about waist height and leans backwards, so that the rope makes a taut circle. The remaining group member climbs onto the rope and walks around the whole circle on it.	

Success criteria	Opportunities for assessment
The stick rises. Individuals can walk around the rope. The participants can explain in a rational way what they think is happening and why. The participants can organise themselves as required for the activities.	These activities lend themselves to continual assessment.

Resources	Timing
A long, thin stick/cane/rod A length of rope, knotted or fastened securely at the ends to form a circle.	Helium stick = 30 minutes Rope circle= 60 minutes

Appendix 2
Survival game scenarios

Aeroplane crash

You and your companions have just survived the crash of a small plane. Both the pilot and co-pilot were killed in the crash. It is mid-January and you are in northern Canada. The daily temperature is 25 degrees below zero and the night-time temperature is 40 below zero. There is snow on the ground, and the countryside is wooded with several creeks criss-crossing the area. The nearest town is 20 miles away. You are all dressed in city clothes appropriate for a business meeting. Your group of survivors managed to salvage the following items:

- A ball of steel wool
- A small axe
- A loaded .45-calibre pistol
- Tub of lard
- Newspapers (one per person)
- Cigarette lighter (without fluid)
- 1 extra shirt and trousers/skirt for each survivor
- 10 × 10 metre piece of heavy-duty canvas
- A sectional air map made of plastic
- One bottle of 100-proof whisky
- A compass
- Family-size chocolate bars (one per person).

Your task as a group is to list the above 12 items in order of importance for your survival. List the uses for each. You *must* come to agreement as a group.

There is a rational explanation for the rankings:

- Mid-January is the coldest time of year in northern Canada. The first problem the survivors face is the preservation of body heat and the protection against its loss. This problem can be solved by building a fire, minimising movement and exertion, using as much insulation as possible and constructing a shelter.

- The participants have just crash-landed. Many individuals tend to overlook the enormous shock reaction this has on the human body and the deaths of the pilot and co-pilot increases the shock. Decision-making under such circumstances is extremely difficult. Such a situation requires a strong emphasis on the use of reasoning for making decisions and for reducing fear and panic. Shock would be shown in the survivors by feelings of helplessness, loneliness, hopelessness and fear. These feelings have brought about more fatalities than perhaps any other cause in survival situations. Certainly, the state of shock means the movement of the survivors should be at a minimum, and that an attempt to calm them should be made.

- Before taking off, a pilot has to file a flight plan, which contains vital information such as the course, speed, estimated time of arrival, type of aircraft, and number of passengers. Search-and-rescue operations begin shortly after the failure of a plane to appear at its destination at the estimated time of arrival.

- The 20 miles to the nearest town is a long walk under even ideal conditions, particularly if one is not used to walking such distances. In this situation, the walk is even more difficult due to shock, snow, dress and water barriers. It would mean almost certain death from freezing and exhaustion. At temperatures of minus 25 to minus 40, the loss of body heat through exertion is a very serious matter.

- Once the survivors have found ways to keep warm, their next task is to attract the attention of search planes. Thus, all the items the group has salvaged must be assessed for their value in signalling the group's whereabouts.

Rankings

1. Cigarette lighter (without fluid): The gravest danger facing the group is exposure to cold. The greatest need is for a source of warmth and the second greatest need is for signalling devices. This makes building a fire the first order of business. Without matches, something is needed to produce sparks, and even without fluid, a cigarette lighter can do that.

2. Ball of steel wool: To make a fire, the survivors need a means of catching the sparks made by the cigarette lighter. This is the best substance for catching a spark and supporting a flame, even if the steel wool is a little wet.

3. Extra shirt and trousers/skirt for each survivor: Besides adding warmth to the body,

clothes can also be used for shelter, signalling, bedding, bandages, string (when unravelled), and fuel for the fire.

4   Tub of lard: This has many uses. A mirror-like signalling device can be made from the lid. After shining the lid with steel wool, it will reflect sunlight and generate 5 to 7 million candlepower. This is bright enough to be seen beyond the horizon. While this could be limited somewhat by the trees, a member of the group could climb a tree and use the mirrored lid to signal search planes. If they had no other means of signalling than this, they would have a better than 80% chance of being rescued within the first day. There are other uses for this item. It can be rubbed on exposed skin for protection against the cold. When melted into oil, the shortening is helpful as fuel. When soaked into a piece of cloth, melted shortening will act like a candle. The empty can is useful in melting snow for drinking water. It is much safer to drink warmed water than to eat snow, since warm water will help retain body heat. Water is important because dehydration will affect decision-making. The can is also useful as a cup.

5   20 × 20 foot piece of canvas: The cold makes shelter necessary, and canvas would protect against wind and snow (canvas is used in making tents). Spread on a frame made of trees, it could be used as a tent or a windscreen. It might also be used as a ground cover to keep the survivors dry. It's shape, when contrasted with the surrounding terrain, makes it a signalling device.

6   Small axe: Survivors need a constant supply of wood in order to maintain the fire. The axe could be used for this as well as for clearing a sheltered campsite, cutting tree branches for ground insulation, and constructing a frame for the canvas tent.

7   Family-size chocolate bars (one per person): Chocolate will provide some food energy. Since it contains mostly carbohydrates, it supplies the energy without making digestive demands on the body.

8   Newspapers (one per person): These are useful in starting a fire. They can also be used as insulation under clothing when rolled up and placed around a person's arms and legs. A newspaper can also be used as a verbal signalling device when rolled up in a megaphone-shape. It could also provide reading material for recreation.

9   Loaded .45-calibre pistol: The pistol provides a sound-signalling device (the international distress signal is three shots fired in rapid succession). There have been numerous cases of survivors going undetected because they were too weak to make a loud enough noise to attract attention. The butt of the pistol could be used as a hammer, and the powder from the shells will assist in fire building. By placing a small bit of cloth in a cartridge emptied of its bullet, one can start a fire by firing the gun at dry wood on the ground. The pistol also has some serious disadvantages. Anger, frustration, impatience, irritability and lapses of rationality may increase as the group awaits rescue. The availability of a lethal weapon is a danger to the group under these conditions. Although a pistol could be used in hunting, it would take an expert

marksman to kill an animal with it. Then the animal would have to be transported to the crash site, which could prove difficult to impossible depending on its size.

10 Bottle of 100 proof whisky: The only uses of whisky are as an aid in fire building and as a fuel for a torch (made by soaking a piece of clothing in the whisky and attaching it to a tree branch). The empty bottle could be used for storing water. The danger of whisky is that someone might drink it, thinking it would bring warmth. Alcohol takes on the temperature it is exposed to, and a drink of minus 30 degree whisky would freeze a person's oesophagus and stomach. Alcohol also dilates the blood vessels in the skin, resulting in chilled blood being carried back to the heart, resulting in a rapid loss of body heat. Thus, a drunken person is more likely to get hypothermia than a sober person is.

11 Compass: Because a compass might encourage someone to try to walk to the nearest town, it is a dangerous item. Its only redeeming feature is that it could be used as a reflector of sunlight (due to its glass top).

12 Sectional air map made of plastic: This is also among the least desirable of the items because it will encourage individuals to try to walk to the nearest town. Its only useful feature is as a ground cover to keep someone dry.

How to score: Each team should list its top five choices in order prior to seeing the answer sheet. To award points, look at the ranking numbers on this answer sheet. Award points to each team's top choices according to the numbers here. For example, the map would earn 12 points, while the steel wool would earn 2 points. The team with the lowest score wins (and survives).

Lost at sea

You and your team have chartered a yacht. None of you has any previous sailing experience, and you have hired an experienced skipper and two-person crew. As you sail through the Southern Pacific Ocean a fire breaks out and much of the yacht and its contents are destroyed. The yacht is slowly sinking. Your location is unclear because vital navigational and radio equipment has been damaged. The yacht skipper and crew have been lost whilst trying to fight the fire. Your best guestimate is that you are approximately 1000 miles South West of the nearest landfall.

You and your friends have managed to save the following 15 items, undamaged and intact after the fire:

- A sextant
- A shaving mirror
- A quantity of mosquito netting

- A 5 gallon can of water
- A case of army rations
- Maps of the Pacific Ocean
- A floating seat cushion
- A 2 gallon can of oil/petrol mixture
- A small transistor radio
- 10 square metres of plastic sheeting
- Shark repellent
- One litre of 160 per cent proof rum
- 15ft nylon rope
- Two boxes of chocolate bars
- A fishing kit.

In addition to the above, you have salvaged a four-man rubber life craft. The total contents of your combined pockets amounts to a packet of cigarettes, three boxes of matches and three £5 notes.

Your chances of survival will depend upon your ability to rank the above 15 items in their relative order of importance. Good luck!

Rationale: According to the experts (US Coastguard), the basic supplies needed when a person is stranded mid-ocean are articles to attract attention and articles to aid survival until rescue arrives. Articles for navigation are of little importance since even if a small life raft were capable of reaching land, it would be impossible to store enough food and water to survive for the requisite amount of time.

Without signalling devices, there is almost no chance of being spotted and ultimately rescued. Furthermore, most rescues occur within the first 36 hours and a person can survive with only a minimum of food and water during that period.

Therefore, the following is the order of ranking the items in their importance to your survival:

1   Shaving mirror. Critical for signalling.

2   2 gallon can of oil/petrol mixture. Critical for signalling. The mixture will float on water and could be ignited with one of the £5 notes and a match. What the experts don't say is how you get away from this conflagration or what to do if the wind should push the life raft into the flames!

3   5 gallon can of water. Necessary to replenish fluids lost through perspiration (that's sweat!).

4   One case of army rations. Basic food intake.

5   20 square metres of plastic. Can be utilised to collect rainwater and provide shelter from the elements.

6   Two boxes of chocolate bars. Reserve food supply (what were you going to do with that much chocolate?).

7   Fishing kit. Ranked lower than the chocolate as 'a bird in the hand is worth two in the bush'! There is no guarantee you will catch any fish.

8   15 metres of nylon rope. Could be used to lash people or equipment together to prevent it being washed overboard.

9   Floating seat cushion. A life preserver if someone fell overboard.

10 Shark repellent. Enough said!

11 One litre of 160 per cent proof rum. Contains 80% alcohol, which is enough to be used as an antiseptic for any injuries, otherwise of little value as would cause dehydration if ingested (that's drunk to you and me)!

12 Small transistor radio. Of no use without a transmitter, you would also be out of range of any radio station.

13 Maps of the Pacific Ocean. Worthless without navigation equipment; it doesn't matter where you are but where the rescuers are!

14 Mosquito netting. There are no mosquitos in the mid-pacific ocean. As for fishing with it? Stick to the fishing kit.

15 Sextant. Useless without the relevant tables and a chronometer.

Nuclear holocaust: who should survive?

World War 3 has just occurred and you and nine other people find yourselves to be the only people left on the earth. You manage to all make it to a bunker, however, you all realise that if three of you wish to survive for many years, seven of you will have to leave soon because there are not enough resources for all of you to survive.

If all of you stay, then you will all live only for a maximum of 2 years.

In your bunker, you have the following facilities:

- Sewage system
- Water
- Seeds
- Some clothes
- A few books
- Some medical facilities but no operating material
- A greenhouse.

In your group, each of you has a chance to speak and you must present your case to explain why you think you should live. Argue for your life unless you really want to sacrifice for others. Listen to others arguments as well.

In the bunker, the following roles will be played out. Each person in the group will play one of the following roles:

- Scientist
- Priest
- Married couple who are hippies and drug addicts
- Single pregnant woman with a 5-year-old girl
- Army officer who has mental instability of some sort but is useful nonetheless
- Elderly woman
- Disabled person
- Lawyer
- Benefits claimant
- Policeman
- Doctor.

You have ten to fifteen minutes as a group, to:

- allow each person to speak
- decide whether some will leave and the others stay
- decide who will leave and who will stay

When that is complete, you are to answer the following question in your journal.
Debrief: Explain why you feel the choice was made. What influenced your decision? Did anyone emerge as a leader? Why? How did this influence the choices?

Reasons for your group's decision

Character	Reasons to keep alive	Reasons to sacrifice them
Scientist		
Priest		
Married couple who are hippies and drug addicts		
Single woman, pregnant woman with a 5-year-old girl		
Army officer who has mental instability of some sort but is useful nonetheless		
Elderly woman		
Disabled person		
Lawyer		
Benefits claimant		
Policeman		
Doctor		

Appendix 3
Sample risk assessment

Risk assessment for orienteering event:

Persons at risk: all participants, accompanying staff

Hazard	Risk	Control measures	Comments actions	Risk rating	Tick if in place
			Name and log of organisation managing the event		
Participants poorly prepared for the event	Participants get lost. Participants leave the site without signing out of the event. Participants in pairs split up and leave a person in an isolated area	Participants receive training in first aid and navigation ahead of the event, providing evidence of competence when registering. Established visits and activities procedures are enforced. The progress of participants is monitored throughout the event. An appropriate level of staff are located at each incident location should support be required.	Participants are only allowed to enter the event upon receipt of training and competence evidence. Parental consent forms and medical forms are received for every participant before starting. The layout of the exit is set up to prevent participants leaving without 'signing out'. All participants receive a verbal and written briefing sheet that addresses expected behaviour.	Low	
Exposure to extreme weather	Participants get cold or wet. Possible hypothermia	Equipment is inspected at start of the event. Red Cross first aiders are present around the course throughout the event. A comprehensive weather forecast is obtained prior to commencement. An indoor shelter is established in case of inclement weather or serious injury.	Event guidelines and a required equipment list is issued to all participants. Participants are not allowed to enter the event without proof they carry the appropriate clothing. The event is cancelled if poor weather is predicted.	Low	

Hazard	Risk	Control measures	Comments actions	Risk rating	Tick if in place
Falling branches from ancient trees	Head injuries, concussion, other injuries	Control points are not placed under trees. Advice will be taken from the site rangers.	Control point locations may be moved. Staff setting up the course are provided with safety guidelines. Accident forms will be completed in case of an incident.	Low	
Navigating uneven terrain in the dark.	Injuries from falls, trips, walking into trees, undergrowth and rough terrain	Participants instructed to navigate between control points via paths and tracks, rather than by direct line or compass bearing. Any site gates are opened for the duration of the event.	A visual inspection of the event terrain is conducted during the weeks prior to the event and a final inspection is made once control points are set up.	Low	
Vehicles moving through the area	Accidents between participants and vehicles. Accidents between vehicles	Vehicle movement is prohibited except for emergency vehicles once the event is underway. Emergency vehicles are provided with a staff escort who knows the site to control point or incident locations.	All staff will receive a full briefing ahead of the event commencing.	Low	
Breakdown in communications between incidents and the central control contact	Loss of knowledge of the location of participants	A back-up system of personal mobile phones will operate. Some designated staff will act as 'runners'.	Communications will be tested at the start of the event.	Low	

Hazard	Risk	Control measures	Comments actions	Risk rating	Tick if in place
Interference/ violence from local youths/gangs	Participants/individuals being frightened, physical assaults, injuries	The Police will be informed of the event and all control point locations. Police Special Constables will patrol the area once light starts to fade.	All staff will be instructed to report any threat of disturbance. Staff will patrol the event site.	Low	

Risk assessment completed by: ....   Date: _ _ / _ _ / _ _

255

Appendix 4
Sample route card

Name of organisation:

Date of walk / expedition

Full names of group members:

Names of field supervisors:

Emergency contact numbers:

Base contact and landline number:

OS MAP USED: White Peak
Planned walking speed: 3 km/hr
Time allowed for height gained: 1 min per 10 m height
START TIME: 10.00

Leg of route	Start (place name and grid reference)	Magnetic bearing (degrees)	Distance (km)	Height gained (m)	Rest time (minutes)	Total time for leg (minutes)	Estimated time to arrive	Details of route	Additional note
	Baslow car park 258 721						10.00		
1	River crossing at Chatsworth House 258 702	180	2	15	0	42	10.42	Follow the path past nursery and Chatsworth House until river crossing.	
2	Carlton Lees at junction 258 682	180	2	0	5	45	11.27	Carry on down footpath, along B6012 until car park and picnic site. Follow road around until junction.	5 min break at picnic site

Leg of route	Start (place name and grid reference)	Magnetic bearing (degrees)	Distance (km)	Height gained (m)	Rest time (minutes)	Total time for leg (minutes)	Estimated time to arrive	Details of route	Additional note
3	Ballcross Farm 228 695	315	3.5	45	5	75	12.42	Follow the footpath past Lees Wood and then past Calton Houses on the sharp bend.	5 min break just past Calton Houses
4	Station Farm road crossing 219 706	225	2.5	0	50	100	14.22	Follow the foot path through the woods then cross the road past the cycle hire and follow Monsal Trail.	Lunch at the cycle hire
5	Rowland village school 200 716	270	2.25	0	0	45	15.07	Follow the trail across the orange road and follow the smaller foot path through the village until the school.	
6	Park House Monsall Head 186 712	270	2.5	10	5	56	16.01	Follow same foot path across yellow road until you reach the village. Then turn and follow the Monsal Trail. Take a sharp turn onto the road. Turn on to the foot path to the B road and turn up to the campsite.	Take a break on the Monsal Trail

Indexes

Index of theories

Index of theorists